Confectionery

by
THE EDITORS OF TIME-LIFE BOOKS

TIME-LIFE BOOKS·AMSTERDAM

TIME-LIFE BOOKS
EUROPEAN EDITOR: Kit van Tulleken
Design Director: Louis Klein
Photography Director: Pamela Marke
Chief of Research: Vanessa Kramer
Planning Director: Alan Lothian
Chief Sub-Editor: Ilse Gray

THE GOOD COOK
Series Editor: Gillian Boucher
Series Co-ordinator: Liz Timothy

Editorial Staff for *Confectionery*
Text Editor: Norman Kolpas
Anthology Editor: Josephine Bacon
Staff Writers: Alexandra Carlier, Sally Crawford,
Jane Havell, Thom Henvey
Researcher: Margaret Hall
Designer: Mary Staples
Sub-Editors: Kathy Eason, Charles Boyle,
Aquila Kegan, Sally Rowland
Anthology Researcher: Deborah Litton
Anthology Assistant: Debra Raad
Design Assistant: Sally Curnock
Proofreader: Kate Cann
Editorial Assistant: Molly Sutherland

EDITORIAL PRODUCTION FOR THE SERIES
Chief: Ellen Brush
Quality Control: Douglas Whitworth
Traffic Co-ordinators: Linda Mallett,
Helen Whitehorn
Picture Co-ordinators: Philip Garner, Steven Ayckbourn
Art Department: Julia West
Editorial Department: Theresa John,
Lesley Kinahan, Debra Lelliott, Sylvia Wilson

Cover: A plump grape, half covered with snowy fondant
and dusted with sugar, is lifted from a dish of dipped
confections. Many different sweets can be dipped in
fondant, caramel or chocolate for a smooth finish. The
chocolate-coated selection here includes marzipans,
caramels, nut clusters and fondants.

THE CHIEF CONSULTANT:
Richard Olney, an American, has lived and worked since 1951
in France, where he is a highly regarded authority on food and
wine. He is the author of *The French Menu Cookbook* and the
award-winning *Simple French Food,* and has contributed to
numerous gastronomic magazines in France and the United
States, including the influential journals *Cuisine et Vins de
France* and *La Revue du Vin de France.* He has directed
cooking courses in France and the United States and is a
member of several distinguished gastronomic and oenologi-
cal societies, including *L'Académie Internationale du Vin, La
Confrérie de Chevaliers du Tastevin* and *La Commanderie du
Bontemps de Médoc et des Graves.*

THE STUDIO CONSULTANTS:
Richard Sax, who was responsible for many of the step-by-step demonstrations for this
volume, was for two years Chef-Director of the test kitchens for *The International
Review of Food and Wine.* Trained in New York and in Paris, where he served an
apprenticeship at the Hotel Plaza-Athénée, he has run a restaurant in America, written
articles for a number of publications and conducted cooking courses.
Pat Alburey is a Member of the Association of Home Economists of Great Britain. Her
wide experience includes preparing foods for photography, teaching cookery and
creating recipes. She was responsible for a majority of the step-by-step demonstrations in this volume.

THE PHOTOGRAPHER:
Tom Belshaw was born near London and started his working career in films. He now
has his own studio in London. He specializes in food and still-life photography,
undertaking both editorial and advertising assignments.

THE INTERNATIONAL CONSULTANTS:
Great Britain: *Jane Grigson* was born in Gloucester and brought up in the north of
England. She is a graduate of Cambridge University. Her first book on food, *Charcu-
terie and French Pork Cookery,* was published in 1967; since then, she has published a
number of cookery books, including *Good Things, English Food* and *Jane Grigson's
Vegetable Book.* She became cookery correspondent for the colour magazine of the
London *Observer* in 1968. *Alan Davidson* is the author of *Fish and Fish Dishes of Laos,
Mediterranean Seafood* and *North Atlantic Seafood.* He is the founder of Prospect
Books, which specializes in scholarly publications on food and cookery. **France:**
Michel Lemonnier was born in Normandy. He began contributing to the magazine
Cuisine et Vins de France in 1960, and also writes for several other important French
food and wine periodicals. The co-founder and vice-president of the society *Les
Amitiés Gastronomiques Internationales,* he is a frequent lecturer on wine and a
member of most of the vinicultural confraternities and academies in France. **Germany:**
Jochen Kuchenbecker trained as a chef, but worked for 10 years as a food photogra-
pher in many European countries before opening his own restaurant in Hamburg. *Anne
Brakemeier,* who also lives in Hamburg, has published articles on food and cooking in
many German periodicals. She is the co-author of three cookery books. **Italy:** *Massimo
Alberini* divides his time between Milan and Venice. He is a well-known food writer and
journalist, with a particular interest in culinary history. Among his 14 books are *Storia del
Pranzo all'Italiana, 4000 Anni a Tavola* and *100 Ricette Storiche.* **The Netherlands:**
Hugh Jans, a resident of Amsterdam, has been translating cookery books and articles
for more than 25 years. He has also published several books of his own, including *Bistro
Koken* and *Sla, Slaatjes, Snacks,* and his recipes are published in many Dutch
magazines. **The United States:** *Carol Cutler,* who lives in Washington, DC, is the author
of three cookery books, including the award-winning *The Six-Minute Soufflé and Other
Culinary Delights. Judith Olney* received her culinary training in England and France
and has written two cookery books. *Robert Shoffner* has been wine and food editor of
the *Washingtonian* magazine since 1975.

Valuable help was given in the preparation of this volume by the following members of
Time-Life Books: *Maria Vincenza Aloisi, Joséphine du Brusle* (Paris); *Janny Hovinga*
(Amsterdam); *Elisabeth Kraemer* (Bonn); *Ann Natanson* (Rome); *Bona Schmid*
(Milan).

CONTENTS

Morsels of Delight

Confectionery is food for sheer pleasure. Whether it is offered to satisfy an unexpected pang of hunger, to reward a virtuous child, or as the culmination of a meal, it is an extra, a treat. Its purpose is primarily to delight—with the crystal-clear fruit colours of lollipops or the creamy richness of truffles, the fluffiness of marshmallows or the crunch of a nut and chocolate cluster.

Part of the fun of confectionery lies in making it. The occasion may be part of a family's preparation for Christmas, or an impromptu fudge-making session on a chilly day. The delicious raw materials and the pleasure of eating scraps along the way ensure that the work of preparing the confections is no labour.

That is not to imply that confectionery-making is a carefree, slapdash branch of cookery. To be sure, some confections—uncooked nut pastes (*page 56*) for example, or balls of dried fruit and honey (*page 50*)—are quickly and easily made. However, many other confections require precision and dexterity in their preparation. Boiled sugar sweets, for example, demand hot syrups that must be cooked to exactly the right temperature and handled with due caution. And although dipping in syrup, melted fondant or chocolate is not difficult or dangerous, it takes practice to get good results with a minimum of mess.

This book offers a comprehensive guide to the making of confections. It begins with explanations of the properties of the basic ingredients—sugar, nuts and chocolate—and guidelines on selecting flavourings and colourings, followed by instructions for lining moulds to contain confections while they set.

The book is then divided into four chapters. The first three deal with broad categories of confections, based on the chief ingredient. Chapter 1 covers sweets made from boiled sugar syrups—brittle toffees and chewy caramels, creamy fondants and hard dropped sweets. The second chapter focuses on fruits— how to crystallize pieces of fruit by saturating them with sugar syrup, how to produce firm fruit pastes or clear fruit jellies. The third chapter deals with confectionery pastes formed from nuts or chocolate, including two classic confections: marzipan and chocolate truffles. In the fourth chapter, you will learn the techniques of dipping and moulding—skills that make use of the ingredients and finished confections introduced in the preceding chapters. Having mastered all these lessons, you will be able to prepare any of the 247 recipes in the Anthology beginning on page 87, as well as create a myriad of confections of your own.

Sources of sweetness

Confections are, of their nature, sweet. Generally, the sweetener is refined white sugar, but there are many alternatives with a more pronounced character—brown sugar, honey, treacle, maple syrup and molasses among them. All plants contain some sugar, but for white sugar the primary sources are sugar cane, a tropical grass, and sugar beet, a temperate-climate root vegetable resembling a plump parsnip.

Sugar cane stores sweetness in the sap in its stem; in order to extract the sweet juice, the cane is crushed between rollers. The juice extracted is then purified by being heated with milk of lime. Further processing brings the juices to the point at which sugar crystals begin to form; the juices are then centrifuged to separate the liquid from the crystals. The results are coarse, dark brown granules of raw sugar, the thick, almost black syrup known as molasses and waste molasses, sometimes called blackstrap.

The raw sugar is now ready to be "refined"—that is, rid of all foreign matter. It is first washed and centrifuged again to remove more impurities. At this stage, it is still brown and may be packaged as coarse brown sugar. The best-known variety of brown sugar, Demerara—named after its region of origin in Guyana—is such a product. Nowadays, however, the name Demerara is also applied to fully refined sugar mingled with molasses for flavour and colour. Further processing and filtering gradually remove the sugar's brown colour and residual flavours, resulting in pure white sugar crystals. The size of the crystals can be varied—preserving sugar, for example, has very large crystals, the crystals of granulated sugar may be large or medium-sized, and castor sugar has fine crystals. Crystals may also be ground very finely to produce powdery icing sugar; or they may be moistened and moulded into sugar cubes.

The processing and refining of white sugar yields many by-products. Treacle is a dark syrup produced from molasses. Liquids drawn off during refining may themselves be processed to make soft yellow and brown sugars or a range of light-coloured syrups such as golden syrup.

Sugar beet retains sugar not in its stem but in its stubby root; in order to extract the juice, the root is sliced and placed in hot water. After this, beet sugar is processed in the same way as cane sugar. However, although some of the by-products of the beet are used for animal food, only the end-product—white sugar—is sold for human consumption.

A method of extracting and evaporating the juice of the sugar cane was known in India as early as 3000 B.C. From India, cane-growing and sugar-making spread east to Indo-China and west to the Arab countries, and—eventually—to Europe. The first sugar refineries came into existence in Persia about the seventh century A.D., and by the eighth century sugar cane was grown and sugar made in Spain and the south of France. In 1493, on his second voyage to the Americas, Christopher Columbus carried some cane seedlings to Santo Domingo; the sugar cane industry of the West Indies was born and production increased steeply. But it was not until the 16th century, when sugar refining became a commercial process, that sugar confectionery began to be made.

Beet was cultivated at an early date in southern Europe, but only as a garden vegetable and for cattle fodder. It was in 1747 that a German chemist, Andreas Marggraf, proved that certain kinds of beet contained sugar. The first sugar beet factory was opened in 1802 at Cunern in Silesia. In France, Napoleon awarded the Cross of the Legion of Honour in 1811 to one Benjamin Delessert for his experiments in crystallizing beet sugar.

Honey was almost certainly the first sweetener used by man. Stone Age hunter-gatherers sought out and stole honey from the hives of wild bees: a prehistoric painting in the Araña cave in Valencia, Spain, for example, shows bees buzzing menacingly around a human figure who gingerly reaches into their nest. The Egyptians had certainly discovered how to domesticate bees by 2500 B.C.: a relief in the temple of Neuserre at Abu Sir shows bee-keepers subduing bees with smoke, then gathering honeycombs from neat, cylindrical hives and emptying the honey from the combs into storage jars. Honey was so much the everyday sweetener of the classical world that the Roman historian Pliny described sugar as "a kind of honey".

Today, honey remains the primary ingredient in many Arab and Middle Eastern confections. Elsewhere, its role in confectionery is more one of flavouring than main ingredient. It adds an extra mellowness to nougat (*page 42*) and does the same for caramels (*page 32*). Because the character of a honey—its strength and its particular aroma—is determined by the kind of blossoms visited by the bees that produced it, your choice of honey will have some effect on the confections you make with it. Heather, orange blossom, rosemary, pine, locust and lavender honey are among the most distinctive. The highly prized Hymettus honey from Mount Hymettus in Greece derives its flavour from thyme.

Another source of sweeteners is the maple tree, a native of North America. In the spring, when the sap is rising, the bark is tapped to extract the sap. Although the sap contains only about 3 per cent sugar, when concentrated by boiling it yields an amber syrup or a pale brown sugar with a mellow sweetness.

A more mundane but nevertheless valuable range of sweeteners is derived from maize. The long, chain-like starch molecules that make up maize grains are broken down with acids to yield sugars and syrups of various strengths and degrees of purity. Corn syrup and liquid glucose are examples of such products.

Corn, maple, honey, sugar cane and sugar beet sweeteners have much in common in terms of chemistry. Ordinary white sugar—the chemical name of which is sucrose—is the purest known commercial chemical, being 99.8 per cent pure. Sucrose is a molecule with two distinct parts joined by a chemical bond. The two parts, glucose and fructose, can also exist as independent sugars. Fructose is sweeter than sucrose, glucose rather less sweet than either. Corn syrup and liquid glucose contain a large proportion of glucose (despite its name, liquid glucose is not 100 per cent glucose). Honey owes its sweetness to fructose. Maple sugar, like cane and beet sugar, is composed chiefly of sucrose.

But, unlike white sugar, maple sugar and unrefined cane sugars are not pure sucrose; it is the small proportion of substances other than sucrose that gives them their distinctive flavour.

The intriguing properties of sugar

No less impressive than the varieties of sweetener are the many ways in which sugar can be treated to produce the wide range of textures found in confectionery. The fundamental skill of the confectioner lies in the handling of a sugar syrup—a solution of sugar in water. If you add enough water to sugar to dissolve it completely, the result is, of course, a liquid. However, if the syrup is boiled to drive off most of the water, the syrup will solidify at room temperature. According to how much water you allow to remain in the sugar syrup, you can produce textures ranging from soft to extremely brittle.

A sugar syrup has a strong tendency to return to its original crystalline structure, forming relatively large, jagged granules. This tendency can be the bane of confectioners. Some sweets, such as lollipops, are intended to be clear and glassy, with no crystals at all. Others, such as fondant, are crystalline—but the crystals must be tiny if the confection is to have a smooth texture. To counter the tendency to make large crystals, a sugar syrup is normally boiled with additives known as "interfering agents".

The logic of adding an interfering agent is that before crystallization can occur, molecules must line up in an orderly pattern; any foreign molecule that gets in the way of the sugar molecules will make it difficult for the sugar to crystallize. A sugar other than sucrose will perform the interfering function well: liquid glucose, corn syrup or honey are all good choices. Present in small quantities, these sugars result in the formation of fine, small crystals; in high concentration, they can prevent graining entirely. Other substances, particularly fats such as butter or cocoa fat, can also serve as interfering agents—they inhibit crystallization by making the syrup thicker. And acids such as lemon juice or tartaric acid will also control crystallization, because they break sucrose down into its component glucose and fructose (a mixture often described as "invert sugar"), thus providing an interfering agent at second hand. It is largely through the assistance of interfering agents that home confectioners can ensure that their lollipops will set clear and brittle, their fudge fine-grained and creamy, and their caramels smooth and chewy.

The glamour of chocolate

If sugar is the staple of confectionery-making, chocolate is the ingredient that for many people symbolizes the sheer luxury of confectionery. Its smoothness, its richness and its intense flavour can be appreciated in chocolate coatings, moulded confections and combinations of chocolate with cream. It is perhaps surprising to find that this archetypal confectionery ingredient derives from hard and extremely bitter little beans.

The beans grow in pods on the cacao tree, a native of the equatorial regions of the Americas. After harvesting, the beans are allowed to ferment for several days—a process that tempers their bitterness and turns them a light brown colour. The beans are cleaned, then dried and roasted, which darkens their colour and develops their aroma. Crushing and grinding of the roasted beans then reduces them to a thick, fatty paste.

Rich in the aroma of chocolate though the beans may be at this point, they do not have a confectionery sweetness or smoothness. The smoothness will be conferred in part by extra cocoa fat—obtained by pressing other batches of beans. (The dry cakes of brown solids that remain after the fat has been extracted are ground up into cocoa powder). To make chocolate, the pale yellow cocoa fat is combined with the cocoa bean paste and the mixture is sweetened with large quantities of sugar—from 40 to 60 per cent of the total weight. Milk may be added for a milder flavour. The chocolate mixture then passes through a series of rollers that grind its particles ever more finely.

Although microscopically small, the particles that remain after rolling are still very rough-textured and grainy. To refine the chocolate to perfect smoothness, it undergoes a process called "conching", after the shell-like curve of the trough in which the process takes place. The trough is heated to keep the chocolate mixture molten, and a roller moves back and forth through the liquid, turning it over in continuous waves. Over the course of several days, the small, rough particles rub against each other and gradually become polished and fine. After cooling and moulding, the result is perfectly smooth chocolate, ready to eat or to use in the preparation of confections.

In South America, the cacao plant was cultivated more than 3000 years ago by the Mayas, Toltecs and Aztecs. They used the beans as currency and consumed chocolate in the form of a thick, slightly bitter drink produced from a mixture of cocoa nibs,

water, maize and spices. Columbus brought cocoa beans back to Spain after his fourth voyage in 1502, but it was his fellow countryman Hernando Cortéz who recognized the commercial potential of the plant. Cortéz was introduced to drinking chocolate at the court of the Aztec emperor Montezuma in 1519, and he sent back to Spain not only beans but also recipes for the preparation of chocolate. The Spaniards sweetened the drink, and in this form it gained high esteem. For a long time—it is said for almost a hundred years—they managed to keep the details of the cultivation of the plant and the preparation of chocolate secret. However, chocolate was introduced into Italy during the first decade of the 17th century, and it became popular in France after the marriage of the Spanish princess Maria Theresa to Louis XIV in 1660. At about the same time, chocolate was gaining popularity among the wealthy in England—it is mentioned in the *Diary* of Samuel Pepys in 1664—and chocolate-houses serving the drink soon became favourite meeting places throughout Europe. Until

the end of the 17th century, chocolate was still an expensive luxury, but early in the 18th century, commercial manufacture began and prices dropped. It was not until the 19th century, however, that processes for preparing eating chocolate were developed. Today, cocoa bean products are available to the consumer in many different forms, from cocoa powder and simple bars to luxurious, elaborately flavoured and moulded sweets.

Essential confectionery equipment

Confectionery is a specialized branch of cookery, but the novice should not be deterred by the fear that a great deal of specialized equipment will be needed. The prime requisites, in fact, are a dextrous pair of hands and a cool, dry atmosphere: humidity can interfere with the preparation of many boiled sugar confections.

However, there are a few essential pieces of equipment—and a few additional items that will improve the quality of your output. First of all, you need a cool, smooth work surface—marble is ideal, but you can use a metal baking sheet—for working with hot confectionery mixtures. Good quality, deep saucepans are necessary, particularly for cooking sugar syrup. Heavy vessels of unlined copper or brass, or of stainless steel or aluminium, are best, because they will cook syrups evenly and will safely withstand the high temperatures involved. To measure sugar temperatures accurately, buy the best sugar thermometer available. It should be clearly marked for ease of reading.

Well-stocked kitchenware shops or professional confectioners' suppliers carry more specialized confectionery equipment, but it is also easy to improvise such equipment from materials readily at hand in the home kitchen. To dip delicate centres in chocolate, for example, most confectioners use specially designed fine forks (*pages 74-77*). But you could do some dipping with an ordinary table fork. For starch-casting, a process used to form thin, hard sugar shells round liquid centres, confectioners have special trays, moulds and pouring equipment. As shown on pages 80-83, however, you can achieve professional results using a baking tray, some wood and modelling clay, a kitchen funnel and a wooden spoon. A set of four steel bars (*page 19*) to enclose confections as they set will save guessing about volumes—but you will produce an acceptable result with a baking tray.

Confections and health

There was a time when confections were believed to have medicinal value. Marshmallows, for example, were originally made with an extract of the roots of the marshmallow plant, sold by apothecaries as a remedy for chest ailments. The traditional Irish country confection called yellow-man (*recipes, page 96*)—a simple honeycomb toffee—enjoyed a folk reputation as a cure-all. And the 19th-century French epicure Jean Anthelme Brillat-Savarin observed that takers of chocolate "enjoy unvarying health, and are least attacked by a host of little illnesses which can destroy the true joy of living".

Nowadays, quite different feelings prevail. Sweets are often spurned as "junk food", which should be avoided. But provided moderation is observed, there is no reason why confectionery should not be enjoyed. And one of the most compelling reasons for making your own confections is that it allows you complete control over the choice of ingredients. First-class ingredients, treated with respect, promise wholesome and delicious results.

Understanding How Syrups Behave

The transformation of sugar and water into syrups and caramel is the foundation of confectionery-making. When a sugar and water solution is boiled (*below*), the water evaporates and the sugar concentration steadily increases. The higher the sugar content, the higher the boiling point—so you can check the concentration by taking the temperature with a sugar thermometer (*box, far right*). By curtailing the boiling at different stages, you can produce syrups with a range of moisture contents. When no water is left, the molten sugar will turn to caramel, amber in colour and rich in flavour.

The less moisture a syrup contains, the harder it will set when it cools. Thus the degree to which the syrup is cooked has a marked effect on the texture of the finished confection. Syrup boiled to a relatively low temperature yields soft sweets such as fudges or chewy caramels; syrup boiled to a high temperature yields hard sweets such as lollipops. The tests demonstrated on pages 10-11 are reliable guides to the consistency of the cooled syrup.

Since the ultimate concentration of the syrup is controlled by evaporation of the water, the initial proportions of water and sugar are not crucial. However, good proportions are about 15 cl (¼ pint) of water to 500 g (1 lb) of sugar. That ratio provides enough water to dissolve the sugar easily, but the resulting syrup will not be excessively watery and so will need only fairly brief cooking to reach the desired temperature. To make caramel, you can either boil a sugar syrup until all the water evaporates, or carefully melt the sugar without any water at all (*box, right*).

Because boiling water can dissolve more sugar than water at lower temperatures, a syrup becomes "super-saturated" with sugar as it cools and the excess sugar tends to re-form into crystals. For some confections, the tendency to crystallize or "grain" is discouraged; for others it is encouraged. The basis for hard, smooth sweets such as barley sugar is a clear, glassy syrup with no crystals. For soft, opaque sweets such as fudges and fondants, on the other hand, you will need a syrup in which crystals are suspended.

One way to discourage crystallization is to boil the syrup until only a minimum of water remains. As the concentrated syrup cools, it becomes so viscous that the molecules cannot line up in preparation for crystallization. Another technique for controlling graining is to add to the syrup a substance that will interfere with crystallization (*page 6*). Milk solids and fats, for instance, by making the syrup thicker, impede crystallization. Any sugar other than sucrose—the constituent of white sugar—can be used either to prevent crystallization altogether or to ensure that only fine crystals are formed. Acids such as lemon juice and cream of tartar have a similar effect because they break sucrose down into other sugars. The most reliable and commonly used interfering agent is powdered or liquid glucose (*Step 1*).

The way to promote a syrup's natural tendency to grain is to beat it. If you want large crystals, for a sweet with a coarse, granular consistency—a firm fudge, for example—begin to beat the syrup while it is still hot. To create smaller crystals and a smoother texture—for fondant or a creamy fudge—the syrup must be partially cooled before it is beaten.

1 **Adding liquid glucose.** Warm a sugar thermometer by placing it in a jug of hot water (*box, far right, above*). Put required amounts of cold water and granulated sugar into a heavy saucepan. To regulate crystallization, add an interfering agent—in this case, liquid glucose—to the syrup ingredients (*above*).

2 **Dissolving the sugar.** Stir the syrup over a medium heat until the sugar dissolves (*above*). Imperfectly dissolved sugar may cause the mass to crystallize—so, if the mixture begins to boil before all the sugar has dissolved, remove it from the heat. Continue to stir. When the syrup has cooled a little, return it to the heat.

3 **Removing stray crystals.** Stir the syrup gently, so that it does not splash up on to the pan sides and crystallize. To remove any stray drops, wipe down the sides of the pan with a pastry brush dipped in hot water (*above*). Alternatively, place a tight-fitting lid on the pan so that any crystals are washed down the sides of the pan by the steam that condenses.

Caramel Made without Added Water

Melting sugar without water. Put sugar into a heavy pan set over a low heat—on a fireproof mat if the cooker controls are not very sensitive. Add a few drops of lemon juice to flavour the caramel and to inhibit crystallization. Stir continuously until the sugar has melted. Add more sugar (*above, left*); stir until all the sugar is melted and the caramel is clear (*above, right*). Still stirring, continue to add sugar in small amounts until you have the desired quantity of caramel.

Using a Sugar Thermometer

Protecting against shock. If a sugar thermometer is subjected suddenly to boiling syrup, it may crack. So first warm the thermometer in hot water. After use, replace the thermometer immediately in hot water to dissolve any sugar crystals that cling to the bulb.

4 **Boiling the syrup.** When the syrup is completely clear, stop stirring. Place a warmed thermometer in the pan and bring the syrup to the boil (*above*). Adjust the heat so that the syrup maintains a steady, light boil.

5 **Arresting the cooking.** Have ready a bowl of cold water. When the syrup has reached the temperature you require (*pages 10-11*), take the thermometer out of the pan. Remove the pan from the heat and immediately dip it in the cold water to cool it quickly and to prevent further cooking (*above*).

6 **Testing for hardness.** With a spoon, take a small amount of syrup from the pan and submerge it in some iced water to cool it quickly (*above*). By testing this small amount in your fingers (*pages 10-11*), you can judge how the whole quantity of syrup will set. If the syrup is not hard enough, return the pan to the heat and continue cooking. □

Testing the Hardness of Syrups

The softness or hardness of a plain sugar syrup after it cools is determined by the temperature to which it is cooked (*page 8*). As it cooks to progressively higher temperatures, a syrup goes through a wide range of stages: tests for these are shown on the right with a plain sugar syrup.

Other ingredients added to a syrup alter the temperature to which it must be cooked to reach each stage. Some, such as honey, cause the syrup to boil at a higher temperature; others, such as milk or fat, at a lower one. Hence, a range of temperatures—shown in the chart below—applies to each stage.

Most syrups fall within these ranges, but certain ingredients used in high proportions may have so marked an effect that temperatures outside the given ranges will apply. So it is advisable always to test the consistency of a syrup, rather than to rely on temperature alone.

Thread 106°-113°C (223°-236°F)

A thin filament. Dip the pan in cold water to stop the syrup cooking (*page 9*). Take a teaspoonful of syrup and tip it out over a dish. If the syrup forms a fine, thin thread (*above*), it has reached the thread stage. If the syrup is too liquid, return it to the heat and test again when the temperature has increased by a few degrees.

Using Temperature to Assess Consistency

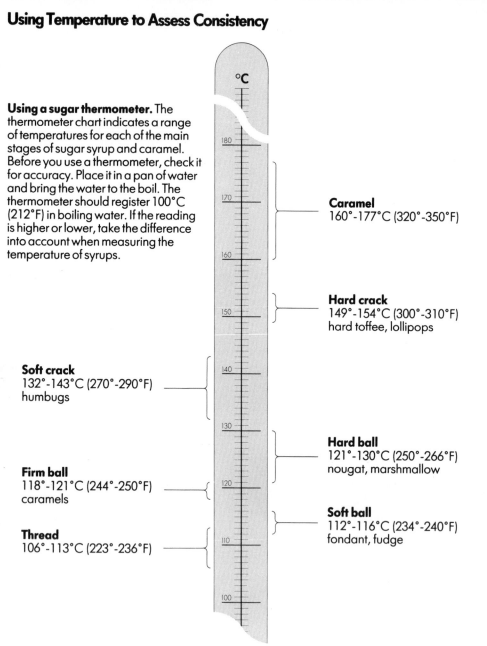

Using a sugar thermometer. The thermometer chart indicates a range of temperatures for each of the main stages of sugar syrup and caramel. Before you use a thermometer, check it for accuracy. Place it in a pan of water and bring the water to the boil. The thermometer should register 100°C (212°F) in boiling water. If the reading is higher or lower, take the difference into account when measuring the temperature of syrups.

°C

Caramel
160°-177°C (320°-350°F)

Hard crack
149°-154°C (300°-310°F)
hard toffee, lollipops

Soft crack
132°-143°C (270°-290°F)
humbugs

Hard ball
121°-130°C (250°-266°F)
nougat, marshmallow

Firm ball
118°-121°C (244°-250°F)
caramels

Soft ball
112°-116°C (234°-240°F)
fondant, fudge

Thread
106°-113°C (223°-236°F)

Soft Crack 132°-143°C (270°-290°F)

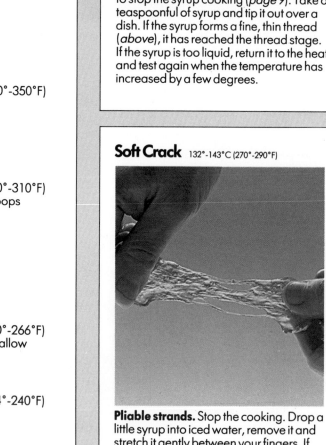

Pliable strands. Stop the cooking. Drop a little syrup into iced water, remove it and stretch it gently between your fingers. If the syrup separates into strands which are hard but elastic (*above*), then it has reached the soft-crack stage. The syrup will now feel only slightly sticky.

Soft Ball 112°-116°C (234°-240°F)

A rapidly flattening lump. Dip the pan in cold water. Drop some syrup into a bowl of iced water. In the water, mould it with your fingers into a ball. Take the ball from the water. If it holds its shape while under water but immediately loses shape and flattens between your fingers (*above*), the syrup is at the soft-ball stage. At this stage, the syrup feels very sticky.

Firm Ball 118°-121°C (244°-250°F)

A pliable globe. Dip the pan in cold water. Drop a little syrup into iced water and mould it into a ball. Remove it from the water. If the syrup has reached the firm-ball stage (*above*), it will feel firm but pliable and still fairly sticky. At this stage, the syrup retains its shape for longer than at the soft-ball stage, but it will lose shape quite quickly at room temperature.

Hard Ball 121°-130°C (250°-266°F)

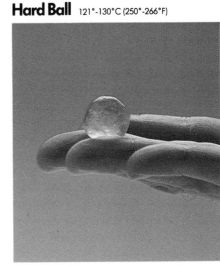

A rigid globe. Dip the pan in cold water. Drop some syrup into iced water. If the syrup has reached the hard-ball stage, it will mould easily into a ball. Take the ball out of the water. It should hold its shape (*above*) and feel resistant to pressure. It will still be quite sticky.

Hard Crack 149°-154°C (300°-310°F)

Brittle strands. Dip the pan in cold water and drop some syrup into iced water. Remove the solidified syrup from the water and bend it. If it snaps easily (*above*), it has reached the hard-crack stage. It will have a yellowish tinge and will no longer feel at all sticky.

Light Caramel 160°-170°C (320°-338°F)

A honey-coloured liquid. Dip the bottom of the pan in cold water to arrest the cooking. Take a spoonful of liquid from the pan and pour it on to a white plate. If the molten sugar has become light caramel, it will be honey-gold in colour.

Dark Caramel 165°-177°C (330°-350°F)

An amber liquid. As for light caramel, spoon a little liquid on to a plate. If it is a reddish-amber colour, it is dark caramel. Do not cook beyond this point, or the caramel will become bitter tasting.

Handling Nuts with Assurance

Nuts are employed in a variety of forms in confectionery: whole, halved, chopped, grated or ground to a flour. They may be plain, lightly roasted or cooked further—toasted—to colour and flavour the kernels. One of the simplest confections is a whole nut dipped in chocolate (*page 74*). Roasted or plain nuts, mixed with caramelized sugar, produce brittles (*page 31*). Coarsely chopped nuts vary the texture of fudges and nougat (*pages 38 and 42*); balls of fondant may be given a coating of finely chopped nuts (*page 36*). Grated nuts can be used in fillings (*page 72*) and ground nuts, combined with sugar and egg, yield a wide range of pastes (*pages 56-63*).

Preliminary shelling is necessary for all nuts, in whatever form they are to be used, and skinning is desirable to relieve nuts of their dark, bitter inner coat. Coconuts, which are exceptional in size and structure, need special treatment (*opposite page, below*). Most other nuts are easily shelled, by hand or with a nut-cracker, but need to be parboiled or roasted before the skin can be removed from the kernels.

Nuts with fairly loose skins—almonds and pistachio nuts, for example—are easy to peel if they are first parboiled (*right, above*). The boiling water penetrates the porous fibres of the skins, temporarily softening them and separating them from the kernels. However, when the nuts cool, the skins harden and cling again, so the skinning must be completed while the nuts are still warm. Nuts with tighter skins, such as Brazil nuts or hazelnuts, need to be roasted in a moderate oven until their skins become parched and flaky (*opposite page, above*).

Once shelled and skinned, nuts can be used whole or halved, or may be chopped with a heavy knife (*right*), or ground with a pestle and mortar or in an electric food processor (*far right*). A food processor transforms nuts into a fine, barely moist powder very suitable for most confectionery purposes. Pounding in a mortar gives a much wetter paste; if you pound oily nuts such as almonds, it is essential to add a little egg white to prevent oil from separating out of the nuts.

Blanching Loose-Skinned Nuts

1 Parboiling nuts. Put a small quantity of shelled nuts—in this case, almonds—into a pan of boiling water and parboil them for about 2 minutes. Turn off the heat and retrieve the nuts with a skimmer (*above*) or with a perforated ladle; alternatively, remove the pan from the heat and drain the nuts in a colander.

2 Removing the skins. Let the nuts cool slightly. With your fingers, squeeze each nut lightly but firmly to pop it from its skin. Allow the nuts to dry thoroughly before storing them in an airtight jar. They will keep for several months in a cool place.

A Speedy Chopping Technique

Chopping finely. Put the nuts—pistachio nuts, here—on a work surface. Place the blade of a heavy, sharp knife across the nuts. Rest your free hand on the knife tip to steady it against the work surface. Using the tip as a pivot, slowly move the knife in an arc while rocking it up and down to chop the nuts. As the pieces become smaller, increase your speed.

Grinding in a Processor

Processing nuts. Put a small quantity of cooled, skinned nuts—almonds, in this case—into the bowl of a food processor. Turn the processor on and off—initially at four-second intervals, later for longer bursts. If the nuts cling to the sides of the processor, push them down. Grind the nuts to a coarse-textured flour.

Rubbing Off a Clinging Skin

1 Roasting nuts. Spread nuts—hazelnuts are shown here—on a baking sheet. Place the sheet in an oven preheated to 170°C (325°F or Mark 3). Roast the nuts for about 10 minutes. Lay a towel on a work surface and spill the roasted nuts on to one half of the towel (*above*).

2 Skinning the nuts. Fold the uncovered half of the towel over the nuts (*above*). Using the palms of your hands, roll the nuts in the towel; after 1 or 2 minutes, most nuts will have shed their skins.

3 Removing stubborn skins. Rub any partly skinned or unskinned nuts between your fingers so that the skin flakes off. Nuts enclosed in their skins even after being rubbed should be reserved for purposes where appearance is not important. Store the nuts in an airtight jar.

Cracking and Grating a Coconut

1 Extracting liquid. With a large knife, cut off the tuft of fibrous husk at the top of the coconut. Use a skewer to pierce through the three indentations or "eyes" that are exposed by the removal of the husk (*above*). Invert the coconut over a bowl to drain off the milky liquid.

2 Opening the coconut. With a hammer or the back of a cleaver, briskly tap the coconut about one-third of the way from the end opposite the eyes (*above*). The coconut will fracture along a natural seam. Continue tapping until the nut cracks open along this line.

3 Grating the coconut flesh. Use a knife to divide the coconut flesh into portions that can be easily lifted from the shells. Lift out each portion and cut off the brown skin covering the flesh. Grate the flesh into crumbs (*above*) or chop it into fine pieces.

A Guide to Flavourings and Colourings

Many boiled sugar sweets, from lollipops to fondant, take their character chiefly from flavourings added in small quantities. Other sweets, such as toffee and marzipan, derive ample flavour from the main ingredients, but often have extra flavourings added for variety. Some flavourings impart colour too; if you use a colourless flavouring, you can, of course, also add a colour. Convention links certain flavours and colours—peppermint with green, for example—but such associations are by no means binding.

Except for cochineal—a deep crimson derived from insects—almost all natural flavourings and colourings are obtained from plants. Flowers, seed pods, leaves, stalks and roots are all commonly used. Some flavourings are prepared easily at home—coffee or fruit juices, for example. You can also make two vivid plant-based colourings. Spinach produces an intense green if it is pounded and squeezed, and the resulting juice is heated to separate the coloured matter from water (box, right). Saffron, simply dissolved in water, gives a sunny yellow (box, far right, above). In the small amounts needed to dye a confection, these colourings will add no perceptible flavour.

Commercial flavourings and colourings are generally available in easily incorporated liquid form. Commercial flavouring liquids fall into three categories: natural flavourings; nature-identical flavourings, in which a natural flavouring is carefully matched by synthetic means; and synthetic flavourings, which merely approximate to the natural flavour. A commercial flavouring may be labelled "essence", "extract" or simply "flavouring". Generally speaking, "essence" and "extract" should indicate that the flavouring has been obtained from the natural substance. "Flavouring" is a neutral term that does not indicate whether the source is natural or not. If you are seeking natural products, you will usually find that the more you pay for a flavouring, the more likely it is to have a natural base.

Commercial colouring liquids may have either a natural or an artificial source. The choice of colours is often restricted but you can mix the colours to obtain more subtle hues.

Most liquid commercial flavourings and colourings are strong, and so only a drop or two need be added to a confection. This feature is no mere accident: many confections depend for their success on a particular consistency and excessive dilution could spell ruin.

If a dilute flavouring is called for in a recipe, it is often used in place of water. To flavour lollipops, for example, the sugar can be dissolved in fruit juice instead of water, and the combination boiled to make a hard-crack syrup. Ideally, however, flavourings and colourings should be added after cooking, since many are marred by prolonged heat.

Home-prepared flavourings and colourings should be stored in the refrigerator and used within three days. Bottles of commercial flavourings and colourings should be stored in a dark cupboard: light fades the colours and reduces the potency of many flavourings. Once the seals of the bottles have been broken, the contents will slowly deteriorate; so buy the smallest size available—usually 15 g (½ oz). Keep the bottles tightly stoppered, to minimize evaporation.

The following selective list of natural flavourings should give you plenty of ideas for ways to vary your confections.

Fruit flavourings

The strained juice from berries such as strawberries and raspberries, and from citrus fruits such as lemons and oranges can be used to make translucent jellies (page 52) and boiled sugar sweets (pages 22-25). A more concentrated citrus flavour can be obtained from the fruit's zest—the thin, coloured outer skin. To obtain the zest, simply rub the fruit against a grater; take care to leave behind all the bitter white pith.

Spices and herbs

Vanilla, the seed pod of a tropical plant, is the most versatile spice used in confectionery-making. It goes particularly well with fudge (page 38) but is also valuable in fruit and nut confections. Vanilla pods are inedible, but they will readily scent a jar of sugar (box, far right, below); most home confectioners use the vanilla sugar thus made whenever vanilla is called for.

Alternatively, you can boil up a vanilla pod in milk or a syrup—extracting the pod once the cooking is complete—or use vanilla extract. In order to draw the maximum of flavour rapidly from a vanilla pod, split it lengthwise.

Other spices that appear occasionally in confections—particularly fruit confections (Chapter 2)—include ginger, mace, cinnamon, cloves, allspice and nutmeg. Any of these spices may be ground and added in powder form.

The herb used most often in confectionery-making is mint—peppermint or the milder spearmint. Working at home, it is not possible to make a concentrated flavouring from the fresh leaves. But commercial extracts are easily available. Mint is a common flavouring for fondant and other boiled sugar sweets.

Coffee and chocolate

Coffee makes a delicious flavouring for fudge, fondant, nut pastes (page 56) or any chocolate sweet. To prepare coffee as a flavouring, use three times the normal proportion of coffee to water to make a brew of triple strength. Alternatively, make ordinary filter coffee but use only the first few drips, which are always stronger than the rest.

Chocolate is, of course, one of the main ingredients in confectionery (page 16), but grated eating chocolate can also be added in small quantities as a flavouring to such sweets as fudge.

Alcohols

The concentrated flavours of spirits and liqueurs make them ideal last-minute additions for flavouring sweets. Rum and cognac go well with chocolate confections, and fruit liqueurs such as Grand Marnier or apricot brandy will bring out the flavour of fruit confections.

Flower water

Rose-water and orange-flower water are obtained by distilling the blossoms: the "waters" are solutions of the flowers' essential oils. They are fragrant but light flavourings, best suited to delicate confections such as marshmallows (page 40). They can also be used to perfume nougat and fruit pastes, and they have a natural affinity with crystallized flowers.

Extracting Colour from Spinach

1 **Pounding spinach to a pulp.** Remove the stems from spinach leaves. Wash the leaves thoroughly and dry them. Put the leave into a mortar and, with a wooden pestle, pound them (*above, left*) until they form a paste (*above, right*).

2 **Preparing a muslin sieve.** Fold a sheet of muslin into a 30 cm (12 inch) double-layered square. Drape it over a shallow dish and spoon the pulp into it (*above*). Fold the muslin to enclose the spinach.

3 **Wringing out the juices.** Grasp the ends of the muslin and twist the cloth to squeeze the spinach, so that the spinach juice flows into the dish (*above*).

4 **Heating the juice.** Pour the juice into a small, heavy pan and set it over a low heat. After a minute or two, stir the juice to see if it has separated into solid matter and watery liquid (*above*).

5 **Straining the extract.** Pour the juice through a fine sieve over a bowl (*above*). Use the solid matter that collects in the sieve to colour cooked pastes such as fondant or marzipan; discard the liquid.

Dissolving Powdered Saffron

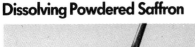

Dissolving the saffron. If you are using saffron threads, dry them out on a baking sheet in a very slow oven for 10 minutes, then pound the dried threads into powder using a pestle and mortar. Put a pinch of powdered saffron into a small shallow dish. Add a teaspoon of cold water (*above*) and stir the mixture until the powder dissolves.

Flavouring Sugar with Vanilla

Distributing flavour evenly. Fill a jar about a quarter full with sugar—here, castor sugar—and stand the pod upright in the sugar. Add more sugar (*above*) until the jar is full. Cover tightly. After a week or two, the sugar will be imbued with flavour. As the sugar is used up, pour more sugar into the jar. The vanilla pod will flavour the sugar for months.

Picking the Right Kind of Chocolate

After sugar, chocolate is perhaps the most valuable and versatile ingredient in confectionery. Melted chocolate alone can be set in polished moulds and decorated, or employed as a coating to enhance other confections. Simply softened and flavoured, chocolate also provides a variety of rich creams and pastes.

Chocolate is a highly processed product, obtained from the beans of the cacao tree. It consists of a combination of cocoa solids and cocoa butter, usually sweetened during manufacture and sometimes mixed with milk or flavourings. A high proportion of cocoa butter—a very hard fat—yields a product with a good flavour and an appealingly brittle texture.

But cocoa butter is an unstable substance made up of a number of individual fats that melt and set at different temperatures. To be melted and set successfully, chocolate with a high proportion of cocoa butter needs to be tempered—a process of repeated heating and cooling that stabilizes the fats. Tempering is too exact-

ing to be performed in the home kitchen. For this reason (and also for economy), manufacturers substitute other, softer vegetable fats for some of the cocoa butter in most chocolate. The more replacement fats in the finished product, the softer it will be and the poorer its flavour.

The hardest chocolate, known as *couverture*, is used only by professional confectioners, since it requires tempering. The various brands of eating chocolate are next in hardness; most contain some replacement fats and all are easy to use for home sweet-making. Milk chocolate is much softer than so-called plain chocolate—that is, chocolate containing no milk. Manufacturers also produce a variety of softer types of chocolate for use in confectionery and baking. Light and dark dipping chocolate, comparable in flavour to milk and plain eating chocolate, are good-quality types of soft chocolate that can be bought from trade suppliers in blocks of about 500 g (1 lb). Baking chocolate is more easily available in shops, but is very soft and greasy, with a poor fla-

vour, and not suitable for confectionery.

The two types of chocolate used in this book are plain eating chocolate and dark dipping chocolate. Eating chocolate can be easily grated (*box, right*) to provide flavouring and also decoration for finished confections. It melts to a thick paste that can either be permanently softened by adding butter or cream (*pages 64-67*) or piped from a small bag to make decorations that will set hard (*below*).

Melted eating chocolate is too thick for coating confection centres and for moulding. Dipping chocolate, made specially for such purposes, melts to a thin consistency and sets with a glossy surface. Before heating it, cut it into pieces (*box, centre right*) so that it melts easily.

Cocoa powder, consisting of the same ingredients as chocolate but with much less cocoa butter, makes an excellent dry coating for sticky bars and sweets, such as truffles (*page 66*). Since cocoa powder often forms lumps in the tin, it should be sieved before use (*box, far right*).

Creating a Miniature Piping Bag of Paper

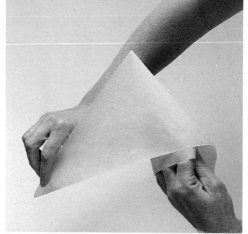

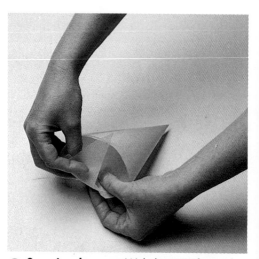

1 **Cutting out the paper.** Cut a rectangle of greaseproof paper 20 by 25 cm (8 by 10 inches). Cut the rectangle of paper in half diagonally: only one triangle will be needed for the bag. Hold the triangle with the right angle at the bottom left-hand side. Take the bottom right-hand corner in your left hand and the top corner in your right hand (*above*).

2 **Shaping a cone.** Bring your right hand down behind your left hand so that the paper begins to make a cone over the fingers of your left hand (*above*). The point of the cone should be about half way down the longest side of the triangle.

3 **Securing the cone.** With the cone formed, the corner held in your right hand will protrude below the cone's lower edge. Tuck this tail up inside the cone (*above*). Make two small tears, through all the layers of paper, at right angles to the folded edge. To prevent the paper from unwinding, fold up the paper between the tears to the inside.

Hard Chocolate for Flavouring

Grating eating chocolate. Chill a bar of eating chocolate so that it is firm and will grate easily. Break the bar into small pieces and grate them finely over a tray placed to catch all the shreds.

A Softer Type for Dipping

Cutting dipping chocolate. With a sharp, heavy knife, cut the chocolate into small pieces so it can be evenly melted. Dipping chocolate is fairly soft and will easily fragment when cut (*above*).

Cocoa Powder for Coating

Sieving the powder. Spoon the powder into a fine-meshed metal sieve held over a bowl. Tap the sides of the sieve firmly with your hand (*above*) until all the powder has fallen through. For a sweeter powder, mix icing sugar with the cocoa and sieve them together.

4 **Fitting a nozzle.** To pipe fine lines (*page 76*), simply snip off the tip of the bag. To pipe decorative shapes such as shells, choose a nozzle of the pattern you want: here a star is used. Snip off the end of the cone so there is just room for the head of the nozzle to come through (*above*). Insert the nozzle and check that it fits securely. If necessary, cut off more paper.

5 **Filling the bag.** Melt some chocolate by breaking it into pieces and putting it in a bowl set over hot water. Stir occasionally until the chocolate is thoroughly melted and smooth. To thicken the chocolate for piping, stir in a few drops of cold water. Spoon the mixture into the piping bag (*above*), not more than two-thirds full.

6 **Piping the chocolate.** Bring the edges of the cone together at the top. Fold the edges over so the bag is securely closed. Pipe out the chocolate—here, the bag is squeezed gently and moved slightly forwards to make a rounded shape with a tail. Each shape slightly overlaps the previous one, producing a string of shells. Work quickly—the mixture sets rapidly.

Choosing and Preparing Moulds

When confections are set as slabs, you must choose moulds that will accommodate the size of the batch. For most recipes, a straight-sided tin, 20 cm (8 inches) square, will do. Larger batches, or thin confections, may require a tin 30 by 20 cm (12 by 8 inches).

If you make confections regularly, you may want to invest in a set of four confectioner's bars. These can be arranged to form a barrier of variable dimensions for any confection. Made of iron or stainless steel about 2.5 cm (1 inch) thick and 5 cm (2 inches) wide, the two pairs of bars usually measure 50 cm (20 inches) and 25 cm (10 inches) respectively. The shorter pair is placed in between and at right angles to the longer pair. One short bar can then be moved back or forth to enclose a rectangle of the required size. Confectioner's bars are best made to order by an ironmonger. They are usually more costly than tins, but for consistently professional results, they are a worthwhile investment.

Because all confections are sticky, any container will have to be prepared in advance for easy unmoulding. The preparation will depend on the type of sweet.

If a mixture is to be cut in its mould, as is toffee (*page 30*) or fudge (*page 38*), just butter or oil the container. Almond oil, mild and slightly sweet, is best; but any flavourless vegetable oil will do.

Flexible sweets such as caramels (*page 32*), are more easily cut after they have been removed from the mould: a lining of oiled greaseproof paper will make it easier for you to unmould the slab without damaging it. In tins, the paper should be tailored for a neat fit (*right, above*). With bars, the paper is simply placed underneath (*opposite page, above*) and the paper and inside edges of the bars are oiled.

A container for fruit jelly (*page 52*) need only be dampened with cold water (*right*). The water forms a film between the mould's surface and the jelly, and the set confection unmoulds neatly.

Some sweets, particularly marshmallows (*page 40*), still have slightly moist surfaces after setting. Dust the tin or the space enclosed by bars with cornflour and icing sugar (*far right*). The sweetened cornflour forms a barely perceptible crust on the confection.

A Paper Lining to Aid Unmoulding

1 **Lining a tin.** Cut greaseproof or wax paper into a rectangle about 2.5 cm (1 inch) wider and longer than the tin. Centre the tin on top of the rectangle of paper. With scissors, cut a diagonal slit from each corner of the paper to the corner of the tin (*above*).

2 **Folding the paper.** Place the paper inside the tin. Crease the paper along the inside edges of the tin; neatly fold and overlap each trimmed corner (*above*), tucking the flaps under the paper. Lightly brush the paper with almond oil or melted butter. Do not trim off any paper above the sides of the tin; it can be used as a handle to lift out the set confection.

A Film of Water for Jellies

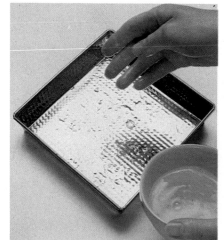

Dampening a tin. Choose a tin large enough for the quantity of jelly you have prepared. Fill a bowl with cold water. To speckle the tin lightly and evenly with water, dip the fingers of one hand into the water and flick your fingertips all over the inside of the tin.

A Dusting of Sugared Cornflour

1 **Oiling the tin.** With a pastry brush or your fingertips, apply a light film of almond oil to the sides and bottom of a tin. Take care to coat all the corners and sides of the tin so that no portion of the confection can stick.

An Adjustable Frame of Metal Bars

1 **Positioning the bars.** Lay a rectangle of paper—in this case, greaseproof paper—on a marble work surface. Position the two bars on top of the paper, parallel to each other. Between them, insert the two shorter bars (*above*); gauging by eye, place the short bars at a distance from each other determined by the volume of paste or syrup to be set and the thickness desired.

2 **Oiling the bars.** With a pastry brush, apply a mild-flavoured oil—almond oil is used in this demonstration—to the inside edges of the confectioner's bars. If you are unsure of where the shorter, adjusting bar must be positioned, oil the entire length of the longer bars. Brush the area of paper bordered by the bars.

2 **Applying cornflour and sugar.** In a bowl, stir together equal quantities of cornflour and icing sugar. Fill a fine-meshed sieve with the mixture. Tap the sieve against the heel of your hand to sprinkle the mixture generously over the bottom of the tin.

3 **Tilting the tin.** Pick up the tin with both hands. Tilt and shake it in all directions so that the mixture of cornflour and sugar is evenly distributed over the bottom and sides of the tin.

4 **Tipping out excess powder.** Place a sheet of paper on the work surface. Invert the tin and tap the bottom to release excess cornflour and icing sugar. Form the paper into a funnel and tip the excess cornflour and sugar into a jar for storage.

1

Boiled Sugar Sweets
Diverse Textures
from Simple Syrups

Clear, hard confections from hot syrups
Pulling and twisting a rope of syrup
Stirring for softness
The versatility of fondant
Incorporating cream and butter
Nougat thick with honey and nuts

Worked in a figure-of-eight to ensure even beating, a soft-ball sugar syrup begins to grain, becoming opaque and acquiring the thick consistency of fondant (*page 34*). After kneading and a resting period, the fondant can be flavoured, coloured and shaped in many ways, or used as an ingredient in other assembled confections.

A plain syrup of sugar and water is the base for an extraordinary variety of sweets—ranging from snowy fondants and pillow-soft marshmallows to glassy sticks of barley sugar. Some of this variety depends on differences in the degree to which the syrup is boiled (*pages 10-11*): a firm-ball syrup, for example, yields chewy caramels, while a syrup boiled to the hard-crack stage acquires the brittle texture needed for lollipops and barley sugar. But the temperature of the syrup is only one variable. The range of confections is further enlarged by different ways of handling the syrup as it sets, and by other ingredients added to the syrup.

Lollipops (*page 22*) are the simplest boiled sugar sweets, in terms of both ingredients and handling. Flavoured simply with fruit juice and poured out in small pools, the syrup sets rapidly to a jewel-like confection. Toffees (*page 30*) and caramels (*page 32*) contain more substantial additions such as cream, honey and butter, but are still merely cooked, poured and left to set undisturbed.

Simple manipulation can effect remarkable changes in a cooked syrup. The traditional corkscrew shape of barley sugar (*page 24*) results from nothing more than cutting and twisting a poured, hard-crack syrup at the crucial moment of pliability just before it sets. A syrup that is slightly softer—hence pliable for longer—can be repeatedly pulled, folded and twisted so that it incorporates tiny air bubbles, becomes lighter in colour and takes on an opaque satin sheen (*pages 26-29*).

Extensive handling can cause a sugar syrup to crystallize or "grain" and acquire a soft, crumbly texture. For pulled confections, graining is only avoided by cooking the syrup to a fairly high temperature—so that it becomes too viscous to crystallize readily—and by adding a generous amount of an interfering agent such as liquid glucose. But for some confections, notably fudge and fondant, graining is deliberately induced by beating a syrup cooked to a relatively low temperature; a small amount of interfering agent may be added to help regulate crystal size.

Soft, light marshmallows (*page 40*) have a texture very different from that of any other boiled sugar sweets; this results from incorporating air, through the agency of beaten egg whites, into a mixture of hard-ball syrup and gelatine. Nougat (*page 42*) is also aerated with egg whites, but the mixture is weighted down as it sets, to produce a more compact confection.

Lollipops in Bright, Sparkling Colours

The simplest boiled sugar sweets are made by cooking syrup to the hard-crack stage (*pages 10-11*), then dropping it in small pools on to an oiled, cold surface—a baking sheet or, preferably, a marble slab. The syrup sets rapidly into hard, sparklingly clear discs of candy. The most popular manifestation of such "dropped sweets" is lollipops (*right; recipe, page 89*). Sticks are set into the pools of syrup as they cool, providing handles with which to hold the lollipops for eating. Smaller discs, without sticks, make equally attractive confections (*box, right, below*).

A hard-crack syrup contains a negligible amount of moisture—two per cent or less—and dropped sweets will readily absorb any moisture from the atmosphere. It is wise, therefore, to make them only on very dry days, otherwise they may fail to set properly and remain sticky.

You can flavour and colour dropped sweets in any way you like (*page 14*), but it is best to choose ingredients that preserve the syrup's sparkle and clarity. In this demonstration, pure, clear juice extracted from raspberries is used. The fruit is heated to draw out the juice; then the juice is strained to remove any pulp that might cloud the syrup. Finally, the juice is boiled with the sugar to make the syrup. You could use other fruit juices to flavour and colour dropped sweets in the same way. Or an ordinary sugar and water syrup can be coloured before cooking and then flavoured, just before pouring, with any concentrated flavouring extract.

When cooking a syrup with juice, you should follow the same procedure as that used for making a syrup with water (*page 8*). To guard against crystallization, glucose is included in the syrup. To prevent graining as the syrup comes to the boil, cover the pan or use a damp brush to wipe any sugar off the sides of the pan; do not stir once the sugar has dissolved.

As soon as the dropped syrup has set hard, the sweets are ready to eat. If you wish to store them, they should be individually wrapped in non-porous material. Cellophane, which does not mask their brilliant colours, is the most attractive wrapper, but sturdy wax paper will also serve. To store the lollipops, pack them in an airtight jar or tin.

1 Preparing the fruit juice. In a small, heavy pan, gently heat soft fruit—here, raspberries—until the juice separates; there is no need to stir. To strain out the juice, set a fine-meshed sieve on top of a bowl and pour the fruit through (*above*). Let the fruit drain without pressing it.

2 Combining the ingredients. Put sugar and glucose in a heavy pan and add the strained juice. Put the pan over a medium heat and stir (*above*) until the sugar dissolves; to dissolve any crystals that form and prevent the syrup crystallizing, cover the pan for a minute or two or brush the sides with a dampened pastry brush.

Fruit Drops: an Alternative Presentation

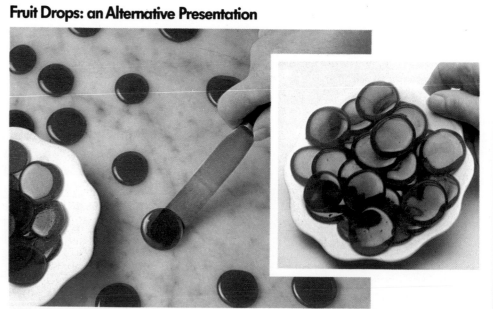

Lifting the set sweets. Prepare a flavoured hard-crack syrup (*Steps 1 to 3, above*). Lightly oil a marble work surface. With a teaspoon, pour out small pools of syrup—about 2.5 cm (1 inch) across—on to the marble. Leave the syrup to cool and set hard. When the drops are cold, use a spatula to loosen them from the marble (*above*); then lift the sweets one by one. If they are to be served at once, pile them on a plate (*inset*). For storage, wrap them individually in cellophane.

3 **Boiling the syrup.** When the sugar has dissolved, place a sugar thermometer in the pan. Without stirring, bring the syrup to a rolling boil and continue boiling until it reaches 143° to 149°C (290° to 300°F)—the hard-crack stage. To arrest the cooking, take the saucepan off the heat at once and dip the base in cold water.

4 **Spooning out the syrup.** Lightly oil a marble slab or other cold work surface. With a tablespoon, pour out four pools of syrup, making them large or small, as you like—in this case, about 5 cm (2 inches) across (*above*). While the syrup is still soft, push a paper or wooden lollipop stick into each drop. Continue to pour four pools at a time, until only a little syrup is left.

5 **Securing the sticks.** To make sure the sticks are firmly secured in the sweets, spoon a few drops of the remaining syrup over the embedded end of each stick. Leave the drops to cool and set hard.

6 **Wrapping the lollipops.** Using a metal spatula, carefully loosen the set lollipops from the oiled surface; lift them up by their sticks. To prevent the lollipops becoming sticky, wrap each one in a rectangle of cellophane (*above and right*). □

Twisted Sticks of Barley Sugar

If hard-crack syrup is poured out in a large pool, there is a brief period during its cooling when the syrup is flexible enough to be folded, cut and twisted. The syrup will then set hard in whatever shape it has been given—be it simple sticks or complicated loops or twists. With a modicum of speed and dexterity, you can fashion the syrup into such handsome sweets as the corkscrew-shaped barley sugar demonstrated here.

Barley sugar is so called because the syrup is sometimes made with water in which pearl barley has cooked—giving the twisted sticks a milky appearance and mellow flavour (*recipe, page 88*). The barley sugar prepared here uses a simpler mixture of sugar and plain water, flavoured with the juice and rind of a lemon (*recipe, page 88*). To produce a brighter lemon colour the syrup may include a very small pinch of saffron. You can also, of course, use alternative flavourings and colourings (*page 14*).

The syrup begins to solidify as soon as it is poured out on to the cold work surface. While it is still warm enough to adhere securely to itself, two opposite sides of the pool are gently lifted and folded to meet in the middle. The result is a double thickness for more substantial sticks.

The folded sheet of syrup must then be cut and shaped at once, before it becomes too brittle. For speed, it is advisable to have someone assisting you, to twist the strips as you cut them. Even if the sheet does solidify before you have finished cutting, however, it need not be wasted. Once hardened, it snaps easily and can be broken into irregular pieces instead of being shaped into sticks.

1 Dissolving the sugar. In a heavy pan, put sugar, glucose and water; for a more intense colour, add powdered saffron dissolved in warm water (*page 15*). Put the pan over a medium heat and, with a wooden spoon, stir until the sugar has completely dissolved. Add thinly pared lemon rind to the syrup (*above*).

2 Adding lemon juice. Put a thermometer in the syrup. Boil the syrup to 116°C (240°F)—the soft-ball stage (*pages 10-11*). Add lemon juice (*above*). Continue to boil the syrup until it reaches 154°C (310°F)—the hard-crack stage. Dip the pan in iced water to arrest cooking. With a fork, lift out the rind.

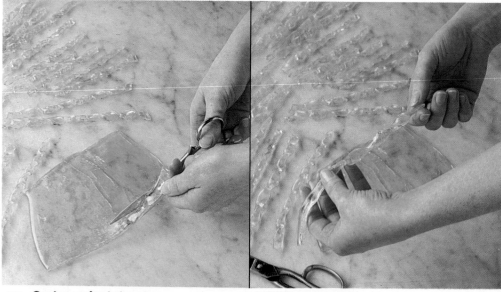

5 Cutting and twisting. As soon as the sheet is folded, use the oiled spatula to free the underside from the work surface. With oiled kitchen scissors, cut the sheet crosswise into strips about 1 cm (½ inch) wide (*above, left*). The unfolded edges of the sheet will harden before the centre does, so cut the strips alternately from opposite ends of the sheet. As each strip is cut, take its ends between your fingers and twist it into a corkscrew-shaped stick (*above, right*).

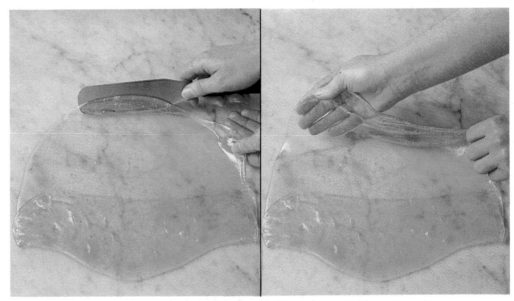

3 **Pouring out the syrup.** Lightly coat a marble work surface with oil. Hold the pan of syrup low over the work surface and tip it slowly; the syrup will spread out into a shallow pool (*above*).

4 **Folding the syrup.** Leave the syrup to cool for a few minutes until it hardens around the edges and a slight skin forms on the surface. Oil a metal spatula to prevent the syrup from sticking to it and use the spatula to ease one edge of the sheet away from the work surface (*above, left*). With your hands, pull up the edge and fold it over to the middle of the sheet of syrup; take care to lay it down evenly to avoid wrinkling it (*above, right*). Immediately fold the opposite edge over to meet the first flap in the middle.

6 **Serving the confections.** Leave the sticks to set hard. For immediate presentation, arrange them in a glass container that shows off their colour and clarity (*right*). To store them and prevent them from sticking together, put the sweets in an airtight container, wrapped individually in cellophane or placed in single layers between greaseproof or wax paper.□

Pulling a Syrup for a Satiny Texture

Repeatedly pulled into a rope, folded and twisted, a hot syrup incorporates many tiny bubbles of air. The bubbles give the syrup an opaque, satiny sheen and a more open texture than lollipops or barley sugar (*pages 22-25*). Here, a syrup flavoured with peppermint is pulled into a satiny rope, then cut with scissors to produce small cushion-like confections.

To make pulled confections, the syrup should be cooked to the soft-crack or the hard-ball stage. A soft-crack syrup is used here: it will cool to brittle confections known as humbugs. A hard-ball syrup will yield a stickier result, the starting point for other sweets, such as Edinburgh rock (*recipe, page 103*). A syrup cooked to any lower temperature would yield too sticky a sweet. A hotter syrup—the hard-crack syrup used for lollipops—is occasionally recommended for pulled sweets but it hardens so fast that it limits the amount of pulling possible.

The extensive handling that the syrup undergoes makes it liable to crystallize, acquiring a crumbly, chalky texture. For certain sweets—Edinburgh rock, for example—this is the intended result. But for humbugs, precautions against crystallization must be taken to achieve a hard, glossy confection. The main precautions are to make the confections only in dry weather and to add plenty of liquid glucose to the syrup. You can also guard against crystallization by making sure the syrup cools evenly: as the syrup cools, begin to turn it with a scraper so that the edges do not cool before the centre.

Because the syrup cools quickly, you must pick it up and start pulling it as soon as you can handle it. But take care not to get burnt: a syrup that is tolerably cool on the surface may still be scorching hot underneath. Oil your hands well to prevent the syrup sticking to them and pick it up with caution, dropping it if it is too hot.

You can repeat the sequence of pulling, folding and twisting as often as you like until the syrup hardens. The twisting helps to keep the syrup in a cohesive mass, but it drives out some of the air incorporated during pulling. The less you twist the syrup strands, the more of the air incorporated during pulling will remain.

1 Turning the syrup. Cook a sugar syrup to the soft-crack stage (*pages 8-10*). Add a few drops of peppermint extract. Using a spiral motion, rapidly pour the syrup on to an oiled work surface. Let the syrup cool until a skin forms—a minute or so. With an oiled metal scraper, turn up the edges of the pool and fold them into the centre.

2 The first stretching. Continue turning the syrup until it is just cool enough to handle. Oil your hands to prevent the syrup from sticking to them. Lift up the syrup with the aid of the scraper, and push the syrup into a sausage shape. Then stretch it between your hands; it will still be very soft and will sag in the middle when pulled.

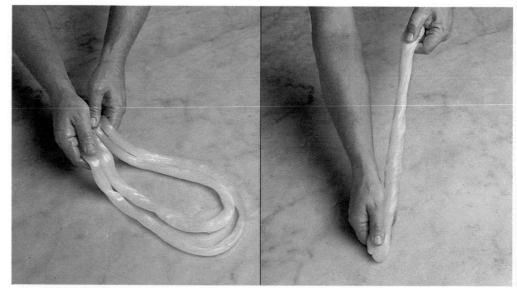

4 The final pulling. The pulled syrup will change from yellowish and translucent to an opaque, creamy white. (If the syrup hardens before it has turned opaque, or crystallizes during pulling, you can rescue it by putting it in a pan with a few spoonfuls of water and liquid glucose, dissolving it over low heat, then boiling it again to the same temperature as before.) To give the rope an even shape, fold it in two and then fold it again (*above, left*). Gently twist the four strands together. Pull the strands again, twisting them gently as you pull, to make a long, thin rope (*above, right*).

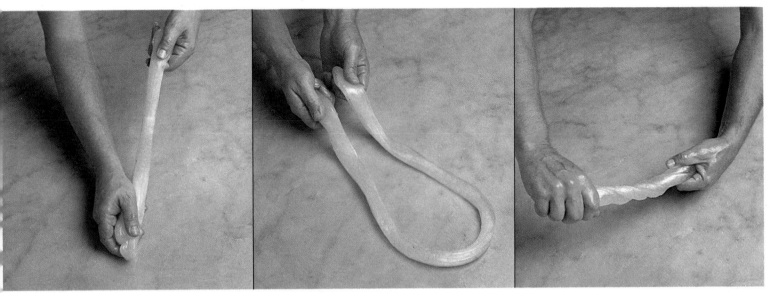

3 **Pulling and twisting.** Gather the syrup back together and continue pulling until it begins to harden and holds its shape when stretched (*above, left*). Fold the pulled syrup in two (*above, centre*) and twist the two halves together. Pull the twisted syrup (*above, right*) to make a long, even rope about 1 cm (½ inch) in diameter. Continue to fold, twist and pull the syrup for as long as it is supple—up to 20 minutes.

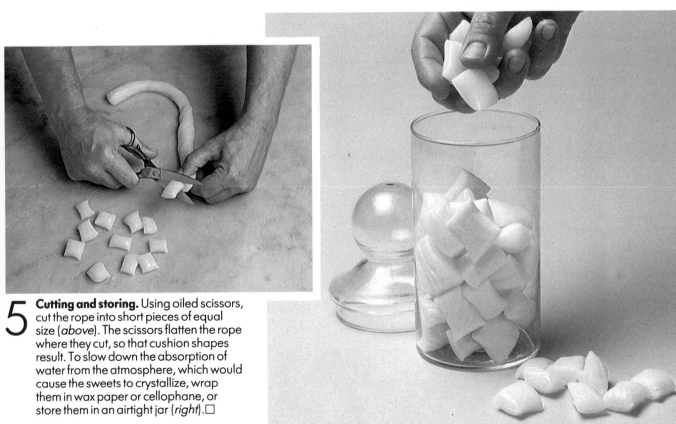

5 **Cutting and storing.** Using oiled scissors, cut the rope into short pieces of equal size (*above*). The scissors flatten the rope where they cut, so that cushion shapes result. To slow down the absorption of water from the atmosphere, which would cause the sweets to crystallize, wrap them in wax paper or cellophane, or store them in an airtight jar (*right*).□

Patterns from Pulled Syrup Combinations

Stretched into ropes or sheets and twisted together, syrups of two different colours yield confections patterned with swirling stripes (*recipes, pages 100-101*). To achieve the contrast, you can exploit the change in a syrup's colour after it has been repeatedly pulled and twisted (*page 26*).

The brown and buff confections in the demonstration on the right have as their starting point a single syrup made from brown sugar. Half the syrup is pulled and twisted until it lightens in colour. The other half is pulled just enough to fashion it into an even rope; it remains deep brown. You can achieve a similar two-tone effect if you pull half a syrup tinted with fruit juice or a colouring agent.

To obtain a stronger contrast of colours, make two syrups—one coloured and one plain. Pull the plain syrup to make it opaque and pearly, but leave the coloured syrup translucent. For the bull's-eyes shown below, a rope of raspberry syrup is enclosed within a sheet of plain pulled syrup; when the combination is twisted, cut and rolled between the palms, gaily patterned spheres result.

Smartly Striped Humbugs

 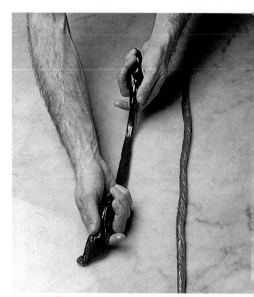

1 **Turning the syrup.** Cook a brown sugar syrup to the soft-crack stage (*pages 8-10*). Pour the syrup out in two pools on an oiled work surface. As the syrup cools, turn up the edges of the pools from time to time with an oiled metal scraper and fold the edges into the centre. Oil your hands well and push one of the pools of syrup into a sausage shape.

2 **Pulling the sugar syrup.** Pull and twist the sausage until it becomes an opaque, creamy brown with a satin finish. Fold the sausage over twice lengthwise to make four strands. Twist the strands together, pulling gently to make a long, even rope (*above*). Scoop up the remaining syrup and push it into a sausage; then pull it into a rope the same size as the first.

Bull's-Eyes with Contrasting Swirls

 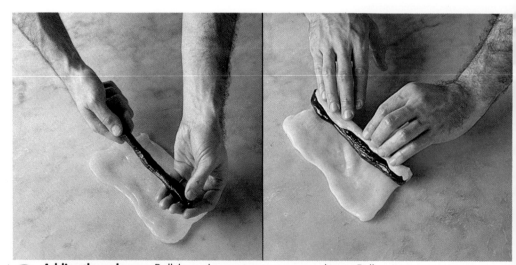

1 **Pulling white syrup.** Make two syrups, one with water and the other with fruit juice—here, raspberry juice. Cook them to the soft-crack stage (*pages 8-10*). Pour them in separate pools on to an oiled work surface. Fold over the edges of the red syrup and let it cool. Pull the plain syrup until it becomes white, satiny and opaque; then stretch it into an oblong.

2 **Adding the red syrup.** Roll the red syrup into a sausage shape. Pull the sausage gently until it is the same length as the sheet of white syrup (*above, left*). Place the red sausage on one long edge of the white syrup sheet. Fold the edge over the sausage (*above, right*) and roll up the sheet so that the sausage is wrapped inside.

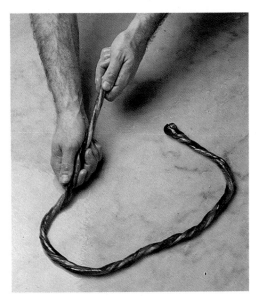

3 **Combining the two ropes.** Lay the two ropes of contrasting colour side by side. Beginning at one end, loosely twist the two strands together (*above*). Then fold the rope over and twist again, to make a short, fat rope of alternating colours.

4 **Pulling and twisting.** Pull the rope gently but firmly, beginning at one end and working your way along its length; use a slight twisting motion as you pull. Work quickly but carefully until you have a long, thin rope with an even cross-section.

5 **Cutting the rope.** Using a pair of scissors with oiled blades, cut a small piece off the end of the rope. Give the rope a half turn towards you and cut again to produce a shape with triangular faces. Continue turning and cutting. Store the confections in an airtight container. □

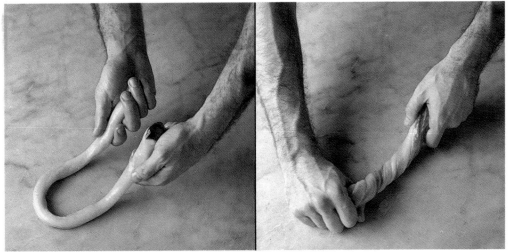

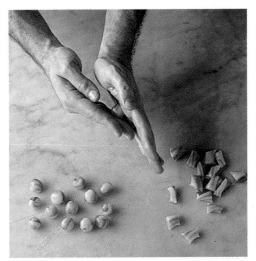

3 **Pulling and twisting.** Pull the wrapped cylinder into a rope and, holding the rope by either end, fold the rope in two (*above, left*). Gently twist the two strands together. Pull the twisted rope gently but firmly (*above, right*) to make an evenly sized rope about 45 cm (18 inches) long, of alternating red and white.

4 **Rolling bull's-eyes.** Using oiled scissors, slice short, equal-sized pieces off the rope. Pinch down the sharp edges of each piece with your fingers and then roll each piece between your palms into a ball. Each ball will have a swirling pattern of red and white. Wrap the bull's-eyes individually in wax paper or cellophane and store them in an airtight jar. □

Additions to a Basic Syrup

Additions to a basic sugar syrup (*page 8*) can go far beyond small quantities of flavourings and colourings; many confections owe their character and texture to the incorporation of generous amounts of other ingredients. Adding a large proportion of butter to a crack-stage syrup, for example, produces a smooth, opaque toffee (*recipes, pages 89-90*). Nuts turn a caramel into the crunchy confection generally known as nut brittle (*opposite page, below; recipe, page 167*).

The richness of a toffee is determined by the amount of butter you include. Among the richest mixtures is the aptly named butter toffee or butterscotch demonstrated here (*recipe, page 90*). Such confections are best appreciated in small, bite-sized pieces. In order to make neat rectangles, the cooked syrup is poured into a buttered tin and scored with a knife while it is still soft. As soon as the mixture has set, the toffee is easily broken along the score lines.

In a brittle, the nuts may make up more than half the confection's total weight. You can select whatever nuts you like: whole, small nuts such as hazelnuts, almonds, cashew nuts or the peanuts used here; or chopped pieces of larger nuts such as brazil nuts or walnuts. Whatever the choice, skin the nuts and warm them for 5 minutes in a 180°C (350°F or Mark 4) oven: if cold nuts are added to a hot syrup, the syrup may begin to congeal and set too quickly to be poured in a thin sheet.

To accentuate the brittleness of the confection, it should be formed into as thin a sheet as possible. To this end, the hot mixture of syrup and nuts is poured straight out on to a cold surface. As soon as the edges of the syrup are firm enough to handle, the sheet is carefully stretched from all sides. Once cooled, the brittle is easily snapped into jagged serving pieces.

Melting in the Flavour of Butter

1 **Adding butter.** Pour cold water into a heavy pan. Add sugar—Demerara is used here for its mellow flavour, but you could substitute white sugar. Cut butter into cubes and add them to the pan (*above*). Put the pan over a medium heat.

2 **Stirring the syrup.** With a wooden spoon, stir the syrup constantly (*above*) until the butter is melted and the sugar dissolved. Remove the spoon and place a sugar thermometer in the saucepan; boil the syrup to 143°C (290°F)—the soft-crack stage (*page 10*). Take the pan off the heat and dip it in cold water to arrest cooking.

6 **Wrapping the toffees.** Run a sharp knife round the edges of the tin to loosen the toffee. Invert the tin and, if necessary, rap the bottom to release the toffee. Lift away the tin (*above, left*). Snap the toffee into pieces along the score lines. Cut wax paper into squares roughly twice the length of the toffee pieces. To keep the pieces from sticking together, fold each toffee in paper and twist the ends (*above*). Store the wrapped toffees in an airtight jar or tin.□

3 **Adding lemon juice.** If you like, add a teaspoonful of lemon juice (*above*) or a few drops of lemon extract to flavour the toffee. The already frothy syrup will foam up with the addition of the liquid, but the foam will subside again after the syrup is poured. Do not stir the mixture—stirring might make the syrup crystallize.

4 **Pouring out the toffee.** Have ready a buttered or oiled tin (*page 18*) large enough to contain the mixture in a thin layer. Pour the toffee into the tin (*above*). It will be fluid enough to spread evenly.

5 **Scoring the toffee.** Leave the toffee to set slightly: it should be firm enough not to flow when the tin is tilted, but should still feel warm to the touch. With a sharp knife, score the toffee into 2.5 cm (1 inch) strips. Score at right angles to the strips to make rectangles slightly wider than they are long (*above*). Leave in a cool place to set.

Producing a Nut-Packed Brittle

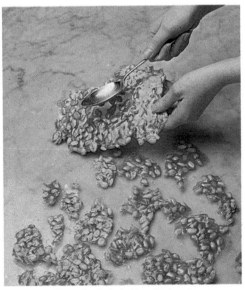

1 **Adding nuts to caramel.** Shell a generous quantity of nuts—peanuts are used here. Skin the nuts (*page 12*) and place them on a baking sheet in the oven to warm. Cook a sugar syrup to a light caramel (*pages 8-11*) and tip the warmed nuts into the caramel (*above*). Stir gently to combine the nuts and the caramel.

2 **Stretching the brittle.** Tip the mixture on to a cold, oiled marble slab or baking sheet. Spread it evenly with an oiled spatula. Coat your hands with oil or butter; when the edges of the syrup are cool enough to handle, grasp one edge and pull it. Continue round the edges until the sheet is too thin to stretch further.

3 **Dividing the brittle.** Let the brittle set hard. Break it into pieces by lifting the sheet and sharply rapping it at intervals with the back of a spoon (*above*). Store the pieces of brittle in an airtight tin, packed in single layers between sheets of greaseproof or wax paper.□

Caramels Enriched with Cream

Caramels—boiled sugar confections that are enriched with milk or cream—get their characteristic mellow flavour and brown colour from a reaction between milk protein and sugar, and from the caramelization of lactose, a form of sugar naturally present in milk products. Lactose caramelizes at a lower temperature than ordinary sugar—at the firm-ball stage (*pages 10-11*). Because the cooking is arrested at an earlier stage than with most toffees, caramels remain relatively moist and set to a chewy consistency.

The moistness of the caramel will vary, however, depending on the temperature it reaches within the firm to hard-ball range. The lower the temperature, the softer the finished caramels will be. If you want harder caramels, boil the syrup to a slightly higher temperature.

Because caramel contains a high proportion of milk products, it needs to be gently stirred from time to time as it cooks, to prevent it from sticking to the bottom of the pan and burning. The thick, creamy syrup resists graining, but to make sure that no crystallization occurs, you should include an interfering agent (*page 8*). In the demonstration on the right, honey is used (*recipe, page 97*).

Honey contributes its own flavour to the caramels. If you like, you can also heighten their flavour with a vanilla pod—used in this demonstration—or, at the end of cooking, you can add a concentrated flavouring (*page 14*), such as peppermint extract. Contrasting texture can be provided by chopped nuts or dried fruit, warmed in the oven and then stirred in at the end of cooking.

Once the caramel has been poured and set, it is easily cut into pieces. With harder caramel the pieces should be bite sized; softer, chewier caramels can be cut into larger pieces. Wrap the caramels immediately in cellophane or wax paper to prevent them from sticking together. Store them in a cool place, where they will keep for up to two weeks.

1 Melting syrup. Pour double cream into a heavy pan. Add granulated sugar, butter and honey. For extra flavour, add half a vanilla pod, split lengthwise. Put the pan over a medium heat. Using a wooden spoon, stir the mixture (*above*) until the butter melts and the sugar dissolves. Place a sugar thermometer in the pan.

2 Testing the consistency. Have ready a bowl of iced water. Stirring occasionally, boil the mixture to 121°C (250°F). Turn off the heat. Dip a spoonful of the syrup into the iced water. Pinch the cooled caramel (*above*) to judge its consistency; it should be just firm enough to mould (*page 11*). For a firmer caramel, boil the mixture a little longer and test again.

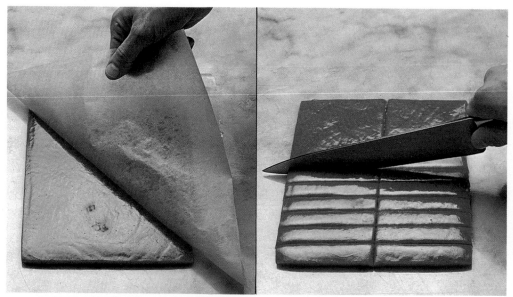

5 Cutting caramel pieces. Peel the greaseproof paper away from the caramel (*above, left*). Soak a piece of kitchen paper with oil and use it to wipe the blade of a heavy knife. Press down firmly on the back of the blade to cut the sheet of caramel in half lengthwise; oiling the blade after each cut, cut across the sheet of caramel to make strips about 2.5 cm (1 inch) wide (*above, right*).

3 **Pouring out the caramel.** Dip the bottom of the pan in the water to arrest cooking. Oil a large sheet of greaseproof paper and lay it on a cold surface—here, marble. Arrange oiled confectioner's bars (*page 19*) in the form of a rectangle on top of the paper. With a fork, remove the piece of vanilla pod from the pan of cooked caramel. Pour out the mixture (*above*) to fill the enclosed space; if necessary, adjust one of the shorter bars to accommodate the caramel.

4 **Unmoulding the caramel.** Leave the caramel to cool and set— about 2 hours. Pull away the bars (*above*); if necessary, use a sharp knife to free any caramel stuck to the bars. Oil another section of the work surface. Grasp two opposite sides of the paper beneath the set caramel and turn the caramel over on to the oiled surface.

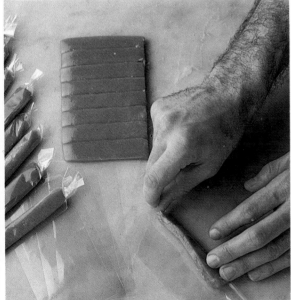

6 **Wrapping the caramels.** Cut cellophane into rectangles three times as wide as and 5 cm (2 inches) longer than the pieces of caramel. Align each caramel along a long edge of a rectangle of cellophane (*above*) and roll up the confection to enclose it. Twist shut the free ends of the cellophane. Pile the caramels on a serving plate (*right*).□

Fondant: a Sugar Paste with Many Uses

When a sugar syrup is cooked to the soft-ball stage (*pages 10-11*), cooled and then worked continuously, tiny sugar crystals form in it and the syrup gradually becomes a firm, snowy-white paste. The paste is known as fondant (*recipe, page 166*)—from the French word *fondre*, to melt—and its name is apt. Fondant has a rich, melting smoothness that makes it a classic confection in its own right, as well as an ingredient of endlessly varied assemblies and dipped confections.

As shown in the demonstration on the right, a fondant paste can be kneaded with concentrated colourings and flavourings, then moulded by hand into individual sweets (*page 36*). Another way to colour and flavour fondant is to melt it and stir in additional liquid ingredients (*page 37*), then pour the melted fondant into individual cups for moulding. In assemblies, hand-moulded fondant is often used as a stuffing for dried fruits (*page 72*) or as a dipped centre (*page 74*). Melted fondant can be poured into moulded chocolate cups (*page 86*) or provide a coating for dipped confections (*page 70*).

Whatever its ultimate use, the way in which fondant is made does not vary. Its texture is only achieved through several stages of careful preparation. This care begins with the addition of liquid glucose to the syrup ingredients; the glucose helps prevent large crystals from forming as the syrup cools and thus ensures that the fondant's texture is not gritty.

As the pool of syrup cools, it should be scooped up around its edges with a metal scraper and folded inwards so that the whole mass cools evenly. As soon as the syrup is glossy and viscous, it is stirred with the scraper or a wooden spatula; a figure-of-eight pattern (*Step 2*) ensures that the syrup grains evenly.

The fondant is next kneaded to make it smooth. It is then left for at least 12 hours to "ripen": its crystalline structure slowly changes and the fondant becomes softer and more pliant. The ripened fondant is then ready for use. However, there is no need to use it at once. Although it dries with prolonged exposure to air, fondant keeps almost indefinitely if it is stored in a sealed jar in the refrigerator.

1 **Cooling the syrup.** Lightly coat a marble slab or a large baking sheet with water. Cook a sugar syrup to 116°C (240°F)—the soft-ball stage (*pages 8-11*); dip the pan in cold water, then quickly pour out the syrup in a spiral on to the prepared surface. Leave to cool for a few minutes. With a dampened metal scraper, lift the edges of the syrup and fold them into the centre. Turn the syrup in this way briefly, just until it is glossy and viscous, with a yellow tinge.

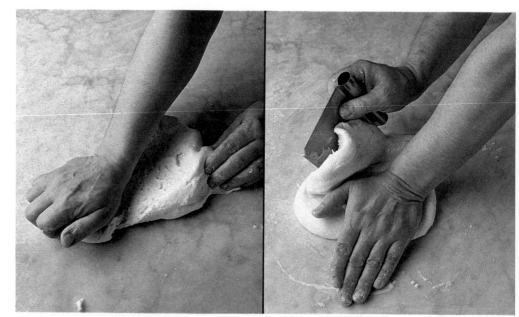

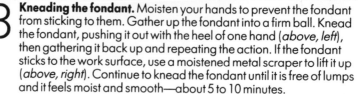

3 **Kneading the fondant.** Moisten your hands to prevent the fondant from sticking to them. Gather up the fondant into a firm ball. Knead the fondant, pushing it out with the heel of one hand (*above, left*), then gathering it back up and repeating the action. If the fondant sticks to the work surface, use a moistened metal scraper to lift it up (*above, right*). Continue to knead the fondant until it is free of lumps and it feels moist and smooth—about 5 to 10 minutes.

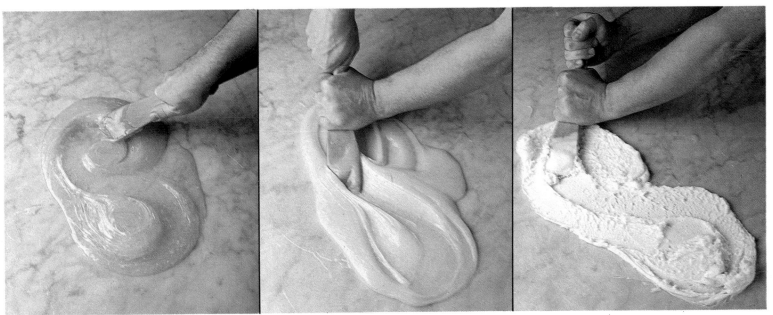

2 **Working the syrup.** Using a dampened wooden spatula, work the syrup continuously in a figure-of-eight (*above, left*). Continue in this way until the syrup becomes thick and opaque; as it stiffens, you will need both hands to push and pull the spatula (*above, centre*). Continue to work the syrup for 5 to 10 minutes, until it suddenly turns white, crumbly and too stiff to stir (*above, right*).

4 **Ripening the fondant.** Lightly moisten a plate with water so that the fondant will not stick to it; with your hands, mould the fondant into a ball and put it on the plate. Cover the fondant with a damp cloth to prevent the surface from drying. Leave it to ripen in a cool place or the refrigerator for at least 12 hours.

5 **Adding colouring.** Dust the work surface with icing sugar and put the ball of fondant on top. With your hands, press the fondant flat. Using a knife or a metal scraper, cut slits along the surface of the fondant and then spoon a concentrated colouring—here, spinach extract (*page 15*)—into the slits.

6 **Kneading in the colouring.** Sprinkle a flavouring extract—here, peppermint—over the fondant. Dust your hands with icing sugar to prevent the fondant from sticking to them; knead the fondant as shown in Step 3, until the colouring and flavouring are evenly distributed. ▶

7 **Rolling fondant balls.** Finely chop nuts—in this case, almonds and pistachio nuts (*page 12*). Spread out the chopped nuts on the work surface. One at a time, pull off small pieces of coloured and flavoured fondant and roll them between your fingers to shape them into neat balls (*above, left*). As each ball is shaped, gently roll it in the chopped nuts to coat it evenly (*above, right*).

8 **Serving the fondant balls.** Let the fondant balls rest on top of the nuts for at least 1 hour, to dry out slightly and firm up. Place each ball in an individual paper case (*above*). For immediate serving, arrange the confections on a plate (*right*). To store the fondant balls, place them in an airtight container, arranging them in single layers between sheets of wax paper. □

Flavoured Creams from Melted Fondant

1 **Melting the fondant.** Place already made fondant (*page 34, Steps 1 to 3*) in a pan with a pouring spout. In a larger pan, simmer water over a moderate heat. Put the small pan of fondant inside the larger pan: the water should reach as high as the top of the fondant. With a wooden spatula, stir until the fondant melts.

2 **Adding colouring and flavouring.** Add a colouring—here, a pinch of powdered saffron dissolved in water (*page 15*)—to the fondant. Add a flavouring—in this case, lemon extract—and stir well. If you use a more liquid flavouring, such as fruit juice, fruit purée or alcohol, it will dilute the fondant sufficiently for pouring and you may omit the liquid used in Step 3.

3 **Adding liquid.** A little at a time, stir in a measured amount of liquid—water, as here, or thin syrup (*page 8*). Place a sugar thermometer in the pan and continue stirring until the mixture reaches 60°C (140°F). At this temperature, the fondant will be fluid enough to pour and will set to a soft consistency; do not overheat the fondant or it will set too hard.

4 **Pouring out fondant.** Pour the fondant from the pan into individual paper cases (*above*): take care to pour into the centre of the cases or they may tip over. For decoration, press pecan nut halves into some of the fondants while they are still warm. Allow the fondants to cool before serving (*right*); store in an airtight tin.

Two Techniques for Fudge

Fudge, like fondant, is a sugar syrup cooked to the soft-ball stage, then beaten to make it grain. Fudge differs from fondant in that its syrup is enriched with milk, butter or cream. Any of a number of flavourings—among them coffee, chocolate, vanilla sugar and honey—can be included before cooking; nuts or candied fruit, folded in just after the fudge has been beaten, give variety of texture.

The diversity of fudges does not end with ingredients. Depending on how you prepare it, it can be either firm and grainy, like the chocolate fudge in the demonstration on the right, or soft and smooth, like the vanilla-flavoured milk fudge below (*recipes, page 107*).

For a firm fudge, the syrup should be beaten just after cooking; beaten while hot, the syrup forms large crystals, which produce a coarse, granular consistency.

For a smoother fudge, leave the cooked syrup to cool. As the syrup cools, it begins to crystallize on its own, forming smaller, more regular crystals. It is then beaten to complete this fine crystallization.

Beating While Hot for a Grainy Result

1 Adding chocolate. Put granulated sugar and milk into a heavy saucepan. Add butter and a flavouring—in this case, chopped plain chocolate (*page 17*). Put the saucepan over a medium heat.

2 Boiling the mixture. To help the sugar dissolve evenly and to combine all the ingredients, stir constantly with a wooden spoon. When the sugar has dissolved and both the butter and chocolate have melted, put a sugar thermometer in the pan (*above*). Bring the mixture to the boil and cook the syrup to 116°C (240°F), the soft-ball stage (*pages 10-11*).

Cooling and Beating for a Fine Texture

1 Heating the ingredients. In a heavy pan, gently heat milk, butter and vanilla sugar (*page 15*), stirring continuously with a wooden spoon until the butter has melted and the sugar has dissolved. Bring the mixture to the boil and cook it to 114°C (237°F), the soft-ball stage (*pages 10-11*).

2 Cooling and beating. Remove the pan from the heat. To arrest cooking, dip the base of the pan in cold water. Leave the mixture to cool to 50°C (122°F), at which point it will be viscous and opaque. Lightly butter a tin. Using a wooden spoon and tilting the pan, beat the syrup (*above, left*) until it thickens and turns paler (*above, right*).

3 **Beating the hot syrup.** To prevent further cooking, remove the pan from the heat and briefly dip its base in cold water. Using a wooden spoon, begin to beat the mixture immediately. To make the syrup deeper and therefore easier to beat, tilt the pan slightly while you work.

4 **Pouring out the fudge.** Continue to beat the syrup for several minutes until it grains and thickens, becoming lighter in colour and less shiny. Before it becomes too stiff to stir, quickly pour and scrape the mixture into a buttered tin (*above*).

5 **Serving the fudge.** Leave the tin of fudge to set in a cool place for 1 to 2 hours. When the fudge is hard, use a greased knife to cut it into 2.5 cm (1 inch) squares. With a palette knife, remove the pieces from the tin and stack them on a plate for serving. To store the fudge, put it in a tin between layers of greaseproof or wax paper; it will keep for several weeks.□

3 **Serving the fudge.** Empty the fudge into the buttered tin (*above*). Leave it to set in a cool place—overnight if necessary. Cut the fudge into small squares and use a palette knife to lift them from the tin. For immediate use, arrange the squares on a serving plate (*right*). Or store the fudge as described in Step 5, above.□

Foamy Marshmallows from Whisked Egg Whites

A very small proportion of beaten egg whites and gelatine transforms a sugar syrup into the light, springy confections known as marshmallows (*recipe, page 120*). The syrup, cooked to the hard-ball stage (*pages 10-11*), gives the marshmallows their sweetness. The air incorporated into the whites makes the mixture fluffy. Gelatine helps prevent the syrup from crystallizing and as the gelatine sets it adds body to the marshmallows.

Prepare the gelatine while the syrup for the marshmallows is cooking. Dry, powdered gelatine does not combine well with other ingredients. It must first be soaked, to soften and swell its granules. At this stage, a small quantity of liquid flavouring is added; orange-flower water—used here—or rose-water will provide the delicate flavour appropriate to such light confections. When the gelatine has been soaked, it is gently heated over boiling water to liquefy it, so that it will mix easily with the sugar syrup.

While the sugar syrup finishes cooking, the egg whites are prepared. Beaten egg whites will be most stable if they are whisked in a copper bowl: a reaction with the metal gives extra strength to the walls of the egg whites' microscopic air bubbles. However, glass, porcelain and stainless steel bowls are also suitable.

As soon as the egg whites hold stiff peaks, the gelatine and syrup mixture is whisked in. The liquid must be poured in a thin, steady stream and the whites must be beaten all the while; otherwise, the weight of the syrup would flatten the whites and the mixture would be heavy. You will find the job easier if you have a helper to pour the liquid while you steady the bowl and do the whisking.

Further beating stiffens and thickens the marshmallow to the point at which it is ready for moulding (*Steps 3 and 4*). Once set and unmoulded, the marshmallow can be cut into cubes with a knife and scissors, as shown here, or stamped with biscuit cutters into whatever shape you choose. Serve the marshmallows plain, dusted with a mixture of icing sugar and cornflour to keep them from sticking together, or dip them in melted fondant (*page 70*) or in chocolate (*page 74*).

1 **Adding gelatine.** Cook a sugar syrup, including glucose, to 127 °C (260°F), the hard-ball stage (*pages 10-11*). While it is cooking, mix powdered gelatine with cold water and orange-flower water; leave for 5 to 10 minutes. Set the gelatine mixture over boiling water to dissolve it. Remove the syrup from the heat and pour in the liquefied gelatine (*above*).

2 **Beating in the syrup.** To prepare a tin for moulding the marshmallow, oil it and dust it with icing sugar and cornflour (*page 18*). In a copper bowl, beat egg whites with a wire whisk until they form fairly stiff peaks. While you continue to whisk, have someone pour the syrup and gelatine mixture in a very thin stream into the egg whites at one side of the bowl (*above*).

6 **Cutting strips.** Lightly oil a large, heavy kitchen knife. Press down on the knife to cut the block of marshmallow into strips 2.5 cm (1 inch) wide (*above*). To stop the marshmallow sticking to the knife, clean and oil the knife after each cut.

7 **Cutting cubes.** With oiled scissors, cut each strip of marshmallow into cubes (*above*). Sprinkle more of the sugar and cornflour mixture over the cut surfaces of the marshmallow cubes to prevent them from sticking together.

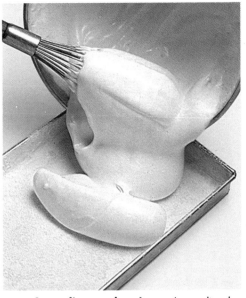

3 **Testing the consistency.** Continue to whisk the mixture until it is light and fluffy and is just beginning to thicken and hold its shape (*above*), while remaining thin enough to flow easily into the tin.

4 **Spreading out the mixture.** Immediately, spread the marshmallow mixture in the prepared tin (*above*). With a palette knife, smooth out the mixture evenly. Leave it to set for several hours.

5 **Unmoulding the marshmallow.** With a small knife, loosen the mixture from the sides of the tin. Sift more icing sugar mixed with cornflour on to a work surface, and invert the tin to unmould the marshmallow on to the powder (*above*). Dust the top and sides of the marshmallow with more powder to coat it evenly.

8 **Serving the confections.** Put the cubes of marshmallow on a wire rack (*above*) and leave them to dry for a few hours. To serve the marshmallows, pile them in a dish (*right*). Store them in an airtight container lined with greaseproof or wax paper; they will keep for about two weeks. □

Nougat Weighted for Firmness

Like marshmallow (*page 40*), nougat is basically a hard-ball syrup aerated with egg whites. Yet the dense texture of nougat could hardly be further from the foamy softness of marshmallows. Nougat owes its firmness to gentle cooking after the whites and syrup are combined; the cooking sets the whites. Weighting overnight then compacts the nougat.

The syrup and egg white mixture that is the basis of nougat traditionally serves as a cement in which nuts are set; almonds and pistachio nuts are used in the demonstration here (*recipe, page 124*). The nuts should be skinned and chopped in advance so that they can be added without delay. Before they are mixed in, they must be warmed in the oven so they do not cool the syrup and set it prematurely.

The choice of ingredients for the syrup will help determine the texture of the finished confection. A plain sugar and water syrup is likely to crystallize when it is beaten, resulting in a dry, crystalline nougat. So, for a chewy, non-crystalline nougat, add an interfering agent such as liquid glucose or honey—or a combination, as in this demonstration.

Liquid glucose is added before the syrup is cooked. Honey's flavour is altered by cooking; to minimize its cooking time, add it to the syrup for just the last few minutes of cooking. A plain syrup should be boiled to the hard-ball stage; to counter the softening effect of glucose and honey, a syrup with these additions should cook a little longer—to the soft-crack stage.

Once the syrup has boiled to the right stage, it is combined very gradually with beaten egg whites: either recruit a friend to pour the syrup while you whisk the whites, or whisk with an electric mixer. The next step is to whisk the mixture over hot water. If you want a chewy nougat, stop whisking the moment the mixture thickens; the longer it is whisked, the more likely it is to crystallize.

As soon as the right consistency is reached, the warmed nuts are folded in. The nougat is then ready to be pressed into thin slabs. For easy unmoulding, nougat is traditionally sandwiched between layers of edible rice paper, which provide dry, easily handled surfaces.

1 Adding honey. Prepare a sugar syrup, with liquid glucose (*page 8*). Put honey in a small pan and stand it in hot water so that the honey becomes warm and runny. When the temperature of the syrup reaches 138°C (280°F), pour in the honey. Bring the mixture to 143°C (290°F). Remove the pan from the heat. Dip the base in cold water to arrest cooking.

2 Whisking egg whites. While the syrup is cooking, use a wire whisk to beat egg whites in a heatproof bowl until they form fairly stiff peaks. As you continue to whisk the egg whites, have a friend pour the syrup into the whites in a slow, thin stream at one side of the bowl.

6 Weighting the nougat. Place another sheet of rice paper over the top to cover both the mixture and the mould. Place a board over the nougat mixture. Weight the board down with heavy weights (*above*) or with bricks. Leave the nougat overnight to set in the mould.

7 Trimming the nougat. The next day, remove the weights, the board and the mould from the nougat. With a sharp knife, trim off the excess rice paper and cut away any uneven edges from the set nougat. Then slice the nougat in half.

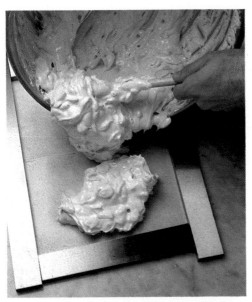

3 **Firming the consistency.** When the syrup has been fully incorporated into the egg whites, place the bowl over a pan of barely simmering water. Continue to whisk the mixture while it thickens and firms. Stop whisking when the mixture can clearly hold its shape on the whisk (*above*) but is still pourable. Remove the bowl from the pan of water.

4 **Adding nuts.** Add halved or chopped almonds and chopped pistachio nuts—first warmed for 5 minutes in a 180°C (350°F or Mark 4) oven—to the egg white and syrup mixture. If you like, add a little vanilla extract or other flavouring. Stir the nuts into the mixture gently but quickly.

5 **Shaping the mixture.** Line a prepared tin or a set of confectioner's bars with rice paper (*pages 18-19*). With the aid of a spoon, transfer the mixture to the tin or bars. Use an oiled palette knife to spread it evenly and smooth its surface. It should fill the mould completely.

8 **Serving the nougat.** Slice the nougat again, lengthwise, to form quarters. Then cut each quarter into bars approximately 2 cm (¾ inch) wide (*above*). The bars may either be served immediately, stacked on a plate (*right*), or they can be wrapped in cellophane and stored in an airtight tin or container for several weeks.□

2
Fruit Confections
Making the Most of Natural Flavours

The luxury of crystallized fruits
Crystallizing peels and petals
Spicy pastes from one fruit or many
Layering syrups for a two-tone jelly

Fruits are nature's own confections. With their sweetness, their bright colours and their pleasing shapes, they need little artifice to transform them into beguiling sweetmeats. In fact, complicated flavourings or excessive cooking would distort the delicate natural flavours of the fruit. Preparation of fruit confections should be simple, and the list of ingredients often does not extend beyond the fruit itself and sugar. The main function of sugar is to sweeten and intensify the flavour of the fruit; but a sugar syrup also gives body to many fruit confections and, in high enough concentration, it acts as a preservative.

For crystallized fruits, sugar plays all these roles. Immersed in a sugar syrup of repeatedly increased concentration, pieces of fruit, or small whole fruits such as the apricots on the left, slowly absorb the syrup. When the fruits are eventually allowed to dry, the sugar in their flesh hardens to give them an appealingly firm texture. And the concentration of the sugar is so high that, properly stored, they will keep indefinitely.

Few other confections, apart from dipped assemblies (*Chapter 4*), are made from whole fruits. Chopped or puréed fruits and juices, however, offer a wide variety of pleasing possibilities. A stiff purée of fresh fruit, cooked with a light sugar syrup, hardens as it cools, yielding a firm paste that can be cut into small shapes. Dried fruits such as dates and prunes, with their denser textures, need only be finely chopped and lightly bound with honey to set to a firm paste.

Fruit juices, carefully extracted to retain their clarity, have little body of their own. But you can use gelatine to set the juices to a solid slab; cut into small pieces, the fruit jelly—firmer than the jellies of dessert cookery—makes a light and refreshing confection. Besides their use in jellies, fruit juices have a minor but indispensable flavouring role in many confections—from lollipops (*page 22*) to fondant. While a particular fruit may be best suited to certain sorts of confections, almost all can be used in some way. Firm fruits that can withstand lengthy soaking in syrup are good for crystallization and will also make the stiffest purées. Juicy fruits such as citrus fruits and berries will give the most transparent jellies. Even citrus peels and flower petals will yield confections: a simple crystalline coating (*page 49*) turns them into crunchy, sugary morsels suitable for eating on their own or for decorating other sweets.

Wearing a decorative coating of castor sugar, crystallized apricots stand ready to be eaten whole or sliced. The fruits were soaked in syrup until saturated with sugar. When dried, the apricots retain much of their natural shape, colour and flavour.

Crystallization: a Slow Transformation

When fruits are saturated with syrup, sugar replaces their moisture, giving them a firm texture, an intensely sweet flavour and excellent keeping properties. This transformation, known as crystallization, must be brought about gradually. If the fruits were suddenly subjected to high concentrations of sugar, they would shrivel and toughen; but if they are left for 14 days in a sugar solution and the concentration of the syrup is regularly stepped up, they keep their shape and tenderness. After they have been impregnated with sugar, the fruits are allowed to dry out so that they will keep well.

Pineapple is crystallized in the demonstration on the right; plums, apricots, peaches, oranges, cherries, apples and pears can be treated in the same way. Soft fruits such as strawberries or raspberries would, however, disintegrate during the prolonged soaking. The fruits used should be ripe but still firm.

Large fruits such as pineapples and oranges are generally skinned and sectioned into sizes easy to eat with your fingers; smaller fruits are often crystallized whole. Any fruits left intact should be pricked all over with a fork or trussing needle to help the sugar to penetrate.

All fruits should be briefly poached in water so they will absorb the sugar readily. Firm fruits need about 15 minutes cooking; soft fruits such as cherries require 4 minutes at most. The cooking water is then combined with sugar to make a syrup in which the fruits are submerged. Part of the sugar may be replaced by liquid glucose, which is absorbed into the fruits more easily than sugar and thus helps to prevent wrinkling.

Almost every day for 10 days, the syrup is concentrated either by the addition of more sugar—as here—or by reduction, and returned to cover the fruits. After a further four days of immersion, the fruits are lifted out and dried. It is important not to hurry the drying process, lest the fruits shrivel. Dry the fruits in a gas oven heated only by its pilot light; or alternatively, near a radiator or sunny window.

Once dried, the fruits are ready to eat. But you can, if you like, alter their appearance by rolling them in castor sugar or glazing them with syrup (*page 48*).

1 **Preparing the fruit.** With a sharp knife, cut off the top and base of a pineapple. Slice off the hard skin. Cut the pineapple crosswise into slices about 1 cm (½ inch) thick. Use a small biscuit cutter to remove the tough core of each slice (*above*).

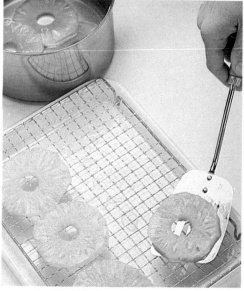

2 **Cooking the fruit.** Weigh the prepared fruit and place it in a large pan. For every 500 g (1 lb) of fruit, add 30 cl (½ pint) of water. Set the pan on a medium heat and cook the pineapple until it is just tender— about 15 minutes. Set a wire rack over a tray. Lift out the fruit with a slotted spatula and place it on the rack to drain (*above*). Reserve the cooking liquid.

6 **Concentrating the syrup.** For every 30 cl (½ pint) of syrup, add 60 g (2 oz) of sugar (*above*). Set the pan over a medium heat and bring the syrup to the boil. Transfer the drained fruit from the rack to the crystallizing dish. Pour the syrup over the fruit. Cover the dish with greaseproof paper and leave the fruit undisturbed for another 24 hours.

7 **Increasing the concentration.** On each of the next five days, repeat Steps 5 and 6. On the eighth day, add 90 g (3 oz) of sugar for every 30 cl (½ pint) of syrup. Boil the syrup and pour it over the fruit. Place greaseproof paper over the fruit; leave it for 48 hours. On the 10th day, again add 90 g of sugar for every 30 cl of syrup. Boil the syrup and pour it over the fruit.

3 **Making the syrup.** For every 30 cl (½ pint) of the reserved cooking liquid, weigh out 175 g (6 oz) of sugar or 125 g (4 oz) of liquid glucose and 60 g (2 oz) of sugar. Put the sugar in the pan with the cooking liquid (*above*); add the liquid glucose if used. Set the pan over a medium heat. Stir regularly until the sugar dissolves.

4 **Immersing the fruit.** Place the fruit in a large, shallow, non-metallic dish. Bring the syrup to the boil and then remove the pan from the heat. Pour the hot syrup over the fruit (*above*). Press a sheet of greaseproof paper on to the surface of the syrup to keep the fruit moist. Leave the fruit undisturbed for 24 hours.

5 **Draining excess syrup.** The next day, set a stainless steel rack over another tray. Remove the greaseproof paper from the fruit. With a slotted spatula, lift out the fruit from the syrup and place it on the rack to drain (*above*). Pour the syrup that drains off into a heavy pan.

8 **Drying the fruit.** Cover the fruit with greaseproof paper and leave it for a further four days. On the 14th day, use a slotted spatula to lift the fruit from the syrup on to a stainless steel rack set over a tray (*above*). Place the tray in an oven heated only by a pilot light for at least 4 hours—or in a warm, dry place for about three days—to dry the fruit.

9 **Serving crystallized fruit.** The fruit is ready when it no longer feels sticky. Cut the slices of pineapple into segments and serve them in a clear glass dish that will display their sparkling colour (*above*). To store crystallized fruits, place them in layers between sheets of greaseproof paper in an airtight box or tin and leave the container in a dry place. The fruits will keep indefinitely. □

A Coating of Fine Sugar

1 **Softening crystallized fruit.** Bring water to the boil in a pan. Remove the pan from the heat. A few pieces at a time, place the crystallized fruit—here, pineapple segments—on a slotted spoon and lower them into the hot water for a second to melt their surfaces. Hold the fruit over the pan to drain off excess water.

2 **Coating the fruit.** Fill a shallow bowl with castor sugar. A few pieces at a time, roll the moistened fruit segments in the sugar until they are evenly coated. Cover a tray with greaseproof paper and place the coated fruit pieces on the tray to dry.

3 **Serving sugared fruit.** When the coating of castor sugar is firm and dry, transfer the pieces of crystallized fruit to a plate for serving. The sugar gives the fruit an attractive frosted appearance.

A Smooth Glacé Finish

1 **Preparing the crystallized fruit.** Bring a pan of water to the boil, then remove it from the heat. In another pan, make a syrup from 15 cl (¼ pint) of water and 500 g (1 lb) of sugar. Pour some of the syrup into a bowl. One at a time, place the segments of crystallized fruit—here, pineapple—on a slotted spoon and dip them in the water for a second to melt their surfaces.

2 **Dipping the fruit in syrup.** Allow the pieces of fruit to drain for a second or two. One piece at a time, quickly dip them in the syrup (*above*). Place the fruit on a rack to drain. When the syrup in the bowl becomes cloudy, replace it with a fresh supply from the pan of reserved syrup.

3 **Serving glacé fruit.** Leave the segments of fruit until their surfaces have dried. They are then ready to be served. The final coating of syrup gives them an especially smooth, glossy appearance.

Preserved Flowers and Peels for Adornment

Stiffened and Sugared Petals

Preserved with sugar, flower petals and citrus fruit peels make attractive garnishes for many confections. Preserved peels can also be dipped in chocolate to become sweets in their own right (*recipe, page 166*). For both flowers and peels the preserving process is known as crystallization, although the method for flowers (*recipe, page 129*) bears little resemblance to the classic crystallization of fruit.

Roses, violets, freesias and the geranium variety known as "rose geranium" have edible petals and are the commonest choices for crystallizing. Violet flowers are crystallized whole; larger flowers are first separated into petals. The petals are first painted with a solution of gum arabic—a natural resin, sold in chemists' shops—which stiffens them and prevents them from shrivelling; they are then sprinkled with sugar and gently dried.

Peels can be crystallized in the same way as whole fruits (*page 46*); but because of their toughness and strong flavour, they can also be simply parboiled to rid them of their bitterness, then simmered in syrup for 3 hours and dried.

1 Brushing the petals. In a small bowl, mix one part of powdered gum arabic with two parts of rose-water. Sprinkle castor sugar on to a plate. Pull the petals from flowers—roses, freesias and geraniums are used here. Using a soft brush, coat three or four petals gently and evenly with the solution. Place each coated petal in the sugar on the plate.

2 Sieving sugar. Sift castor sugar over the petals (*above*). Transfer the petals to a wire rack. Paint and sugar the remaining petals in the same way. Leave them in a gas oven heated by the pilot light for 2 to 4 hours, until brittle; turn them every hour so that they dry evenly. Or place them near a radiator to dry for three days. □

Citrus Peels Simmered in Syrup

1 Peeling fruit. Slice off the top and the bottom of the fruit—grapefruit is used in this case. Slice the peel from the fruit in spirals. Here, the peel is sliced thinly with a sharp knife to obtain the rind with no pith attached, but you can crystallize rind and pith together if you prefer.

2 Softening the rind. Boil water in a pan. To soften the rind and to extract bitter juices, simmer the rind for about 3 minutes, until soft. Use a skimmer to transfer the rind to a bowl of cold water (*above*). Repeat this process twice more, changing the water in both the pan and the bowl each time. Then drain the rinds well.

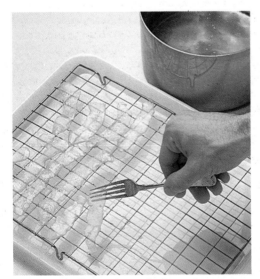

3 Crystallizing the rinds. Prepare a syrup from sugar, glucose and water (*page 47*). Bring the syrup to the boil, add the drained rinds and cook at a bare simmer for 3 hours. Using a fork, lift out the rinds on to a wire rack set over a tray. Place the rack in an oven heated only by its pilot light; the rinds will dry in about 3 hours. □

Puréeing for a Firm Paste

Both fresh and dried fruits can be made into firm pastes with concentrated flavours. These pastes are easily shaped into individual confections and, stored between sheets of wax paper in an airtight tin, will keep almost indefinitely. When based on fresh fruit, pastes are made by simmering a sweetened and seasoned purée until it is so thick that it will set when cooled (*right; recipe, page 156*). If you use dried fruit, which is low in moisture and firm in texture, you can make a paste simply by mincing the fruit and binding the pulp with syrup, egg white or honey (*right, below; recipe, page 148*).

For a cooked fruit paste, you can use any kind of fresh fruit except citrus fruits, which do not form stiff purées. Firm fruits—such as the apples used here, quinces, pears or apricots—need preliminary cooking to make them soft enough to purée. Soft fruits—strawberries and raspberries, for example—are effortlessly puréed while raw.

Once puréed, the fruit is cooked with a large amount of sugar—usually a quantity equal in weight to the fruit. During cooking, the fruit's natural moisture partially evaporates and the purée thickens. At the same time, the sugar forms a dense syrup which, when the paste is spread out to cool, hardens and helps the purée to set firmly. Some recipes give an alternative method of preparation, in which a soft-crack or hard-crack syrup is combined with a thick fruit pulp; the paste is then left to cool and set (*pages 153-155*).

Once set, the paste can be shaped by hand or cut into individual pieces. Here, the apple paste is cut into simple squares.

Fruit pastes can be made from one type of fruit or a combination of different fruits. Spices and chopped nuts may also be included. In the dried fruit paste here, equal quantities of minced dates, prunes and apricots are used. Any thick syrup will do to bind a dried fruit paste—a stock syrup (*page 8*), rich molasses or, as in this case, honey. For a less sweet taste, you can omit the syrup and bind the minced fruit with lightly beaten egg white.

Pastes of dried fruit are most easily shaped by hand into small balls. All you need do then is coat them in sugar and leave them to dry overnight.

Fresh Apples Concentrated by Cooking

1 **Preparing the fruit.** Choose ripe fruit—here, apples. Wash the apples and slice them into a heavy pan (*above*): their peels and cores are rich in pectin, a substance that will help the paste to set more firmly. Add a little water to prevent the apples from sticking to the pan. Over a gentle heat, cook the fruit until just soft—apples take 20 to 30 minutes.

2 **Making a purée.** Remove the pan from the heat and leave the fruit to cool. Set a fine-meshed sieve over a large bowl. With a pestle, force the apples through the sieve (*above*). Discard the peel and the pips left behind in the sieve.

An Uncooked Mixture of Dried Fruits

1 **Stoning fruit.** Set any stoned fruit to one side. To remove the stones from unstoned fruit—in this demonstration, dates and prunes—slit each piece of fruit with a small, sharp knife. Pull back the flesh (*above*) and pick out the stone.

2 **Mincing the fruit.** Fit a meat grinder with a medium or coarse disc. Push the dried fruit—in this case, the stoned prunes and dates, and apricot halves—through the meat grinder (*above*).

3 **Cooking the purée.** Transfer the purée to a large, shallow pan and stir in an equal weight of sugar (*above*). Over a low heat, cook the purée, stirring continuously, for about 40 minutes—until it is so thick that the spoon, when drawn across the base of the pan, leaves a permanent trail.

4 **Firming the paste.** Remove the pan from the heat. If you like, you can season the paste with spices—cinnamon, ground cloves or nutmeg—and add grated orange or lemon rind. Lightly coat a tin with butter and pour the purée into the tin (*above*); tilt the tin to distribute the paste evenly. Leave the paste for several hours or overnight, until it is set.

5 **Cutting and serving the sweets.** With a sharp knife, cut the set paste into squares about 2.5 cm (1 inch) across. Sprinkle a tray with icing sugar. With a spatula, transfer the squares of paste to the tray. To coat the tops of the sweets, sift more icing sugar over them (*above*). Before serving, leave the paste standing in the tray of sugar to dry for about 1 hour. □

3 **Binding the mixture.** Transfer the minced fruit to a large mixing bowl. Spoon in a binding ingredient—in this case, honey (*above*). Mix the ingredients until they are thoroughly blended. If the paste feels too dry to cohere, work in more honey. If the paste is too moist and sticky, add a dry ingredient—sugar, finely ground nuts or some more minced fruit.

4 **Shaping the sweets.** To shape the fruit paste into balls, roll small pieces of the mixture between the palms of your hands. As each ball is shaped, roll it in granulated sugar (*above*) and transfer it to a rack.

5 **Serving the sweets.** Leave the fruit paste balls overnight to firm up and dry slightly. Put each sweet into a fluted paper case, and arrange the sweets in piles on small serving dishes (*above*). □

Sparkling Jellies Based on Fresh Juice

Confections that have a firm texture, fresh flavour and jewel-like translucency are produced by warming together fruit juice, sugar and gelatine, then leaving the mixture to cool and set. Following this procedure, you can make either simple jellies in single flavours or—with a little extra effort—layered combinations of two or more flavours, exemplified by the orange-and-raspberry jellies demonstrated here (*recipe, page 133*). For layered creations, one jelly is allowed to set and another warm jelly is poured on top; the warmth of the second layer melts the top of the first so the layers bind together.

Fruits that will easily yield a clear juice include berries such as blackcurrants, strawberries and raspberries, and citrus fruits—especially oranges and lemons. To extract the juice from berries, heat them gently in a saucepan until their juice flows out; then strain the fruit through a fine-meshed sieve, discarding the pulp (*page 22*). Citrus juice, squeezed by hand or with a juice extractor, may be similarly strained; or it can be used as it is for a deep, opaque colour.

Once the juice is ready, sugar and glucose are dissolved in it—over a gentle heat that will not affect the juice's flavour. In combination with gelatine, glucose gives jellies a chewy texture.

The next step is to add the gelatine that sets the confections. The gelatine must first be soaked in cold water to soften its granules so that they will dissolve easily in the sugared juice.

You can mould the jelly in a single slab to be cut up once it is set, or pour the liquid into small, individual moulds. As the jelly sets, a slight skin forms on its surface; this skin prevents it from absorbing moisture from the air and thus keeps it firm and intact. If you are layering two or more jellies, each layer must be set before the next is added, so that they form distinct bands.

Once set and turned out, the jellies should be kept in a cool place and served as soon as possible. The skin on the jellies will begin to toughen after about 24 hours; however, a light coating of sugar will help keep them a few days longer.

1 **Preparing the first jelly.** Measure out enough powdered gelatine for the entire quantity of juice—about 30 g (1 oz) for every 15 cl (¼ pint). Sprinkle the powder into a bowl; add a little cold water and leave the gelatine to soften in the water for 5 to 10 minutes. Put sugar and liquid glucose in a pan. Extract the juice from raspberries and add it to the pan (*above*).

2 **Adding the gelatine.** Put the pan over a low heat; stir frequently with a wooden spoon until all the sugar has dissolved completely. With the pan still on the heat, add half the soaked gelatine (*above*).

5 **Pouring the second layer.** Remove the pan from the heat; leave the liquid to cool for a few minutes. By this time, the jelly in the tin should have set firmly enough to support another layer: touch it gently to make sure it is firm. In a thin, even stream, pour in the hot orange mixture (*above*). Leave the layered jelly for at least 6 hours in a cool place to set it completely.

6 **Turning out the jelly.** To loosen the jelly from the tin, run the tip of a small, sharp knife along the inside edges. Invert the tin over a cool, level cutting surface; the jelly should slip out easily, but if it sticks, flex the tin slightly to release it.

3 **Pouring the first layer.** Stir the contents of the pan until the gelatine dissolves and the liquid is clear; a little scum may form on the surface, but it will disappear when the jelly sets. Dampen a tin (*page 18*) and set it on a cool surface. Remove the pan from the heat and pour the hot liquid into the prepared tin (*above*). Leave the raspberry jelly undisturbed for a few hours until it is set.

4 **Making the second jelly.** In a small pan, put sugar, glucose and freshly squeezed orange juice—in this case, unstrained. Put the pan on a low heat and stir the mixture frequently until the sugar has dissolved. Add the remaining gelatine and continue stirring until the gelatine dissolves and the liquid is clear.

7 **Cutting cubes.** With a heavy, sharp knife, cut the slab of jelly into strips about 2 cm (¾ inch) wide; then cut across the strips to form squares (*above*). Serve the sweets plain (*right*), or roll them in sugar. □

3
Nut and Chocolate Pastes
A Repertoire of Rich, Smooth Blends

Using any combination of nuts
Layered marzipan for patterned confections
Colour and crispness from baking
Truffles rolled in cocoa
Chocolate buttercreams enlivened with spirits

Pastes made from nuts or chocolate are among the least difficult and most rewarding sweets to make at home. The basic preparation requires nothing more than combining ground nuts or melted chocolate with liquid or fat to achieve a soft consistency. Such amalgams are valued for their luxurious texture and because they can be moulded into different shapes.

For nut pastes, egg is the essential binding and moistening element; egg whites serve most often, but egg yolks or whole eggs are also used. The simplest nut pastes are made by kneading ground nuts with sugar and egg. A smoother, more pliable paste is made by cooking the mixture. One method is to cook the nuts with the sugar until the mixture is thick and smooth, then firm it, if necessary, with more sugar (*recipe, page 134*). Alternatively, you can use a soft-ball syrup in place of sugar and briefly cook the syrup with the nuts and some egg white (*page 58*). Cooked pastes made from ground almonds are known as marzipan; the title is sometimes extended—albeit incorrectly—to uncooked almond pastes.

Nut pastes are an excellent modelling material. Uncooked pastes can be rolled out or cut and stamped into simple shapes. Cooked pastes, with their greater cohesiveness, offer further possibilities. Differently coloured and flavoured sheets of paste may be stacked, bound with egg white and sliced into gaily striped bricks (*opposite*). If the bound sheets are cut and re-stacked, chequered designs result; if they are rolled into a cylinder, bull's-eyes are produced (*page 60*). Miniature fruits, vegetables and animals can be fashioned from differently coloured pastes and decorated with pistachio nuts or almond splinters. For a different texture and appearance, you can bake any nut paste confection lightly and glaze it with icing, or coat it with a sparkling film of sugar crystals (*page 62*).

For a chocolate paste, butter, cream or milk is incorporated into the melted chocolate. Chocolate pastes are too soft and too easily melted to be handled much, and they cannot be formed into such elaborate designs as nut pastes. But you can make spheres or logs by rolling the paste between your palms, or create a variety of scalloped shapes by piping the mixture from a bag fitted with a plain or decorative nozzle. For further variety, the sweets can be finished in different ways—dusted with icing sugar or cocoa powder, for example, coated with chopped nuts or enclosed in a nut paste.

A long rectangle of pastel-coloured marzipan is sliced to make individual sweets (*page 58*). Rolled-out sheets of marzipan, two coloured pink, have been stacked and bound with egg white to produce a simple striped pattern.

A Simple Nut Mixture that Needs No Cooking

Finely ground nuts sweetened with sugar and bound with egg produce a soft, smooth paste that is easily rolled and cut into small pieces. When made entirely from almonds, it is sometimes called marzipan.

Almonds are not the only choice for this sort of confection. Walnuts, hazelnuts, pistachio nuts and chestnuts all contribute distinctive qualities. The paste made here has equal quantities of almonds and hazelnuts (*recipe, page 167*).

Whatever nuts you choose, they must be skinned (*page 12*), and chestnuts must be cooked, first partially to loosen their shells and skins, then fully to soften their flesh and develop its flavour. Slit a cross in the flat surface of each chestnut. Boil the nuts for 10 minutes, then peel them. Simmer the skinned nuts for a further 40 minutes, until they are tender.

Once skinned, the nuts selected are finely ground—or, in the case of chestnuts, puréed. They are then mixed with sugar—at least an equal weight or, for a sweeter paste, up to twice that amount. The sugar not only acts as a sweetener, but also affects the texture of the paste. Icing sugar—used here—yields a smooth paste; castor sugar or granulated sugar makes a grainier product. Brown sugar produces a dark, rich paste but it is best to use this only with strong-flavoured nuts such as walnuts or chestnuts.

Once the nuts and sugar are combined, all that remains is to bind them with egg. The proportions of white and yolk are a matter of taste. Egg whites alone produce a light, mild paste. Yolks alone will yield a denser, richer and more yellow paste. And whole eggs balance the extremes.

The paste is kneaded until smooth, then flavoured and coloured—here, crystallized orange peel and an orange liqueur are used. Citrus zest, spirits, cocoa powder and coffee are all good alternatives. But use only a little flavouring; the taste of the nuts can easily be masked.

You can mould the paste into small balls by hand or roll out and cut it, as shown here. Packed between layers of wax paper in an airtight tin, the sweets will stay fresh for a week; the kneaded paste, wrapped in plastic film or foil, can be refrigerated for up to two months.

1 Mixing nuts and sugar. Blanch almonds and grind them finely in a food processor (*page 12*). Lightly toast an equal quantity of hazelnuts and rub off their skins; grind the nuts. In a large bowl, mix together the ground almonds and hazelnuts with a quantity of sieved icing sugar equal to their combined weight (*above*).

2 Adding egg white. In a small bowl, lightly beat the egg whites until they begin to foam. A little at a time, cut the egg whites into the nuts and sugar (*above*), adding just enough to make the mixture cohere.

6 Rolling out the paste. With your hands, roughly mix in the crystallized peel and liqueur and lightly knead the paste until the flavourings are evenly distributed. If the liqueur has made the paste too wet, work in a little more icing sugar. Dust a rolling pin with icing sugar to prevent it from sticking and roll out the paste to a thickness of about 5 mm ($\frac{1}{4}$ inch) (*above*).

7 Cutting out shapes. Select a small cutter and dust its edge with icing sugar. Cut the paste into individual sweets, leaving them on the marble surface. After each cut, dust the cutter edge with more icing sugar to prevent sticking and to ensure neat edges for the finished confections.

3 **Combining the ingredients.** With one hand, gently work the mixture together. If it feels too dry, add a little more egg white to moisten it—the amount of egg white needed will vary with the moistness of the nuts. Continue to work the mixture until it forms a thick paste.

4 **Gathering up the paste.** Knead the paste lightly until it comes away cleanly from the sides of the bowl. Do not overwork it; you might draw out too much oil from the nuts and make the paste greasy. With your hands, gather up the paste (*above*).

5 **Adding flavouring.** Lightly dust a cool marble surface with icing sugar and turn the paste out on to it. Flatten the paste slightly with your hands and sprinkle it with about 2 teaspoonfuls of orange liqueur. Coarsely chop some crystallized orange peel (*page 49*) and scatter it over the flattened paste (*above*).

8 **Serving the sweets.** Cut crystallized orange peel into small wedges and lightly press one into the centre of each piece of paste (*above*). Put the sweets on a rack and leave them for about 1 hour to harden slightly. Serve the sweets the same day (*right*), or store them in an airtight tin for up to one week. □

Marzipan: a Cooked Almond Paste

Marzipan, the classic almond paste, combines a sweet, pronounced flavour of nuts with a smooth, firm texture. Like a simple nut paste (*page 56*), it is made from sugar, ground nuts and egg, but heat plays a key role in the preparation: the sugar is boiled first to form a syrup, and then the syrup, nuts and egg are briefly cooked together (*recipe, page 134*). Cooking alters the consistency of the paste: while a simple nut paste can be rolled and cut into designs, marzipan is markedly more cohesive and pliable. Indeed, it is the best medium in confectionery for fanciful shaping. Miniature fruit and vegetables, animals and geometric patterns are all within the scope of the home sweet-maker.

To make marzipan, begin by combining the ingredients off the heat. Then stir the paste over a gentle heat for about 3 minutes. During this time, the egg whites coagulate, firming the paste slightly. The marzipan becomes even firmer when it is left to cool and its syrup hardens.

The cooled marzipan is then kneaded for smoothness. At this point, the marzipan can be coloured. A single batch may be given several different colours: simply divide the marzipan into portions and knead colouring into each. You can, of course, add flavourings to some of the portions—but avoid combining more than two flavours in the same sweet. Once kneaded, the mixture is ready to shape. If you do not want to use it immediately, wrap the portions in plastic film, put them in a plastic bag or box and refrigerate; the marzipan will keep indefinitely.

Here, sheets of coloured marzipan are stacked, stuck together with egg white and cut to make small, striped sandwiches. On page 60, two designs of greater complexity are shown. In the first demonstration, a pair of differently coloured marzipan sheets are stacked, cut, then re-stacked and cut again to make eye-catching chequerboards. In the second, two sheets of marzipan are rolled round a coloured cylinder so that, when the roll is sliced, bull's-eye patterns emerge.

Before you serve any marzipan, leave it to dry and firm up briefly. To store the confections, arrange them in a tin between layers of wax paper. They will keep for up to three weeks.

1 Adding ground almonds. Blanch and finely grind almonds (*page 12*). In a heavy pan, cook a sugar syrup to the soft-ball stage (*pages 8-11*), then dip the bottom of the pan in cold water to arrest cooking. Off the heat, stir the syrup with a wooden spoon for a minute or so until it clouds. Add the almonds (*above*).

2 Blending the ingredients. With the wooden spoon, stir the almonds into the syrup until they are well incorporated and the mixture forms a loose paste (*above*). Stir in lightly beaten egg whites.

6 Rolling the marzipan. Colour and shape the remaining portions. Here, one ball has been coloured green with spinach extract, one yellow with saffron and one has been left uncoloured. Dust a rolling pin with icing sugar and roll out one of the balls—in this case, the coffee-coloured one—into a rectangle. Roll out the other balls in the same way.

7 Stacking the layers. To make its surface sticky, brush the coffee-coloured sheet with lightly beaten egg white. Lay the green sheet on top (*above*) and brush it, too, with egg white. Add the uncoloured sheet to the stack; brush it with egg white. Finally, add the yellow sheet. With a rolling pin, lightly roll over the top of the stack to press the layers together.

3 **Cooking the marzipan.** Set the pan over a low heat and, with the spoon, blend the egg whites thoroughly into the paste (*above*). Continue to stir for a couple of minutes, until the paste thickens. Remove the pan from the heat. Lightly sprinkle a cold work surface with icing sugar.

4 **Kneading the marzipan.** Turn out the marzipan on to the work surface. To cool the paste, spread it out with your hands and turn it over a few times. When it is cold and firm, it is ready to knead. Dust your hands with icing sugar. Gather up the marzipan into a ball (*above*) and knead it gently (*Step 4, page 57*) until it is smooth and pliable—about 5 minutes.

5 **Colouring the marzipan.** Prepare the flavourings and colourings of your choice (*page 14*). Divide the marzipan into as many portions as you have colours. One by one, flatten each portion and spoon an additive—such as the strong black coffee used here—into it (*above*). Knead the marzipan until it is evenly coloured, then shape it into a ball.

8 **Cutting the marzipan stack.** To make a neat rectangular shape, trim away the uneven edges of the marzipan. If you like, divide the trimmings into small pieces and roll them between your palms to make multi-coloured balls. With a long, sharp knife, cut the rectangle lengthwise into equal-sized strips (*above*).

9 **Finishing the sweets.** Slice the marzipan across at 1 cm (½ inch) intervals (*inset*). Line a tray with wax paper; transfer the sweets to it. If any icing sugar clings to them, brush it off. Leave them to dry, uncovered, for a few hours or overnight. Serve the sweets piled on a dish. □

A Complex Chequerboard Design

1 **Assembling the marzipan.** Prepare the marzipan (*page 58*) and divide it into two equal portions. Colour one half—here, with spinach extract (*page 15*). Sprinkle a work surface with icing sugar and roll out each portion into a rectangle about 5 mm (¼ inch) thick. Brush one rectangle with lightly beaten egg white; lay the second rectangle on top (*above*).

2 **Cutting wide strips.** Dust a rolling pin with icing sugar and roll it over the surface of the top layer of marzipan. Trim off any uneven edges. With a long, sharp knife, cut the layered rectangle lengthwise into three strips of equal width (*above*).

3 **Stacking the strips.** Brush the top of one strip with lightly beaten egg white. Place another strip on top, aligning the edges carefully. Brush its upper surface with egg white and add the third strip to the stack.

Concentric Circles of Colour

1 **Assembling the marzipan.** Make some marzipan (*page 58*) and divide it into two portions, one twice the size of the other. Dust a work surface with icing sugar. Knead some colouring—here, cochineal (*page 14*)—into the larger portion and divide it in two. Leave the rest uncoloured. With your palms, roll out one pink portion into a long, even log (*above*).

2 **Enclosing the centre.** Roll the remaining portions out into narrow rectangles the length of the pink log; roll the pink sheet slightly thinner and wider than the plain sheet. Brush the plain sheet with egg white; place the pink log along one long edge. Roll the plain sheet round the pink log (*above*) and trim off any overlap.

3 **Cutting the roll.** In the same way, roll the pink sheet round the log; cut off any overlap. Trim the ends, then slice the log at 1 cm (½ inch) intervals (*above*). Line a tray with wax paper and put the slices on the tray. When the marzipans have hardened and dried slightly—after 1 to 2 hours—they are ready to eat or store. □

4 **Cutting narrow strips.** Dust a rolling pin with icing sugar and roll it over the top of the stack. With a long, sharp knife, cut the long marzipan sandwich lengthwise into four narrow strips (*above*).

5 **Alternating the colours.** Lay one strip flat and brush it with egg white. Take a second strip, turn it upside down so that its uncoloured stripes rest on top of the green stripes of the lower layer and lay it on top of the other strip. Brush the upper strip with egg white. Stack the remaining strips in the same way, making sure that the colours alternate.

6 **Cutting the chequerboards.** Lightly roll over the top of the stack with a rolling pin. To make individual chequerboards, cut the block of marzipan into slices about 5 mm (¼ inch) in thickness (*above*).

7 **Serving the marzipan.** Line a tray with wax paper. Put the chequerboards on the tray and leave them to dry for a few hours or overnight. To serve the confections, arrange them on a dish to show off their chequerboard design (*left*). □

Appealing Finishes for Nut Pastes

By varying the methods of finishing a nut paste confection, you can achieve different textures and decorative effects. If you immerse pieces of paste in a sugar syrup, they will acquire a fine, sparkling coat (*right*). Or, for a crisper texture, you can bake them (*below; recipe, page 137*). Both methods are suitable for either cooked or uncooked nut pastes.

A sugar coating not only looks attractive, it also helps to seal in the paste's natural moisture. Confections that are to be immersed in syrup should be made a day in advance; they will then be dry and firm enough to keep their shape in the syrup. The longer you leave them immersed, the more sugar crystals will be deposited and the thicker the coating will be.

The texture of baked nut paste will vary according to oven temperature and baking time. Brief baking in a hot oven will crisp the outside and leave the inside moist and chewy. Longer baking in a cool oven will dry the sweets right through. For a crunchy surface, brush them with icing sugar half way through baking.

A Fine Coating of Sugar Crystals

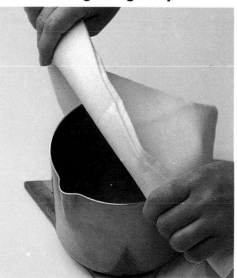

1 Preparing a syrup. Prepare sufficient sugar syrup (*pages 8-11*) to cover the confections completely. Boil the syrup to a temperature of 105°C (221°F), then dip the bottom of the pan in cold water to arrest cooking. Cover the pan with a napkin (*above*) or greaseproof paper. Leave until cold—about 6 hours.

2 Pouring the syrup. Arrange the sweets—here, two-tone marzipan sandwiches (*page 58*)—in a shallow dish. Cover them with the cold syrup (*above*). Separate any that slide together. To keep the sweets submerged, press a sheet of greaseproof paper on to the surface of the syrup. Leave undisturbed for 8 to 10 hours.

A Crisp Surface from Baking

1 Cutting out shapes. Make a nut paste—a plain marzipan (*page 58*) is shown here. Line a baking sheet with greaseproof paper. On a flat surface dusted with icing sugar, roll out the paste 5 mm (¼ inch) thick. With a knife or biscuit cutter, cut out shapes—here, circles; place them on the lined baking sheet. Gather up any scraps of paste into a ball and roll it out again.

2 Turning the marzipans. Put the shapes in an oven preheated to 200°C (400°F or Mark 6). After 5 minutes, remove the sheet of marzipans from the oven; let them cool for 2 to 3 minutes, until the upper surfaces are no longer sticky to the touch. Using a small spatula, turn the marzipans over (*above*).

3 Decorating the tops. You can use a fork to mark a design on the tops of the marzipans. Holding each sweet steady with one hand, prick holes in the marzipan with the prongs of the fork or, as here, gently drag the prongs across the surface to make lines (*above*).

3 **Draining and serving.** Place a wire rack on a sheet of greaseproof paper. With a slotted spoon, lift the marzipans on to the rack. Loosely cover them with more paper (*above*); leave them in a dry, warm place for a few hours, turning them occasionally by hand. When their surfaces are dry, serve the confections (*right*) or store them in a tin between layers of wax paper.□

4 **Glazing the confections.** Put some icing sugar in a bowl. With a spoon, stir in enough cold water to form a liquid glaze that is thin enough to drip easily from the spoon. Use a pastry brush to coat the surface of each marzipan (*above*); return the marzipans to the oven for 5 to 10 minutes, until they are lightly coloured.

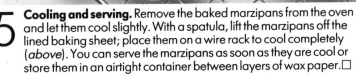

5 **Cooling and serving.** Remove the baked marzipans from the oven and let them cool slightly. With a spatula, lift the marzipans off the lined baking sheet; place them on a wire rack to cool completely (*above*). You can serve the marzipans as soon as they are cool or store them in an airtight container between layers of wax paper.□

A Chocolate Mixture Softened with Butter

When melted chocolate is combined with softened butter and sugar, the mixture sets to a thick paste that has none of the hardness of the original chocolate. The paste is easily moulded by hand, or it can be piped into individual confections, as shown on the right (*recipe, page 142*).

The first step in making the paste is to soften the butter and mix it with a flavouring and sweetener. Chocolate pastes are best flavoured with strong tasting ingredients that can hold their own with the richness of the chocolate and fat. Strong black coffee, sherry, whisky, brandy and liqueurs such as cointreau and maraschino are effective flavourings—but all liquids must be added in small quantities that will not dilute the paste too much. Extracts and oils, such as vanilla or peppermint, are also appropriate.

The flavour of the paste may be affected by the sweetener. Honey and brown sugar contribute their own particular flavours; castor sugar, icing sugar, fondant and sugar syrup sweeten without flavouring. The sweetener will also affect the paste's texture: syrups produce a silky smoothness, while uncooked sugars give the paste a grainy edge.

You can make the paste with any kind of chocolate, milk or plain. Whatever you use, the chocolate must be melted with care. Chocolate melted over direct heat, even at the gentlest setting, may scorch. It is safest to melt chocolate slowly, in a bowl or pan set over hot water. Once melted, the chocolate should be left to cool to room temperature, so that it does not melt the flavoured and sweetened butter.

While the paste is still fairly loose, you can pipe it into foil cases (*opposite page*) or in small free-form shapes on a lightly oiled tray. Alternatively, you can chill the paste first, to firm it up, and then mould it into balls by hand, or shape it into a log and slice it into pieces. Once the confections have set, they should be covered and stored in the refrigerator, where they will keep for up to two weeks.

1 Mixing butter and sugar. Put butter in a large bowl. Using the back of a wooden spoon, mash the butter against the sides of the bowl; when it becomes supple enough, beat it until it is smooth and creamy. Gradually stir sugar—here, icing sugar—into the butter. Beat until both ingredients are thoroughly mixed.

2 Adding flavourings. Measure the liquid flavourings into a spoon and add them to the butter and sugar mixture. In this case, strong black coffee and rum (*above*) are included. Thoroughly stir the mixture to incorporate the flavourings.

5 Stirring the paste. Vigorously stir the melted chocolate into the butter and sugar mixture until all the ingredients are thoroughly blended. Continue to stir the paste until it is thick and firm.

6 Filling a piping bag. Fit a cloth piping bag with a decorative nozzle and fold down the top of the bag over your hand. Hold the bag above the bowl. Spoon the paste into the bag, squeezing each addition towards the nozzle, until the bag is filled up to the level of the fold. Unfold the top of the bag and twist it to enclose the paste.

3 **Melting the chocolate.** Put pieces of chocolate—here, plain chocolate—into a small pan. In a slightly larger pan, boil water; remove the pan from the heat. Place the smaller pan over the larger pan—its base should be close to, but not touching, the water. Stir the chocolate until it is thoroughly melted.

4 **Incorporating the chocolate.** Remove the smaller pan and let the melted chocolate cool and thicken for about 5 minutes; stir occasionally so that the chocolate cools evenly. Pour and scrape the chocolate into the bowl of butter and sugar (*above*).

7 **Piping the paste.** Pipe the paste into small foil cases until each is about two-thirds full. Swirl more paste on top to give each sweet a spiralled finish (*left*). Leave the sweets to harden at room temperature for a few hours, or cool them more quickly in the refrigerator. Before serving, allow them to return to room temperature. □

Truffles: Chocolate and Cream Confections

The lightest, freshest-tasting chocolate pastes are made by whisking together cream and melted chocolate. Moulding the paste into balls yields confections often known as truffles (*recipes, pages 142-146*)—a name inspired by their resemblance to the prized fungi.

To make the paste, stir warmed cream into melted chocolate, or melt grated chocolate gently in cream. When the two ingredients are blended and cooled, you can add flavouring (*page 14*). Then whisk the paste to make it light and fluffy.

Truffle pastes are fairly loose and require careful moulding. As a preliminary step, chill the whisked paste to firm it. Next, to prevent the warmth of your hands from melting the paste during moulding, the sweets should be given a dry surface of cocoa powder. Spoon or pipe the paste on to a tray of the powder. The truffles can then be shaped by hand. If you like, give them a further coating of grated chocolate, icing sugar or nuts, or dip them in chocolate (*page 74*). Store them in the refrigerator and eat them within a few days, while they are fresh.

1 **Melting chocolate.** Break chocolate—here, plain chocolate—into a bowl. In a pan smaller in diameter than the bowl, heat water to boiling point. Remove the pan from the heat. Set the bowl over the hot water and, with a wooden spoon, stir occasionally as the chocolate melts. Continue stirring until the chocolate is smooth, then lift out the bowl.

2 **Adding cream.** Gently warm cream until it is tepid. Trickle the cream into the melted chocolate, stirring it continuously to incorporate the cream smoothly. Let the mixture cool to room temperature.

5 **Forming truffles.** Sieve a generous layer of cocoa powder on to a tray. Remove the bowl of paste from the refrigerator. Take out spoonfuls of the paste and, with another spoon, push the lumps of paste on to the cocoa powder (*above, left*). Dust your fingertips with some of the cocoa powder and quickly roll each piece of paste between your fingertips to form a ball (*above, right*).

3 **Flavouring the paste.** Add flavouring to the paste. Here a spoonful of cognac is used, but you could substitute rum or a liqueur. With the wooden spoon, lightly stir the flavouring into the paste.

4 **Whisking the paste.** Steady the bowl with one hand and vigorously whisk the paste (*above, left*). Continue whisking until it becomes fluffy, lightens in colour and holds soft peaks when the whisk is lifted above the bowl (*above, right*)—the paste should reach this stage after about 5 minutes of whisking. Remove any paste clinging to the whisk. Place the bowl in the refrigerator. Leave it until the paste thickens and is firm enough to shape by hand, about 5 to 10 minutes.

6 **Coating the truffles.** Fill separate bowls with grated chocolate, finely chopped nuts—walnuts, in this case—and icing sugar. Hold each truffle in one hand and, with your free hand, apply a coating of chocolate, nuts or icing sugar (*above*). Put each truffle in a paper case, arrange them on a dish and serve them (*right*). □

4
Dipping and Moulding
Acquiring the Professionals' Skills

Moulded in two pieces which are then joined together, a chocolate Easter egg (*page 84*) is carefully balanced on fingertips and thumb to be decorated. The piped design of melted chocolate (*page 16*) will cover the join between the two halves, leaving the rest of the egg's glossy surface untouched. Once decorated, the egg should be placed on wax paper to dry.

Confectionery's sweetest rewards await the cook who acquires skill in handling a bath of molten sugar or chocolate. Dipped into the warm liquid, any fruit, nut or ready-made confection emerges with a thin, smooth coating that—once set—becomes an integral part of the sweet. The chief gains from dipping are a contrast of texture and flavour, and a sophisticated appearance. But the outer coating serves in addition as protection. It keeps caramels, for example, from being damaged by humidity, and it provides a strong encasement for the fragile sugar walls and liquid centre of a liqueur chocolate (*page 80*). Furthermore, a coating will unify a confection whose centre is made up of several different elements—whether layered or mixed together.

For dipping, you can use hard-crack syrup or caramel, fondant or chocolate, according to the appearance and flavour you prefer. Chocolate is valued especially highly because of the possibilities for decorating it before it sets (*page 76*). Whatever dipping medium you choose, the principles of dipping are the same. The medium should be melted to a completely smooth liquid and, if necessary, kept over a water bath so that it does not solidify during the dipping process. The confections should be dry and firm enough not to disintegrate in the warm liquid: make soft confections a day ahead so that they have the chance to harden. Use your hands if you only want to immerse part of a confection or fruit (*page 70*) or if you want a rough-textured finish (*page 78*). Otherwise, the amateur confectioner will get best results using an ordinary table fork or, for greater precision, a confectioner's fork—either straight-pronged or with a ring-shaped tip. Gently submerged and turned in the dipping liquid, confections will emerge gleaming and perfect on the fork's prongs or ring.

While molten syrup and fondant rival chocolate as a dipping medium, melted chocolate has properties that make it uniquely suitable for moulding. Poured to coat the inside of a mould, chocolate will shrink as it dries and can easily be detached from the mould. Separately moulded shapes can be welded together with more melted chocolate; two half-ovals, for example, are joined to make the Easter egg opposite. On a miniature scale, a foil cup can serve as a mould for chocolate (*page 86*). The chocolate container formed against the cup's base and sides can be filled with whatever soft centre you like, and sealed with a lid of chocolate.

Applying a Gleaming Coat of Fondant

A delicious sweet in its own right (*pages 34-37*), fondant also makes a decorative and protective coating for just about any other firm confection—marzipan, caramel and crystallized fruits included. You can even, as in the demonstration on the right, coat a fondant centre with fondant, choosing a contrasting colour and flavour for the outer layer. Or, as in the demonstration below, you can dip pieces of fresh fruit into fondant, then coat them with sugar for a frosted effect.

To melt fondant to coating consistency, warm it slowly over hot—not boiling—water, stirring it constantly. If it is too thick to form an even coat, add a little hot water or other liquid (*page 37*). As it cools, the fondant will set to a firm finish with a high gloss. Take care not to heat the fondant above 66°C (150°F), or it will become brittle when it sets.

You can coat the whole of a confection or just part of it. In either case, melted fondant will slide off a moist surface, so make sure confections are quite dry before dipping them. Partly covering a confection is very simple; hold it in your fingers at one end—or, with such fruits as cherries and strawberries, by the stalk—and immerse the part to be covered in the melted fondant. Confections that are to be given a complete covering must be entirely submerged and carefully turned in the fondant. To avoid marking the surface, use a fork—a table fork or, better still, a fork with straight prongs specially designed for dipping—to turn the confection and to lift it out. If you keep the sweet near the end of the prongs as you lift it out, you will be able to slip it easily off the fork. When working with a small quantity of fondant, tilt the bowl in the pan of hot water and hold the fork almost parallel to the fondant's surface: there is less risk that the sweet will fall back into the fondant. Let the dipped sweet slip from the fork on to wax paper, nudging it off with the tip of a knife blade if necessary.

The sweets can be served as soon as the fondant coating is firm. Stored between sheets of wax paper in a box, fondant balls will keep almost indefinitely; fresh fruit dipped in fondant, however, should be eaten on the same day.

Contrasting Surface for Fondants

1 **Making fondant balls.** To shape fondant balls, pull small pieces off a slab of ripened fondant (*page 36*) and roll each piece between your fingers (*above*). Put the shaped balls on a tray lined with wax paper and leave them overnight at room temperature to firm. If the balls flatten a little, reshape them before dipping.

Partly Dipped Fruits with a Frosted Appearance

1 **Dipping fruit.** Wash grapes, cherries and strawberries, leaving their stalks on; pat the fruits dry. Separate tangerines into segments, taking care not to puncture the membrane that covers each piece. Melt fondant over hot water. Holding each piece of fruit by its stalk or by one end, dip it into the fondant (*left*); allow the excess fondant to drip off (*above*).

2 **Dipping.** Colour and flavour melted fondant (*page 37*)—here, cochineal and vanilla extract have been added—and tilt the bowl. Drop one ball at a time into the bowl; turn it over with a dipping fork and lift it out (*above*). Tap the dipping fork against the bowl and wipe the underside of the fork on the bowl's rim, then slip the ball on to wax paper. When the coating of fondant is firm—after 5 to 10 minutes—serve the sweets in paper cases (*right*).□

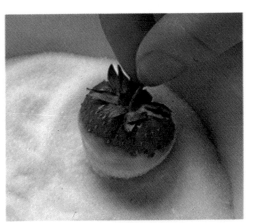

2 **Coating with sugar.** When all the excess fondant has run off the piece of fruit, dip the fondant-coated tip of the fruit into a bowl of sugar. Put the sugar-dipped fruit on to a tray lined with wax paper.

3 **Presenting the fruits.** Allow the fondant coating to set and harden completely—5 to 10 minutes. Arrange the pieces of dipped fruit in individual paper cases with their sugared tips visible, and serve.□

A Translucent Finish for Assemblies

Nuts and dried or crystallized fruits combine particularly well with sweet pastes such as fondant and marzipan; these assembled confections take on lustrous elegance when given a brittle syrup coating. Two such sweets are demonstrated here: stoned dates and prunes stuffed with a mixture of fondant and grated coconut, then dipped in a hard-crack syrup (*right*); and walnut halves filled with flavoured and coloured marzipan, and dipped in caramel (*below, right; recipes, page 159*).

The cavities that are left when the stones are removed from fruits such as dates, prunes and crystallized cherries are natural pockets for fillings. Fruits without stones, such as figs, are simply slit open for the filling to be placed inside. Nuts can be pressed into or round a filling: halved walnuts and pecan nuts and whole or split almonds are suitable choices.

The combinations of fruits, nuts and paste fillings, and the way the pastes are coloured and flavoured, may be extensively varied. The marzipan shown here is flavoured with Grand Marnier, but other liqueurs, or spirits such as rum or brandy, could be substituted. If you use a liquid flavouring, you may need to add a little icing sugar or other dry ingredient to firm up the paste. You may also need to include sugar when using moist, freshly grated coconut to flavour a paste. Desiccated coconut, on the other hand, may make the paste too dry; if so, add a little water or some other liquid.

For a nut or fruit to be successfully dipped, the surface must be dry; otherwise, the syrup will not stick. Make only small quantities of syrup at a time: the agitation of the syrup when the confections are dipped will eventually cause the syrup to crystallize. If the syrup in the pan becomes too shallow for easy dipping, prop the pan up inside another, so that it is tilted at an angle. Use an oiled dipping fork to turn each confection in the syrup and lift it out. If a hard coat of syrup begins to build up on the fork, wash the fork in hot water, then oil it again.

Once the syrup coating has hardened, it will rapidly absorb moisture from the atmosphere and become sticky. These confections should therefore be eaten on the day they are made.

Fruits with a Stuffing to Replace the Stone

1 Preparing a filling. Place some fondant (*page 34*) in a mixing bowl. Add a handful of freshly grated coconut to the fondant and knead together (*above*). Continue until the coconut is fully incorporated. Gather the mixture into a ball.

2 Filling the fruit. Stone prunes and dates (*page 50*). For each fruit, pull off a piece of fondant slightly larger then the fruit stone and roll it into an oval. Squeeze the fruit open and insert the fondant oval into the cavity (*above*); press the fruit round the filling to re-create the original shape.

Walnuts Sandwiched with Marzipan

1 Preparing a filling. Select perfect walnut halves. Colour some marzipan (*pages 14 and 58*); here, green colouring was used. Make a hollow in the paste and add a flavouring—in this case, a little Grand Marnier (*above*). Knead until the flavouring is thoroughly incorporated.

2 Filling the walnuts. Pull off small pieces of the marzipan and roll them in your hands to form balls. Take two walnut halves and press a marzipan ball firmly between them. Continue in this way until you have used up all the walnuts.

3 **Dipping.** Oil a baking sheet. Cook a sugar syrup to the hard-crack stage (*pages 8-11*), then dip the bottom of the pan in cold water to stop the syrup from cooking further. Place the pan on a trivet on a work surface. Drop one filled fruit at a time into the hot syrup; turn the confection over with an oiled fork to coat it. Lift the fruit out on the fork, wiping the underside of the fork on the pan rims to remove drips. Ease the confection from the fork on to the baking sheet.

4 **Serving.** Leave the dipped fruits on the baking sheet to cool until their syrup coating has hardened. Then arrange the confections in individual paper cases (*above*). You can serve the dipped fruits at once or store them for up to 12 hours in a cool, dry place.□

3 **Dipping and serving.** In a pan, cook a sugar syrup to a light caramel (*pages 8-11*); dip the pan in cold water and place it on a trivet on a work surface. Add the balls one at a time to the caramel, coat them and lift them out with a fork on to an oiled baking sheet. Leave the balls to cool until the syrup hardens; arrange them in individual paper cases and serve.□

Chocolate: the Classic Coating

Coating nuts and sweets with chocolate is one of the classic accomplishments of the confectioner. Professionals use a special chocolate called *couverture* for this purpose, but its high content of cocoa fat demands special handling techniques that are beyond the scope of the home cook. Nevertheless, amateurs can achieve admirable results with either a milk dipping chocolate or the dark variety used in this demonstration. Both varieties will melt to the thin, fluid consistency ideal for dipping and both will set quickly to form a thin, glossy coating.

Since chocolate will not stick to a wet or sticky surface, whatever confection you dip should be firm and dry on the outside. Nuts such as Brazil nuts or hazelnuts need no preparation other than skinning (*page 12*). Other confections, such as the marzipans (*page 58*), caramels (*page 32*) and fondant balls (*page 70*) shown here, should be made a day in advance to allow their surfaces to dry thoroughly.

Unlike eating chocolate that is heated simply to soften it—to blend it with cream, for instance (*page 66*)—dipping chocolate must be heated until all its fat has melted and the chocolate is completely fluid. However, overheating chocolate scorches its cocoa solids, permanently impairing both the flavour and texture. In order to guard against scorching, melt the chocolate over a water bath and use a sugar thermometer to check that the temperature never exceeds 49°C (120°F).

After the chocolate is fluid, it will need to be cooled slightly so that it begins to thicken. If the chocolate were too hot, it would run off the centre and not form a thick coating. Also, there is a danger that, as the coating cooled, the cocoa fat would appear as an unattractive greyish bloom on the surface. Once the chocolate has reached the right consistency—neither too thick nor too thin—it must be kept over a water bath so that it remains at a fairly constant temperature.

The method of handling a dipping fork and coating the centres is the same as that used for dipping in fondant (*page 70*). But you can, if you like, decorate the chocolates with the dipping fork before their surfaces dry (*page 76*).

1 **Putting the chocolate to melt.** Cut some dipping chocolate into pieces (*page 17*). Boil water in a pan; remove the pan from the heat. Put the chocolate into a wide bowl and set the bowl over the pan of water: the water should not touch the bottom of the bowl. Cover the bowl with a lid to keep the heat inside (*above*).

4 **Dipping the centres.** Place a tray of confection centres on one side of the bowl of chocolate; line a tray with wax paper and place it on the other side of the bowl. Drop one centre at a time into the melted chocolate. Touch the centre lightly with the dipping fork to submerge it (*above, left*); turn the centre over with the fork. Lift out the coated centre, tapping the fork on the bowl's edge (*above, centre*) to shake off excess chocolate. To remove any drips, wipe the bottom of the fork on the rim of the bowl (*above, right*).

2 **Stirring the chocolate.** Lifting the lid at intervals, use a wooden spoon to stir the chocolate as it melts (*above*). When the chocolate is no longer lumpy—after about 10 to 15 minutes—remove the lid from the bowl and stir the chocolate continuously until it is completely smooth.

3 **Testing the consistency.** The optimum temperature for dipping is 32° to 43°C (90° to 110°F). Check the temperature; then, to ensure that the chocolate is thick enough, pick up a blob between your thumb and forefinger (*above*). The chocolate should shrink and set almost immediately. If it remains liquid for several seconds, leave it until it cools a little.

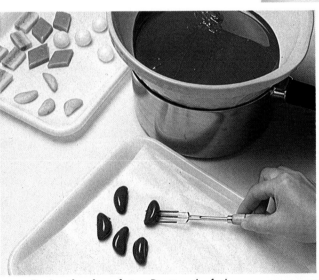

5 **Drying the chocolates.** Position the fork over the paper-lined tray. Angling the fork slightly, allow the chocolate to slide off the fork's prongs (*above*). Space the chocolates well apart. Allow them to dry completely before serving (*right*). To store the chocolates, place them in individual paper cases to protect their surfaces, and keep them in a cool place.□

Embellishments for a Chocolate Coating

Adding decoration varies the appearance of dipped chocolates and gives them a professional finish. The decoration could be a nut, a crystallized flower or a twist of crystallized citrus peel (*page 49*) pressed into the chocolate coating before it dries. You can also make designs in the chocolate coating itself while it is still liquid, or pipe on extra chocolate when the coating has dried. Some of the most ele-

gant decorations are done with the fork used to dip the confection. By lightly touching the newly dipped chocolate with the fork's prongs, you can create a raised pattern. A straight-pronged fork will make parallel ridges (*below, left*) or a tailed design (*opposite page*) that neatly finishes straight-sided confections. For rounded confections (*below, right*) use a ring-fork first to dip the centres and then to mark circles. Instead of a dip-

ping fork, the tip of a finger can serve to trail chocolate over the confection—a method particularly suitable for uneven shapes such as Brazil nuts (*bottom, left*). For a piped design, use a chocolate of contrasting colour to emphasize the design. Snip a tiny hole in the piping bag to make fine lines (*bottom, right*) or thicken the chocolate (*page 17*) and attach a small nozzle to pipe shells.

Decorating a straight-sided shape. Using a straight-pronged dipping fork, dip three confections (*page 74*); decorate them before dipping three more. Holding the fork parallel to the edges of a confection, lay the prongs across the wet surface of the chocolate. Keeping the fork in the same position, lift it slightly so that the fork's prongs create raised ridges. To remove the fork, draw it towards yourself, following the path of the ridges.

Decorating a round shape. Using a fork with a ring-shaped tip, dip three confections (*page 74*); remove each one from the fork by inverting the fork and allowing the confection to drop on to wax paper. To decorate a confection, lay the fork on the wet surface of the chocolate and raise it slightly so that the chocolate forms a circular ridge. Lift the ring-fork off vertically.

Decorating an irregular shape. Using a ring-fork or a pronged fork, dip three confections (*page 74*). To decorate a confection, dip the tip of a forefinger into the dipping chocolate and draw your fingertip along the length of the confection; the liquid chocolate will trail along the surface to form a raised ridge.

Decorating with piped lines. Dip some confections in dark dipping chocolate (*page 74*) and space them out on wax paper to dry. Melt a small quantity of light dipping chocolate. Prepare a small paper piping bag (*page 16*); spoon in the light chocolate and snip the end of the cone to make a hole. Slowly pipe lines back and forth over the confection, piping beyond the edges.

Dipping to Unify a Three-Layer Sandwich

By layering different confections, you can create original combinations of flavour and texture. Cut into individual pieces, the assembly can then be dipped in chocolate (*page 74*) for a unifying coating.

To form the base of the sandwich, use confections that are firm enough to roll out. A plain marzipan (*page 58*) is the choice in this demonstration, but you could use a fondant (*page 34*) or a flavoured nut paste (*page 56*). Confections such as a chocolate and cream paste (*page 66*) or a chocolate buttercream paste (*page 64*), which are too soft to roll out, can then be spread on top of the solid base to form a thick, even layer. For variety of texture, you can sandwich between the layers a more solid ingredient—such as pieces of nut, or the crystallized fruit used here.

To decorate the confections, use a dipping fork (*below, right*), or sprinkle a dry ingredient such as finely chopped nuts (*page 12*) or grated chocolate (*page 17*) on to the chocolate coating before it sets.

1 **Pressing in pieces of pineapple.** Cut a slice of crystallized pineapple (*page 46*) into small slivers. Flavour the pineapple with a few drops of kirsch. Dust a marble slab and a rolling pin with icing sugar; roll marzipan—here, a plain marzipan (*page 58*)—into a rectangular shape 5 mm ($\frac{1}{4}$ inch) thick. Press the slivers of pineapple firmly into the marzipan (*above*).

2 **Spreading chocolate paste.** Prepare a chocolate paste. This one is made from chocolate and fresh cream (*page 66*). With a spatula, spread the paste firmly over the pineapple-studded marzipan to form an even layer. Allow the chocolate paste to harden until it is firm to the touch—about 1 hour.

3 **Cutting into pieces.** With a sharp knife, cut the layered sheet into even-sized pieces; square, triangular or diamond shapes are all suitable. Separate the pieces and arrange them on a tray to allow the cut surfaces to harden.

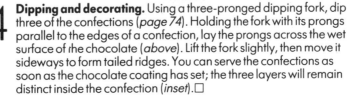

4 **Dipping and decorating.** Using a three-pronged dipping fork, dip three of the confections (*page 74*). Holding the fork with its prongs parallel to the edges of a confection, lay the prongs across the wet surface of the chocolate (*above*). Lift the fork slightly, then move it sideways to form tailed ridges. You can serve the confections as soon as the chocolate coating has set; the three layers will remain distinct inside the confection (*inset*). □

A Rough Finish Reached by Different Routes

Rough-surfaced chocolates make a pleasing change from smooth cubes or spheres and are especially welcome in a mixed presentation. Because any chocolate coating follows the form of the underlying confection, you must ensure that the confection has an undulating surface. You can give a rough exterior to a smooth sweet by rolling it in chopped nuts or fragments of hardened syrup. On the right, truffles are rolled in pieces of nut brittle.

If the confection to be coated has a naturally uneven shape, there is, of course, no need to endow it with a rough surface. The confections prepared below are simply clusters of dry ingredients—hazelnuts, raisins and crystallized orange peel—bound together with chocolate.

Either type of uneven confection can be dipped in melted chocolate with a fork in the usual way (*page 74*). But to emphasize their free-form appearance, you can dip them by hand in chocolate that is just beginning to set (*Step 4, right*). The thick chocolate will coat them unevenly.

Hand-Dipping in Extra Thick Chocolate

1 **Crushing nut brittle.** Prepare a brittle (*page 31*), using one kind of nut or a combination; here, hazelnuts are chosen. Put a few pieces of brittle at a time into a plastic bag. With a rolling pin, crush the brittle to make a coarse powder (*above*). Tip the crushed brittle on to a shallow tray, spreading it out in an even layer.

2 **Shaping truffles.** Sieve a thick layer of cocoa powder on to a tray. Prepare a chocolate and cream paste (*page 66*). Taking teaspoonfuls of the paste at a time, use another spoon to push the paste on to the cocoa. Dust your hands with cocoa and roll each piece of paste into a ball between your fingers (*above*); place the balls on the crushed brittle.

Following the Contours of an Uneven Centre

1 **Assembling the ingredients.** Melt some plain eating chocolate until it is smooth (*page 65*). Remove the chocolate from the heat. Put equal quantities of nuts—here, lightly toasted hazelnuts—and raisins into a bowl. Finely chop some crystallized orange peel (*page 49*) and add it to the nuts and fruit (*above*).

2 **Binding with chocolate.** With a wooden spoon, ease the chocolate out of the bowl into the nut and fruit mixture. Using one hand to steady the bowl, stir the mixture to blend the chocolate thoroughly with the rest of the ingredients.

3 **Shaping the confections.** Line a tray with wax paper. Remove teaspoonfuls of the chocolate mixture and, with another teaspoon, push the spoonfuls of mixture on to the wax paper (*above*). Leave the confections in a cool place until they have completely set—about 1 hour.

3 **Rolling in brittle.** Pick up some of the crushed brittle. Roll each ball between your fingers, gently pressing the larger crumbs of brittle into the ball's surface (*above*). Place the truffles on the tray of brittle; chill them. Remove the tray from the refrigerator a short while before you want to use the confections, to allow their surfaces to return to room temperature.

4 **Dipping in chocolate.** Line a tray with wax paper. Melt chocolate (*page 74*)—here, a dark dipping chocolate. Remove the chocolate from the heat and leave it to cool slightly. Using the fingers of one hand, submerge the truffles one at a time in the chocolate. Lift out the coated truffles (*above, left*); with both hands, pull the surface of the chocolate into tails before it sets. Place the truffles on the tray. When the confections have set, serve them in paper cases (*above, right*). □

4 **Dipping in chocolate.** Line another tray with wax paper. Melt some chocolate (*page 74*)—a dark dipping chocolate is used here. Use a dipping fork to dip the confections (*above*), slipping them off the fork on to the wax paper to dry. Place the confections in paper cases to serve them (*right*), or store them in a cool place. □

Perfect Liqueur Chocolates Formed with Simple Equipment

Encasing a sweet, syrupy liquid in chocolate is one of the most dazzling accomplishments of the confectioner. The secret is first to allow some of the sugar in the syrup to crystallize, thus forming a shell that will trap the rest of the syrup within. Protected by the walls of its shell, the syrup can be dipped like any other centre.

Making such centres at home requires special preparation. To form the shell into a pleasing shape, the centres must be moulded in cornflour that has been dried in a slow oven so that it will not absorb the syrup. The cornflour is placed in a tray and uniform depressions are made in its surface with the help of a simple home-made modelling block (*box, below*). These hollows are filled with syrup, which is then covered with more cornflour.

The surrounding cornflour promotes crystallization—for two reasons. First, the grains of cornflour provide a large surface area against which the sugar molecules of the syrup will align; secondly, the cornflour draws a little moisture out of the syrup, concentrating it to the point where it crystallizes very readily. After

the wall of sugar crystals has formed, it prevents further moisture from being drawn out of the syrup within, so the centre remains liquid.

The syrup used for the centres of these confections must be prepared with great care. Only a fairly light syrup, cooked to a temperature of 108°C (227°F), will produce a fine, even shell. A thick, lumpy shell would result from too concentrated a syrup. Traditionally, the syrup is flavoured with a liqueur or, as here, with brandy (*recipe, page 163*). Then it is cooled to 49°C (120°F). As the syrup cools it becomes "supersaturated" (*page 8*) and ready to crystallize.

When the shell begins to form, the top is thinner than the walls and base. To promote even thickening, the centres should be turned in the bed of cornflour. It takes about 24 hours to develop a shell of an even thickness that is strong enough to be dipped without cracking. Once they are fully formed, the finished centres can be given a single coating of chocolate, as here, or dipped two or three times to build up a thicker surface.

1 **Filling a tray with cornflour.** Spread cornflour in a 1 cm (½ inch) layer on several trays and place them in an oven at its lowest setting for about 1 hour. Using a tray 4 to 5 cm (1½ to 2 inches) deep, sift in the warm, dry cornflour through a fine drum sieve until it forms a mound that rises above the rim of the tray (*above*).

A Home-Made Modelling Block

1 **Forming the shapes.** Roll out a modelling compound—such as the children's clay used here—into a rectangle 1 cm (½ inch) thick. With a biscuit cutter, stamp shapes out of the damp clay (*above*). To allow for the clay's shrinkage as it dries, cut out shapes slightly bigger than you wish the finished centres to be.

2 **Smoothing the shapes.** Pick the shapes out of the excess clay and dry them according to the instructions given by the manufacturer. To smooth the surfaces of the dried clay shapes, rub them lightly on sandpaper (*above*).

3 **Glueing the shapes to a block.** Cut a strip of wood 2.5 cm (1 inch) wider than the shapes and 10 cm (4 inches) longer than the length of your tray. Glue the shapes to the wood. Space the shapes about 2 cm (¾ inch) apart, leaving about 5 cm (2 inches) clear at each end of the strip of wood.

2 **Levelling the surface.** Use one straight side of the modelling block (*opposite page, below*) to smooth the surface of the cornflour and make it level with the rim of the tray. To do this, push away from you with the side of the block so that excess cornflour is swept forward and spills over the edge of the tray (*above*).

3 **Casting the cornflour.** To make a row of hollows, press the moulded side of the modelling block into the cornflour until the wooden ends of the block rest on the edges of the tray. Smoothly lift the block straight upwards and out of the cornflour. With a dry pastry brush, remove any cornflour that clings to the block. Continue to make rows of hollows, leaving a 4 cm (1½ inch) space between the rows (*above*). Very gently, transfer the tray to an oven at its lowest setting. Pile the excess cornflour into a bowl and put it in the oven.

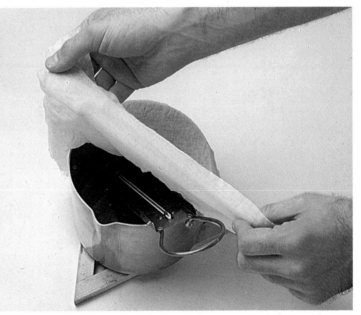

4 **Making a flavoured syrup.** In a heavy pan, dissolve sugar and water over a medium heat, stirring occasionally. When the sugar has completely dissolved, put a sugar thermometer into the pan, turn up the heat and boil the syrup to a temperature of 108°C (227°F). Dip the pan in cold water, remove the thermometer and leave the syrup to cool for 5 minutes. Add brandy (*above*), or a liqueur; blend the mixture by pouring it into a clean pan and then back into the first pan. Do not stir the syrup, lest it crystallize.

5 **Cooling the syrup.** Return the sugar thermometer to the pan. Leave the flavoured syrup until it has cooled to a temperature of 49°C (120°F). To encourage the alcohol that escapes during cooling to recondense, drape a damp cloth over the pan (*above*). Lift the cloth every few minutes to check the falling temperature of the liquid. ▶

6 **Transferring the syrup to a funnel.** To pour the syrup accurately into the hollows, select a funnel with a tube that is narrower at its tip than the hollows, and make a stopper for it by putting the handle of a wooden spoon in the tube. Pour enough of the cooled syrup into the funnel to fill it about half full (*above*). Leave any excess syrup in the pan, covered with the cloth, until you need to refill the funnel.

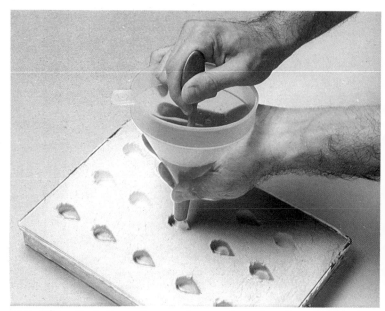

7 **Filling the hollows.** Remove the tray of cornflour from the oven and set it on a work surface. To fill a hollow, centre the tube of the funnel over it and raise the spoon slightly so that the syrup drips slowly on to the cornflour. When the hollow is full, stop the syrup by pushing the spoon back into the tube. Fill the other hollows in the same way.

10 **Removing the centres.** Set the tray on a work surface. With your fingers, carefully lift the centres one by one from the tray. To remove any excess cornflour, brush the centres with a soft pastry brush (*above*) before putting them on a plate. If you intend to re-use the cornflour, sift it both before and after re-baking it.

11 **Coating with chocolate.** Line a tray with wax paper. Melt dipping chocolate in a bowl set over hot water (*page 74*). One at a time, put each centre into the bowl of chocolate and turn it over with a dipping fork—here, a loop-shaped type. With the fork, lift the coated centre out of the bowl; to remove excess chocolate from the base of the centre, wipe the fork against the bowl's rim (*above*). Set the chocolates on the prepared tray.

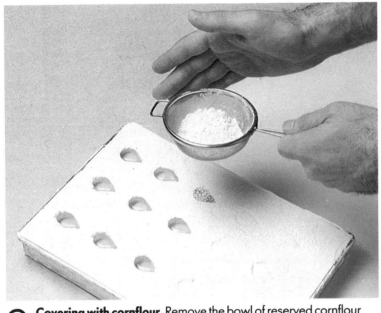

8 Covering with cornflour. Remove the bowl of reserved cornflour from the oven. With a fine-meshed sieve, gently sift the cornflour evenly over the whole tray to a depth of about 3mm ($\frac{1}{8}$ inch) in order to encourage crystallization for the formation of the "lids".

9 Turning over the centres. To allow the syrup to form complete shells, leave the tray in a warm place for at least 6 hours. To ensure that the shells thicken evenly, gently flip the centres over with a spoon or fork (*above*). Leave the tray in a warm place for another 6 hours.

12 Decorating and serving. Immediately after dipping three chocolates—before their surfaces set and harden—add any decoration you want. Here, the dipping loop is briefly pressed against each chocolate (*above*). When their surfaces are firm, put the chocolates on a serving dish (*right*). □

Moulding a Hollow Easter Egg

By pouring melted chocolate round the inside of two halves of a mould to set, you can produce identical chocolate shapes. Because chocolate shrinks as it cools, once the shapes have set they can easily be removed from the mould and joined to form decorative figures. Moulds are most commonly used to make Easter eggs, such as the one shown in this demonstration, but they are also found in other shapes—various animal forms, for instance.

The moulds are available in both metal and plastic. The easiest to use are made of semi-transparent plastic, which enables you to see when the chocolate has shrunk away from the sides. Whatever material you choose, polish the mould's interior well before you pour in the chocolate; the glossier the inside of the mould, the glossier the moulded chocolate's surface will be. To clean the mould after use, rub it with a soft, dry cloth.

The chocolate must be firm enough to unmould cleanly once it has set, so choose a chocolate with a hard consistency, such as dipping chocolate or a dark eating chocolate (*page 16*). The amount of chocolate you need will, of course, depend on the size of your mould. The larger the confection you are making, the thicker the chocolate shell will need to be to withstand unmoulding and handling. But chocolate will not set evenly in a thick layer, so always apply the melted chocolate in thin layers. The 20 cm (8 inch) high Easter egg shown here was made with 350 g (12 oz) of chocolate, applied in two layers. For a larger object, three layers might be needed. After completing each layer, invert the mould; the soft chocolate will drain downwards before it sets to form a sturdy, flat rim. When the chocolate halves are unmoulded, the two rims can be joined securely. If you like, you can fill the confection with small sweets before you bond the two halves together.

To decorate an Easter egg, fill a piping bag fitted with a star nozzle (*Step 9*) with melted eating chocolate and pipe a design round the egg's join. If you want the decoration to stand out you can use chocolate of a contrasting colour.

Stored in a cool place, chocolate shapes will keep indefinitely.

1 Polishing the moulds. Holding each half of a metal or plastic mould in turn by its outer edge, use a soft, dry cloth—here, a square of muslin—to polish the inner surface to a high gloss.

2 Spooning in chocolate. Line a tray with wax paper. Melt some chocolate (*page 74*). To keep the chocolate liquid as you work, leave it over hot water; stir it from time to time with a wooden spoon. Coat each half of the mould separately. Supporting a mould in the palm of your hand, spoon in enough chocolate to coat the entire inside surface.

6 Freeing the edges. When the chocolate has set hard—usually about 2 hours, but it may take much longer—it will shrink away from the mould. Use a plastic scraper to trim away any dry chocolate round the outer edge of the mould. Run your thumbnail around the rim between the chocolate and the mould to free any chocolate stuck to the mould.

7 Unmoulding the chocolate. To detach the chocolate shell from its mould, press downwards at one end of the shell's rim. Placing the fingers of one hand inside the chocolate shell, balance the shell on your fingertips (*above*) and lift it free of the mould; place the chocolate shell rounded side down on the wax paper.

3 **Coating the mould.** Holding the outer edges of the mould with both hands, tilt the mould slightly and rotate it so that the melted chocolate runs round the inside, coating it completely (*above*).

4 **Tipping out the excess.** Tip the mould to allow the excess chocolate to run back into the bowl (*above*). When no more chocolate drips out, invert the mould on the tray; leave it until the chocolate is firm to the touch—for the egg shown, about 20 minutes, but the time taken will vary according to the thickness of the layer and external conditions.

5 **Spooning in a second layer.** Pull away the mould from the wax paper. Spoon in sufficient melted chocolate to form a second layer (*above*). Rotate the mould so that the chocolate runs round to coat the set chocolate layer. Tip the excess chocolate back into the bowl. Invert the mould and place it on the tray.

8 **Assembling the Easter egg.** Cut out two rectangles of wax paper. Stir the melted chocolate. Using the wax paper, pick up one of the chocolate shells. With a small spatula, spread some melted chocolate round the shell's rim (*above*). Use the second piece of wax paper to pick up the other chocolate shell. Press the two shells together to seal them.

9 **Finishing the egg.** Melt some chocolate and prepare a piping bag (*page 16*); fit the bag with a star nozzle. Hold the egg in a horizontal position, balancing it on the fingertips of one hand or supporting it with a piece of wax paper to avoid marking the surface. Pipe over the join. Pipe a small circle on the egg's rounded end to form a base. Stand the egg on a sheet of wax paper.□

Soft-Centred Chocolate Cups

Using the basic technique of moulding (*page 84*), you can fashion individual cups of chocolate and fill them with a variety of centres. For such small shapes, rigid moulds are not necessary; little confectionery cups give enough support. The foil moulds are decorative enough to be left on the finished chocolates, or you can peel them off once the chocolate has set.

A chocolate cup may be given either a soft centre, such as the fondant in this demonstration (*pages 34-37; recipe, page 162*), or a stiffer, creamy centre, such as a nut or chocolate paste (*pages 56 and 66*). For extra flavour and a varied texture, you can add pieces of nut or crystallized fruit peel, a single nut or half of a small fruit—such as the raspberry halves used here. Use a teaspoon to handle liquid or textured fillings. Fondant, which has to be melted over heat, should be allowed to cool slightly before it is spooned into a cup, or it may melt the chocolate. Creamy fillings can be either spooned or piped into the cups; if they are piped, they will set with decorative tops. Alternatively, top the confection with a layer of chocolate.

1 Lining foil cups. Melt some chocolate (*page 74*). Using a teaspoon, half fill a foil cup with melted chocolate. Gently rotate the foil cup to coat the sides and bottom (*above*); invert the cup over the bowl of chocolate to tip out the excess. Place each chocolate-coated cup on a tray to set until firm—2 to 5 minutes.

2 Adding the centres. Melt some fondant (*page 37*). Drain and halve brandied raspberries. Spoon a little melted fondant into a chocolate cup (*above*). Place a raspberry half on top of the layer of fondant. To seal in the raspberry's juice and provide a solid surface for a final layer of chocolate, cover the raspberry with another layer of fondant.

3 Sealing the sweets. When the surface of the fondant is firm to the touch, spoon over a little more chocolate (*above*). Tilt the chocolate cup so that the chocolate spreads evenly over the fondant. Serve the chocolates as soon as they are hard (*right*), or pack them in a box between sheets of wax paper. Stored in a cool place, they will keep for a few days.□

Anthology of Recipes

The 247 confectionery recipes in this Anthology have been selected by the Editors and consultants from among the best ever published. The 128 authors whose work is represented include such early masters as Nostradamus, whose book about confectionery was written in 1555 at a time when sugar was becoming less expensive and more widely available to the average cook. And, of course, there is an extensive selection of recipes by modern authorities in this specialized branch of cookery—among them Walter Bachmann and Mary Norwak.

The confections presented here are drawn from the cooking literature of 29 countries; they include the traditional toffees and taffies of England and Wales, the divinities and penuches of the United States, the nougats of France and marzipans from central and eastern Europe. There are also exotic, cardamom-spiced pastes from the Indian sub-continent and halvas from the Middle East and the Balkans. The recipes range in complexity from uncooked sweets made with icing sugar and egg white, such as cinnamon stars and peppermint cushions, to more elaborate creations such as crystallized brandy liqueurs and caramel-dipped stuffed fruit.

Throughout the Anthology, as in the first half of the book, the emphasis is on techniques fully accessible to the home cook. You will be able to produce professional-looking, hand-made chocolates and sweets by carefully following the instructions. Since many early cookery writers did not specify quantities, lacked sugar thermometers and gave minimal instructions, the missing information has been judiciously included. Where appropriate, references to the sugar-boiling stages given on pages 10-11 have been inserted in square brackets in the recipe text. You are strongly advised to use a sugar thermometer for all recipes involving sugar-boiling. Cooking terms and ingredients that may be unfamiliar to the reader are explained in the combined Index and Glossary at the end of the book.

The recipes follow the order of the techniques section in the front of the book with the exception of fruit paste confections, which are combined with the other types of confectionery paste, such as chocolate pastes, marzipan and uncooked sugar paste.

Metric and imperial weights for each ingredient appear in separate columns. The use of either metric or imperial weights and measures will produce equally good results, but the two systems should not be mixed in one recipe. All spoon measures are level. Butter and oil for greasing tins or work surfaces are not included in the ingredients list; no specific quantities are given for icing sugar and cornflour used for dusting work surfaces or utensils.

Boiled Sugar Sweets

Barley Sugar

The technique of making barley sugar is shown on page 24. Be especially careful in this recipe to remove the pan from the heat and stop the cooking as soon as the syrup reaches the hard-crack stage—otherwise the syrup will caramelize. Since this mixture cools and hardens rapidly, it may be advisable to ask a friend to help you twist the barley sugar into strips, or the last strips may become too stiff to twist. If the mixture does harden too fast to make twisted strips, it can be broken into small pieces for eating. One tablespoon of liquid glucose may be substituted for the cream of tartar.

To make about 500 g (1 lb)

500 g	granulated sugar	1 lb
15 cl	water	$\frac{1}{4}$ pint
$\frac{1}{2}$	lemon, juice strained, rind thinly pared in one continuous strip	$\frac{1}{2}$
	cream of tartar	

In a heavy pan, heat the sugar and water until the sugar has completely dissolved. Add the strip of lemon rind and a pinch of cream of tartar. Boil the syrup until it reaches the soft-ball stage [*pages 10-11*]. Add the lemon juice and boil the syrup until it reaches the hard-crack stage [*pages 10-11*]. Stop the cooking by dipping the base of the pan into iced water; remove the lemon rind. Pour out the syrup in a thin layer on to a lightly oiled work surface. Leave the mixture to cool for a few minutes, then use a palette knife to fold the sides to the middle. Oil some scissors and use them to cut the mixture into strips. Twist the strips rapidly while they are still warm.

GOOD HOUSEKEEPING INSTITUTE (EDITOR)
GOOD HOUSEKEEPING'S PICTURE COOKERY

Old-Fashioned Barley Sugar

The quantity of barley water used in this recipe can be halved; this will reduce the cooking time of the syrup.

To make about 1 kg (2 lb)

1 kg	lump sugar	2 lb
125 g	pearl barley	4 oz
1	lemon, half the rind thinly pared, juice strained	1
1.25 litres	cold water	2 pints

Butter a large dish or marble slab. Into a saucepan, put the barley and the rind of half the lemon. Pour in the cold water, bring the mixture to the boil and simmer it, covered, for 2 hours. Remove the pan from the heat and leave the barley water to stand and settle for about 30 minutes. Ladle off enough clear liquid from the top of the barley water to make 60 cl (1 pint) of liquid.

Pour the barley water into a saucepan and add the sugar. Stand the pan over a gentle heat, stirring until the sugar has dissolved; then let it boil without stirring. Add the lemon juice and boil up the syrup again until it begins to crack [*hard-crack stage, pages 10-11*]. Pour the syrup on to the buttered dish or marble slab; when it is cool enough to handle cut it quickly into strips with oiled scissors, then hold each strip at both ends and twist the ends in opposite directions.

MAY BYRON (EDITOR)
PUDDINGS, PASTRIES AND SWEET DISHES

Horehound Candy

Horehound is a herb that grows wild throughout Europe, Asia and America. Although indigenous to warmer climates, it is also found in northern Europe. It can be bought dried from herbalists. If corn syrup is not available, you can substitute 2 tablespoons of liquid glucose.

Horehound has been prescribed for many generations for chest, nasal and sinus congestion and it was often used as an ingredient in snuff.

To make 850 g (1$\frac{3}{4}$ lb)

850 g	soft brown sugar	1$\frac{3}{4}$ lb
35 cl	water	12 fl oz
60 g	fresh horehound leaves or 30 g (1 oz) dried horehound	2 oz
4 tbsp	corn syrup	4 tbsp

Butter a 30 by 20 by 3 cm (12 by 8 by 1$\frac{1}{4}$ inch) tin. Put the water into a stainless steel saucepan with a lid and bring it to the boil. Reduce the heat, add the horehound, cover and simmer it for 15 minutes. Remove the pan from the heat and let the mixture stand for 1 hour to infuse. Strain the liquid and discard the horehound. Add the sugar and the corn syrup to the liquid and boil it to the hard-crack stage—149°C (300°F) on a sugar thermometer [*pages 10-11*]. Pour the syrup into the buttered tin and when it begins to set, mark it into squares. Cut the candy into pieces when cold.

DOROTHY HALL
THE BOOK OF HERBS

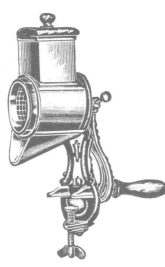

Clear Fruit Drops

The technique of making these fruit drops and transforming them into lollipops is shown on page 22. Lollipops can also be made from any boiled sugar mixture cooked to the hard-crack stage. Flavourings and colourings are discussed on page 14. If fruit juice is substituted for the water, additional flavouring and colouring may be omitted and the syrup should be boiled to a temperature a few degrees lower.

To make 250 g (8 oz)

250 g	granulated sugar	8 oz
6 tbsp	water	6 tbsp
2 tsp	liquid glucose	2 tsp
	flavouring and colouring	

Butter or oil moulds, a large tin or a marble slab. Dissolve the sugar in the water with the glucose over a medium heat. Bring this syrup to the boil and boil it to a temperature of 147° to 148°C (296° to 298°F). Add the flavouring and colouring and boil to 149°C (300°F) [*hard-crack stage, pages 10-11*].

Remove the pan from the heat at once. Pour the syrup immediately into the moulds or tin, or by spoonfuls on to the marble slab. If the mixture is poured into a tin, mark it at once into squares and break it into pieces when it is cold. The mixture sets very quickly.

D. F. HUTTON AND E. M. BODE
SIMPLE SWEETMAKING

Butterscotch

To make about 500 g (1 lb)

500 g	Demerara sugar	1 lb
15 cl	water	¼ pint
60 g	butter	2 oz

Butter a 15 cm (6 inch) square tin. Pour the water into the pan and bring it to the boil. Add the sugar and the butter. Heat the mixture slowly, stirring constantly, until the sugar dissolves and the butter melts. Bring it to the boil, cover the pan and simmer it for 2 minutes. Uncover the pan and continue to boil without stirring for about 12 minutes, or until a little of the mixture dropped into a cup of cold water separates into hard, brittle threads. The temperature on the thermometer should be about 149°C (300°F) [*hard-crack stage, pages 10-11*].

Pour the mixture into the tin. When the butterscotch is almost set, butter a knife and use it to mark the butterscotch into squares or bars. When the butterscotch has hardened, break it up and wrap it in wax paper.

SONIA ALLISON
THE DAIRY BOOK OF HOME COOKERY

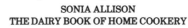

Old-Fashioned Butterscotch

To make about 500 g (1 lb)

500 g	granulated sugar	1 lb
15 cl	double cream	¼ pint
15 cl	water	¼ pint
	cream of tartar	
90 g	butter, cut into small pieces	3 oz
½ tsp	vanilla extract	½ tsp

Butter a tin 17.5 cm (7 inches) square and 10 cm (4 inches) deep. Dissolve the sugar in the cream and the water, add a pinch of cream of tartar and boil the mixture very slowly to 116°C (240°F) [*soft-ball stage, pages 10-11*]. Add the butter and boil the mixture until it reaches 138°C (280°F) [*soft-crack stage, page 10*]. Add the vanilla extract and remove the pan from the heat. Pour the mixture into the tin.

When the butterscotch is nearly cold, use the point of a buttered or oiled knife to mark it into bars or squares. When it is quite cold and set, break it up, wrap it in wax paper and keep it in an airtight tin.

SONIA AGNEW
SWEET-MAKING FOR EVERYWOMAN

Everton Treacle Toffee

To make about 500 g (1 lb)

300 g	Demerara sugar	10 oz
4 tbsp	water	4 tbsp
2 tbsp	golden syrup	2 tbsp
1 tbsp	black treacle	1 tbsp
100 g	butter	3½ oz

Butter a 15 cm (6 inch) square tin. Put all the ingredients into a pan. Heat the mixture slowly, stirring, until the butter melts and the sugar dissolves. Bring the mixture to the boil. Cover the pan. Boil gently for about 2 minutes. Uncover the pan and continue to boil the mixture, stirring it occasionally, for 10 to 15 minutes or until a little of the mixture dropped into a cup of cold water separates into hard and brittle threads [*hard-crack stage, pages 10-11*]. The temperature on the sugar thermometer should read about 149°C (300°F). Pour the mixture into the tin. Leave it until it is hard. Turn it out on to a board and break it up with a small hammer.

SONIA ALLISON
THE DAIRY BOOK OF HOME COOKERY

Everton Toffee

The technique of making toffee is shown on page 30. The lemon juice may be added at the end of cooking to minimize loss of flavour by evaporation.

To make about 600 g (1¼ lb)

500 g	granulated sugar	1 lb
125 g	butter	4 oz
1 tsp	strained lemon juice	1 tsp
30 cl	water	½ pint

Put all the ingredients into a heavy pan. Stir them over a medium heat until the sugar has dissolved, about 10 to 15 minutes. Then, without stirring, boil until the mixture reaches a temperature of 143°C (290°F) [*soft-crack stage, page 10*]. Dip the base of the pan briefly in cold water. Pour the mixture into a buttered or oiled 30 by 20 by 3 cm (12 by 8 by 1¼ inch) tin and leave it to cool until it is almost firm to the touch. Then mark it into 2.5 cm (1 inch) squares with a very sharp knife. When it is completely cold, break the toffee into pieces and wrap them in wax paper.

WINIFRED GRAHAM
CHOCOLATES AND CANDIES FOR PLEASURE AND PROFIT

Hopjes

Haags Hopje

Confectioner's bars are shown on page 19.

This typically Dutch sweet, originating from the Hague, is mostly made commercially, but can also be prepared at home.

To make about 300 g (10 oz)

200 g	granulated sugar	7 oz
75 g	golden syrup	2½ oz
8 cl	strong coffee extract	3 fl oz
50 g	butter	2 oz
4 tbsp	double cream	4 tbsp

Butter a stone or marble slab and arrange four confectioner's bars on it in a 15 cm (6 inch) square. In a large saucepan, dissolve the sugar with the golden syrup and coffee, and bring the syrup to the boil. Add the butter and cream, taking care not to let the mixture boil over as it will bubble up quickly to the top of the pan. Cook, stirring constantly, until the mixture reaches 137 °C (278°F), the soft-crack stage [*page 10*].

Pour the mixture on to the slab between the bars. As soon as the mixture begins to harden, in about 15 to 20 minutes, mark it into 2 cm (¾ inch) squares. When the mixture has cooled completely, break it into the little squares.

C. A. H. HAITSMA MULIER-VAN BEUSEKOM (EDITOR)
CULINAIRE ENCYCLOPÉDIE

Swedish Cream Toffee

Knäck

To make about 850 g (1¾ lb)

400 g	granulated sugar	14 oz
30 cl	double cream	½ pint
30 cl	golden syrup	½ pint
4 tbsp	sieved dry breadcrumbs	4 tbsp
150 g	almonds, blanched and finely chopped	5 oz

Butter a 30 by 20 by 3 cm (12 by 8 by 1¼ inch) tin. Pour the sugar, cream and golden syrup into a saucepan, stirring until the mixture reaches the hard-ball stage [*pages 10-11*]. This will take about 15 to 20 minutes. Add the breadcrumbs and boil the mixture for a further 5 minutes [*soft-crack stage*]. Stir in the almonds and let the mixture come to the boil again quickly. Pour into little fluted paper cases.

INGE NORBERG (EDITOR)
GOOD FOOD FROM SWEDEN

Farfel Candy

Matzo farfel is obtainable at Jewish grocers. It is made from matzo meal, a flour obtained by grinding unleavened bread. The meal is bound with water, separated into small lumps and roasted or fried. Farfel is usually used as a soup garnish.

To make about 1 kg (2 lb)

125 g	granulated sugar	4 oz
500 g	honey	1 lb
90 g	matzo farfel	3 oz
350 g	nuts, chopped	12 oz

Dissolve the honey and the sugar over a low heat. Bring to the boil, and boil until they are light brown or until a sugar thermometer registers the soft-crack stage [*page 10*]. Stir in the farfel and nuts. Turn the mixture out on to a wet marble slab or board. Wet your hands with iced water and pat the candy into a square 2 cm (¾ inch) thick. Let it cool slightly. Cut it with a sharp, wet knife into about 50 squares or diamonds.

SARA KASDAN
LOVE AND KISHKES

Toffee Butter Crunch

If corn syrup is not available, use half the quantity of liquid glucose. The techniques of blanching and toasting nuts are demonstrated on page 12.

To make about 1 kg (2½ lb)

350 g	granulated sugar	12 oz
250 g	almonds, blanched	8 oz
250 g	butter	8 oz
3 tbsp	water	3 tbsp
1 tbsp	white corn syrup	1 tbsp
500 g	milk chocolate, broken into pieces	1 lb

Thoroughly butter a 32 by 23 cm (13 by 9 inch) flexible metal tin. Chop half the almonds coarsely, the other half finely and toast them lightly in an oven preheated to 180°C (350°F or Mark 4) for 5 minutes or until lightly browned. In a large saucepan, melt the butter. Add the sugar, water and corn syrup. Cook the mixture over a medium heat, stirring occasionally, until it reaches the hard-crack stage—149°C (300°F) [*pages 10-11*]. Quickly stir in the coarsely chopped almonds. While it is still hot, spread the mixture in the tin. Cool the mixture thoroughly. Turn it out on to wax paper.

In a basin over a saucepan of hot water, melt the chocolate. Spread the cooled mixture with half of the melted chocolate and sprinkle it with half of the finely chopped almonds. Cover the top with wax paper. Flip the mixture over and spread the other side with the remaining chocolate and sprinkle it with the remaining almonds. Chill the mixture to firm it up, then score it with a knife and break it into about 24 pieces.

JUNIOR LEAGUE OF JACKSON, MISSISSIPPI
SOUTHERN SIDEBOARDS

Passover Ginger Candy

Passover Ingberlech

Matzo meal is obtained by grinding matzo—unleavened bread. It can be bought in Jewish grocers.

To make about 750 g (1½ lb)

250 g	granulated sugar	8 oz
200 g	honey	7 oz
60 g	almonds, blanched and chopped	2 oz
1½ tbsp	ground ginger	1½ tbsp
125 g	medium matzo meal	4 oz
2	eggs, well beaten	2
60 g	granulated sugar mixed with 1 tsp ground ginger	2 oz

In a deep saucepan, combine the plain granulated sugar and the honey, stir over a low heat and bring the mixture to the boil. Reduce the heat and simmer for 10 minutes. Remove the pan from the heat. Mix the almonds, ground ginger and the matzo meal with the eggs; mix well, using a fork. Add the mixture to the syrup. Cook over a low heat, stirring constantly until the soft-crack stage is reached [*page 10*].

Turn the mixture out on to a wet marble slab or board. Dip your hands in iced water; use the palms of your hands to flatten the mixture to 1 cm (½ inch) thickness. Sprinkle it with the mixed sugar and ginger and leave it to cool slightly. With a wet, sharp knife, cut it into about 25 squares or diamonds.

SARA KASDAN
LOVE AND KISHKES

Molasses Toffee

La Colle

It is most important to dissolve the sugar thoroughly. The finished toffee should have the glue-like consistency implicit in the French name for this confection—colle, meaning "glue". It was a Creole speciality of New Orleans.

To make about 1 kg (2½ lb)		
1 kg	soft dark brown sugar or ½ litre (16 fl oz) black molasses	2 lb
250 g	pecan nuts or peanuts, coarsely chopped	8 oz

Heat the sugar with 4 tablespoons of water or heat the molasses and bring to the boil. Stir in the chopped nuts and cook the syrup until it reaches the soft-crack stage [*page 10*].

Pour the mixture into 10 by 5 cm (4 by 2 inch) paper cases or moulds, making each sweet about 6 to 12 mm (¼ to ½ inch) thick. Leave the sweets to cool.

THE PICAYUNE'S CREOLE COOK BOOK

Christmas Almond Brittle

Makagigi

The technique of cooking sugar to a caramel without water is shown on page 9.

To make 750 g (1½ lb)		
60 g	granulated sugar	2 oz
150 g	honey	5 oz
150 g	butter	5 oz
500 g	almonds, blanched and chopped, or walnuts, chopped	1 lb

Put the sugar into a heavy frying pan. Heat the sugar over a low heat until it has melted and is delicately browned. Add the honey and butter and simmer slowly for 20 minutes. Stir in the nuts and cook for 10 more minutes. Line a dish or tin with wax paper and drop tablespoons of the mixture on to the paper. Leave the brittle to harden.

SAVELLA STECHISHIN
TRADITIONAL UKRAINIAN COOKERY

Cracknel

Croquante

Originally this recipe, which is similar to nougat, was made only with almonds and honey. This confection is made in Provence at Christmas.

To make about 400 g (14 oz)		
200 g	castor sugar	7 oz
150 g	ground almonds	5 oz
5 tbsp	honey	5 tbsp
1	large potato (optional)	1

Oil a marble slab. Put the castor sugar, almonds and 4 tablespoons of the honey into a saucepan and cook, stirring constantly, until the mixture turns a pale caramel colour [*hard-crack stage, pages 10-11*]. If the mixture is too thick to stir, add another tablespoon of honey during the cooking.

Pour the mixture out on to the marble slab and spread it out with an oiled rolling pin or a large, smooth potato, until it forms an even layer about 5 mm (¼ inch) thick. With a sharp, oiled knife, cut the mixture into 5 cm (2 inch) squares before it has completely cooled.

LOUIS GINIÉS
CUISINE PROVENÇALE

Italian Cracknel

Croccante

The technique of boiling sugar without water to make a caramel is shown on page 9.

To make about 225 g (7½ oz)		
100 g	castor sugar	3½ oz
120 g	almonds, blanched and chopped or slivered	4 oz
30 g	butter (optional)	1 oz
½	lemon	½

Dry the almonds by putting them in a heavy-based pan over a very low heat. Toast them, turning them frequently, until they are yellowish in colour but not browned.

Put the sugar into a heavy-based saucepan and place it over a very low heat, rotating the pan as the sugar melts. When the sugar has completely dissolved, stir in the hot almonds. Add the butter if you want a richer result. Continue cooking the mixture until it turns a cinnamon colour. Stop the cooking immediately by dipping the bottom of the pan quickly into cold water. Then gradually pour the mixture into a buttered or oiled 30 by 20 by 3 cm (12 by 8 by 1¼ inch) tin. Use the cut side of the lemon to spread the mixture evenly and push it into the corners of the tin. Leave the mixture to get completely cold. To unmould it, loosen the edges with a sharp knife, then invert the tin. If unmoulding is difficult, dip the base of the tin in boiling water.

PELLEGRINO ARTUSI
LA SCIENZA IN CUCINA E L'ARTE DI MANGIAR BENE

Black Nougat with Pine Honey

Le Nougat Noir au Miel de Pin

Nougat noir *is a French name for dark nut toffee.*

The pine honey in the title is a speciality of the Chartreuse Valley, but you can use any good flower honey. The candy will have a different flavour for each kind of honey used.

To make about 750 g (1½ lb)

600 g	honey	1¼ lb
500 g	whole almonds	1 lb
1 tbsp	fresh thyme	1 tbsp

If the almonds have been washed, make sure they are perfectly dry before using. Into a 1.75 litre (3 pint) heavy iron saucepan, put the honey and heat it slowly. As the temperature of the honey begins to rise, drop in the thyme and the almonds with their skins on. Continue cooking the mixture slowly, raising the temperature and stirring the contents almost continuously until the honey begins to turn dark brown and the almonds begin to crackle. This will usually take about 30 minutes.

Line a 23 by 23 by 4 cm (9 by 9 by 1½ inch) tin with well-buttered aluminium foil or wax paper. Pour the almonds and honey into the tin. Press another piece of buttered paper or foil on top of the mixture. On top of that, place a light wooden board of a size to fit just inside the tin, and put a 1 kg (2 lb) weight on top of the board so that the mixture will be pressed down and solidified. Let the mixture cool gradually to room temperature. Do not refrigerate it. The mixture will take at least 4 hours to cool.

When the brittle is cold, take it out of the tin, peel off the covering, lay it on a wooden board and with a heavy, sharp knife, cut it up into bite-sized pieces. Store these in a tightly lidded jar. At room temperature they will be chewy. From the refrigerator, they will be crackly.

ROY ANDRIES DE GROOT
THE AUBERGE OF THE FLOWERING HEARTH

Dark Nougat

Nougat Noir

This nougat is traditional in Provence and is one of the 13 desserts for Christmas. Confectioners mould it between two rice paper wafers.

To make 2 kg (4 lb)

500 g	castor sugar	1 lb
1 kg	almonds, blanched and lightly toasted	2 lb
500 g	honey	1 lb
1 tbsp	orange-flower water	1 tbsp

Thoroughly oil two 20 cm (8 inch) square tins. Into a saucepan, put the almonds, honey, sugar and orange-flower water. Stirring frequently, bring the mixture to the boil, on a low heat, until the almonds crackle under the spatula and the honey turns pale golden-brown.

Turn the mixture into the tins and leave it to cool. Unmould the nougat and break it into pieces.

CÉLINE VENCE
ENCYCLOPÉDIE HACHETTE DE LA CUISINE RÉGIONALE

Maine Peanut Brittle

The technique of cooking sugar to a caramel without water is shown on page 9.

To make about 500 g (1 lb)

500 g	granulated sugar	1 lb
150 g	toasted peanuts, chopped	5 oz

Butter a 23 cm (9 inch) square tin. Spread the peanuts in it. Put the sugar in a heavy pan and cook it over a low heat, stirring constantly, until it melts into a thin syrup, about 10 minutes. Pour the syrup over the nuts. When the brittle is nearly cold, mark it into squares.

FANNIE MERRITT FARMER
THE FANNIE FARMER COOKBOOK

Nut Candy

Nuent

To make about 1 kg (2½ lb)

125 g	sugar	4 oz
½ litre	honey	16 fl oz
750 g	walnuts or pecan nuts, finely chopped	1½ lb

Bring the sugar and honey to the boil; boil them for 10 minutes. Slowly add the nuts. Cook the mixture until it is thick or until a sugar thermometer registers the soft-crack stage [*page 10*]. Spoon the mixture out on to a wet marble slab or wooden board. Dip your hands in iced water and pat the mixture into a square about 2.5 cm (1 inch) thick. Leave the mixture to cool slightly. Using a sharp, wet knife, cut the candy into squares or diamonds.

SARA KASDAN
LOVE AND KISHKES

Peanut Candy

The technique of cooking sugar without water to a caramel is shown on page 9.

To make about 600 g (1¼ lb)

500 g	granulated sugar	1 lb
100 g	peanuts, chopped	3½ oz
¼ tsp	salt	¼ tsp

Heat the peanuts and the salt together. Put the sugar in an iron pan, place it over a low heat and stir it constantly until the sugar is changed to a light brown syrup. Add the chopped peanuts and the salt, stirring them in as quickly as possible. Pour the mixture immediately into a hot buttered tin and, with a buttered chopping knife, divide it into squares.

A BOOK OF FAMOUS OLD NEW ORLEANS RECIPES

Chocolate Almond Brittle

If white corn syrup is not available, you can substitute 3 tablespoons of liquid glucose.

To make about 750 g (1½ lb)

500 g	granulated sugar	1 lb
10 cl	white corn syrup	3½ fl oz
15 cl	water	¼ pint
60 g	unsalted butter	2 oz
60 g	semi-sweet chocolate, grated	2 oz
1 tsp	vanilla extract	1 tsp
½ tsp	bicarbonate of soda	½ tsp
175 g ·	blanched almonds, toasted and coarsely chopped	6 oz

In a saucepan, combine the sugar with the corn syrup, cold water and butter. Cook over a medium heat, stirring, until the sugar has dissolved. Continue cooking without stirring until a temperature of 149°C (300°F) is reached on a sugar thermometer—the hard-crack stage [*pages 10-11*]. Remove the pan from the heat. Stir into it very rapidly the grated chocolate, the vanilla extract, the bicarbonate of soda and the toasted almonds. Pour the mixture in a thin layer on to a greased baking sheet. When it is cool enough to handle, pull it outwards at two opposite edges to make the layer thinner, resting the extra width on a second greased baking sheet. Leave it to cool. When the brittle is cold, break it into pieces.

JULIETTE ELKON
THE CHOCOLATE COOK BOOK

Polish Poppy-Seed Candy

Makagigi

To make about 500 g (1 lb)

125 g	granulated sugar	4 oz
300 g	honey	10 oz
150 g	poppy seeds, ground	5 oz

Lightly oil a marble slab or a flat dish. Cook the ingredients, stirring continuously, over a low heat. When the mixture is lightly browned, after about 15 minutes, pour it on to the dish or slab. Use an oiled palette knife to spread the mixture into a thin layer. Leave the mixture to set and, when firm but not cold, cut it into 2.5 cm (1 inch) squares.

JAN CZERNIKOWSKI
CIASTA, CIASTKA, CIASTECZKA

Poppy-Seed Candy

Mohnelech

To make about 1.5 kg (3 lb)

125 g	granulated sugar	4 oz
500 g	poppy seeds, soaked overnight in boiling water and drained	1 lb
600 g	honey	1¼ lb
250 g	pecan nuts or walnuts, chopped	8 oz

Pound the poppy seeds with a pestle or other heavy instrument for at least 10 minutes. Large poppy seeds can be run through a food grinder. (Pounding cracks the seeds and releases the flavour.) Cook the sugar and honey over a low heat until the sugar dissolves. Add the poppy seeds and cook the mixture until it is thick, stirring frequently. This may take 30 to 40 minutes. Test the mixture by dropping a spoonful on to a wet work surface; if it holds its shape, it is ready for the next step. Stir in the nuts. Cook for 1 minute longer.

Turn the mixture out on to a wet work surface. Dip your hands in iced water and pat the mixture to 1 cm (½ inch) thickness. Let it cool for 5 to 10 minutes. With a sharp knife dipped in hot water, cut the candy into about 50 pieces.

SARA KASDAN
LOVE AND KISHKES

Sesame Snaps

Halawet Sumsum

To make about 1 kg (2 lb)

500 g	granulated sugar	1 lb
500 g	sesame seeds	1 lb

Butter a baking sheet or metal tray. Place the sugar and sesame seeds in a saucepan. Allow them to simmer on a very low heat, stirring gently all the time, until the sugar is melted and the whole turns slightly brown, about 10 minutes. Pour the mixture on to the buttered baking sheet or metal tray. Spread it out to 5 mm (¼ inch) thickness. While it is still warm and before it becomes brittle, slice the mixture with a sharp knife. Wrap the pieces separately in greaseproof paper. This sweet keeps indefinitely.

MARGARET JOY PHILIPPOU
101 ARABIAN DELIGHTS

Sesame Squares

To toast sesame seeds, spread them out evenly in a dry frying pan, and cook them over a medium heat, stirring constantly, for about 10 minutes, until they begin to release their aroma.

This candy is chewy, but becomes brittle if the syrup is cooked to 149°C (300°F). After it cools, it can be broken into small pieces and stored in an airtight tin. Remember, moisture is the enemy of brittles!

To make about 600 g (1¼ lb)

350 g	toasted sesame seeds	12 oz
450 g	honey	15 oz
1 tbsp	lemon juice	1 tbsp

Thoroughly oil or butter a 30 by 23 cm (12 by 9 inch) Swiss roll tin. Lightly oil the inside of a 3 litre (5 pint) saucepan. Combine the sesame seeds, honey and lemon juice in the saucepan. Cook the mixture over a medium heat to boiling point. Then, stirring constantly, boil it to 138°C (280°F), the soft-crack stage [*page 10*]. Pour the syrup immediately into the tin. As the mixture cools, flatten it at the edges. When it has cooled completely, cut it into about thirty 5 cm (2 inch) squares or fifteen 5 by 10 cm (2 by 4 inch) bars. Wrap each piece in wax paper or plastic film. Store in an airtight tin.

MIRIAM LOWENBERG
CREATIVE CANDY MAKING

Sesame Candy

Semsemyah

To make about 275 g (9 oz)

3 tbsp	soft brown sugar	3 tbsp
175 g	sesame seeds	6 oz
3 tbsp	honey	3 tbsp

To roast the sesame seeds, spread them evenly in a 25 cm (10 inch) frying pan. Stirring constantly, cook the seeds over a fairly low heat for about 5 minutes. Remove the seeds from the heat and let them stand.

In a small pan, combine the honey and the sugar. Stirring constantly, cook them over a low heat until thick, about 5 minutes. Add the sesame seeds and mix thoroughly. Lay a piece of wax paper on a board or work surface and empty the mixture into the centre. Cover it with another piece of wax paper and roll out the mixture to about 5 mm (¼ inch) thickness with a rolling pin. Remove the paper. Cut the candy into square or diamond shapes. Leave them until cold, then separate the pieces and store them in a tightly covered box or jar.

DAISY INY
THE BEST OF BAGHDAD COOKING

Yellow-Man (Traditional)

The golden syrup can be replaced by treacle. If made with treacle, this honeycomb toffee will be dark brown in colour.

This is a universal favourite in Northern Ireland and to this day is found on stalls at country fairs. It is usually brought to the fairs in one large lump and broken off as it is sold.

To make about 600 g (1¼ lb)

250 g	Demerara sugar	8 oz
30 g	butter	1 oz
2 tbsp	water	2 tbsp
500 g	golden syrup	1 lb
1 tsp	bicarbonate of soda	1 tsp

Butter or oil a marble slab or a large dish. Melt the butter in a pan and tip the pan to grease it evenly. Then add the Demerara sugar, the water and the golden syrup. Stir until the sugar has dissolved. Bring the syrup to the boil and boil without stirring until the syrup is crisp and brittle when tested in cold water [*hard-crack stage, pages 10-11*]. Stir in the bicarbonate of soda and quickly pour the mixture on to the marble slab or large dish. Turn the edges of the mixture to the centre and pull it directly it is cool enough—about 3 minutes. Pull the toffee until it is pale in colour.

FLORENCE IRWIN
THE COOKIN' WOMAN

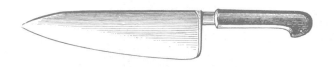

Old-Fashioned Molasses Candy

To make about 500 g (1 lb)

90 g	soft dark brown sugar	3 oz
35 cl	molasses	12 fl oz
15 g	butter	½ oz
1 tbsp	vinegar	1 tbsp
1 tsp	bicarbonate of soda	1 tsp
90 g	peanuts, roughly chopped (optional)	3 oz

Butter a shallow 20 cm (8 inch) tin. Cook the brown sugar, molasses, butter and vinegar together. Boil them to a temperature of 127°C (260°F) or until a drop will form a hard ball in cold water [*pages 10-11*]. Add the bicarbonate of soda and stir rapidly. Turn the mixture at once into the tin. If desired, spread the chopped peanuts over the top. Cool the mixture and break it into pieces for serving.

MILDRED GROSBERG BELLIN
THE JEWISH COOK BOOK

Peanut Molasses Brittle

To make about 850 g (1¾ lb)

500 g	granulated sugar	1 lb
12.5 cl	molasses	4 fl oz
12.5 cl	water	4 fl oz
75 g	butter	2½ oz
1 tsp	bicarbonate of soda	1 tsp
300 g	unsalted peanuts, blanched and roasted	10 oz

Put the sugar, molasses and water into a saucepan and cook them, stirring until the sugar has dissolved. Continue cooking very slowly until a temperature of 149°C (300°F) is reached [*hard-crack stage, pages 10-11*].

Remove the pan from the heat, stir in the butter, and then beat in the bicarbonate of soda. Add the peanuts and mix them in well. Pour the mixture out in a thin layer on a well-greased cold work surface or baking sheet. Smooth the mixture out with a spatula, pulling it into a thin sheet, if desired. If not, mark it into 2.5 cm (1 inch) squares. In any case, loosen the confection from the baking sheet while it is still warm. When cold, break it into squares or into irregular pieces.

MAY B. VAN ARSDALE AND RUTH PARRISH CASA EMELLOS
CANDY RECIPES AND OTHER CONFECTIONS

Yellow-Man (Modern)

To make about 850 g (1¾ lb)

500 g	Demerara sugar	1 lb
125 g	butter	4 oz
2 tbsp	vinegar	2 tbsp
250 g	treacle	8 oz
250 g	golden syrup	8 oz
½ tsp	bicarbonate of soda	½ tsp

Butter a 20 cm (8 inch) square tin. In a saucepan over a medium heat, melt the butter. Add the vinegar, treacle, golden syrup and Demerara sugar. Stir the mixture until the sugar has dissolved. Without stirring, boil the mixture until it is crisp when tested in cold water [*hard-crack stage, pages 10-11*]. Remove the pan from the heat and stir in the bicarbonate of soda. When the mixture foams up, stir it again. Pour the mixture quickly into the tin and leave it to cool. When it is cool, mark it into 2.5 cm (1 inch) squares. Leave it until cold, cut it into squares and store the toffee in a tightly closed tin.

FLORENCE IRWIN
THE COOKIN' WOMAN

Molasses Candies

Knäck

Although Swedish toffees (knäck) are always made with treacle, molasses or golden syrup, some contain cream which gives them a softer, more chewy consistency.

To make about 500 g (1 lb)

250 g	granulated sugar	8 oz
¼ litre	molasses	8 fl oz
60 g	butter	2 oz
¼ litre	double cream	8 fl oz
45 g	almonds, blanched and coarsely chopped	1½ oz

In a heavy saucepan, dissolve the sugar with the molasses, butter and cream. Cook the mixture over a low heat, stirring constantly until the mixture boils, and boil it to 121°C (250°F) [*firm-ball stage, pages 10-11*]. Add the almonds. Pour the mixture into paper confectionery cases and allow it to set.

SAM WIDENFELT (EDITOR)
FAVOURITE SWEDISH RECIPES

Vanilla Cream Caramels

Caramels are soft toffees for which the sugar syrup is cooked to either the firm-ball or hard-ball stage; they are not to be confused with liquid brown caramel—used for dipping or coating—which is sugar cooked to a much higher temperature. The technique of making caramels is on page 32.

To make about 275 g (9 oz)

250 g	granulated sugar	8 oz
¼ litre	double cream	8 fl oz
30 g	butter	1 oz
60 g	clear honey	2 oz
½	vanilla pod, slit lengthwise	½

Line a 20 cm (8 inch) square tin with oiled or buttered greaseproof paper, or oil confectioner's bars and arrange them round a sheet of oiled or buttered greaseproof paper.

Into a medium-sized copper pan, put the cream, sugar, butter, honey and the vanilla pod. Place the pan over a medium heat and stir until the sugar has dissolved, occasionally brushing down the sides of the pan with a wet pastry brush to remove any crystals which form. When the sugar has completely dissolved, set a sugar thermometer in the pan and bring the mixture to the boil. Boil the mixture steadily, stirring occasionally, until the sugar thermometer registers 121°C (250°F) [*firm-ball stage, pages 10-11*]. Quickly test the consistency of the mixture by dropping a teaspoonful of it into a bowl of iced water. Remove the test sample from the bowl with your fingers—it should be cold and firm enough to shape into a ball. The syrup will now have the consistency of the finished sweet. If the syrup is too soft, cook it a little longer. If it is just right, quickly remove the pan from the heat and dip the base in a bowl of cold water to stop further cooking. Use a fork to remove the vanilla pod and quickly pour the syrup into the tin or between the confectioner's bars.

Leave the caramel to cool. It should take about 2 hours at normal room temperature. When it has cooled and set, unmould the caramel and cut it into 2.5 cm (1 inch) strips, using an oiled or buttered knife. Chop the strips into 7.5 cm (3 inch) nuggets. Caramels become sticky if left in contact with the air, so wrap them in pieces of cellophane.

PETITS PROPOS CULINAIRES VI

Ohio Chocolate Caramels

To make about 500 g (1 lb)

200 g	granulated sugar	7 oz
12.5 cl	milk	4 fl oz
100 g	chocolate, grated	3½ oz
¼ litre	molasses	8 fl oz
30 g	butter	1 oz

Butter a marble slab or two large plates. In a saucepan, heat the milk and add the sugar, chocolate and molasses; stir the mixture over a medium heat until the sugar has dissolved and the chocolate has melted. Add the butter. Do not stir the mixture after it begins to boil as that will make it grain. It is done when it hardens and becomes brittle when dropped in cold water [*hard-ball stage, pages 10-11*].

Pour the mixture on to the buttered slab or plates in a layer about 1 cm (½ inch) thick. When the caramel is nearly cold, cut it with a buttered knife into 2.5 cm (1 inch) squares.

THE BUCKEYE COOKBOOK: TRADITIONAL AMERICAN RECIPES

Kinuski Caramels

Kinuskikola

To make about 350 g (12 oz)

175 g	granulated sugar	6 oz
15 g	cocoa powder	½ oz
40 g	black treacle	1½ oz
17.5 cl	milk	6 fl oz
30 g	butter	1 oz
	vanilla extract	

In a heavy-based saucepan, mix the sugar and cocoa. Add the treacle, milk and butter and heat the mixture slowly, stirring until the sugar has dissolved. Without stirring, simmer the mixture over a medium heat until it reaches a temperature of 120°C (248°F)—the firm-ball stage [*pages 10-11*]. Remove the pan from the heat and stir in a few drops of vanilla extract. Quickly pour the mixture into a buttered 20 by 10 cm (8 by 4 inch) shallow baking tin.

When the toffee has cooled to lukewarm, cut it into about thirty-two 2.5 cm (1 inch) squares. Wrap the toffee pieces individually in wax paper.

GUNNEVI BONEKAMP
SCANDINAVIAN COOKING

Swedish Toffee

Knäck

To make about 350 g (12 oz)

125 g	granulated sugar	4 oz
6 tbsp	double cream	6 tbsp
90 g	black treacle	3 oz
30 g	butter	1 oz
30 g	almonds, blanched and chopped	1 oz

In a heavy-based saucepan, heat the sugar, cream and treacle slowly, stirring, until the sugar has dissolved. Without stirring, cook the mixture over a medium heat until it reaches a temperature of 120°C (248°F)—the firm-ball stage [*pages 10-11*]. Remove the saucepan from the heat and stir in the butter and chopped almonds.

Quickly pour the mixture into a buttered 20 by 10 cm (8 by 4 inch) shallow baking tin. When the toffee is lukewarm, use a greased knife to mark it into about thirty-two 2.5 cm (1 inch) squares. Remove the toffee from the tin when it is completely cold and cut or break it into squares. Wrap the squares individually in wax paper.

GUNNEVI BONEKAMP
SCANDINAVIAN COOKING

Chocolate Caramels

To make 1 kg (2½ lb)

650 g	soft light brown sugar	1¼ lb
35 cl	molasses	12 fl oz
175 g	butter	6 oz
45 g	flour	1½ oz
175 g	plain chocolate	6 oz
35 cl	milk	12 fl oz
1½ tsp	vanilla extract	1½ tsp
About 30	almonds, blanched (optional)	About 30

Butter a 23 cm (9 inch) square tin. In a saucepan, combine the sugar, molasses, butter and flour. Dissolve the sugar, stirring over a medium heat, and bring the mixture to the boil. Boil it for 5 minutes, without stirring, then add the chocolate and milk. Cook, stirring occasionally, until a small amount of the mixture forms a firm ball when dropped into very cold water—120°C (248°F) on the sugar thermometer [*pages 10-11*]. Add the vanilla extract and pour the mixture into the buttered tin. Leave the caramel to cool before cutting it into squares. Put the squares into individual paper cases and top each with an almond. Or wrap the caramels in a strip of cellophane, twisting the cellophane and tying it with ribbon to separate the caramels.

WOMAN'S DAY COLLECTOR'S COOK BOOK

Toffee

If the cream is slightly soured, it is just as good or better.

To make about 500 g (1 lb)

300 g	castor sugar	10 oz
30 cl	double cream	½ pint
2 tsp	vanilla extract	2 tsp
2 tsp	whisky	2 tsp

Butter a flat dish or 20 cm (8 inch) square shallow tin. In a clean, untinned copper saucepan, dissolve the sugar in the cream, over medium heat, and bring the mixture to the boil, stirring occasionally. As it boils, the mixture will first become quite liquid, and afterwards it will gradually thicken. When it has thickened, after 10 to 15 minutes, add the vanilla extract and the whisky. When the mixture becomes very frothy and leaves the sides of the pan clean when stirred, a few minutes later, pour it quickly on to the dish or tin—it should set at once. Cut it into 2.5 cm (1 inch) squares. It should be quite smooth and of a creamy white; it should be rich without being at all crisp or crumbly.

THE KING'S COLLEGE HOSPITAL BOOK OF COOKING RECIPES

American Caramels

The author suggests that the vanilla extract can be replaced with strawberry or raspberry flavouring to make raspberry and strawberry caramels.

To make 6 kg (12½ lb)

3 kg	granulated sugar	6 lb
2 kg	liquid glucose	4 lb
2 litres	double cream	3½ pints
750 g	butter	1½ lb
4 tbsp	vanilla extract	4 tbsp

Oil a marble slab or six 20 cm (8 inch) square tins. Put the sugar, glucose and cream into a pan; put the pan on a low heat and stir constantly until the sugar has dissolved. Without stirring, boil the syrup to the firm-ball stage [*pages 10-11*]. Add the butter, stir until the butter is well mixed into the syrup, then remove the pan from the heat. Flavour the caramel mixture with the vanilla extract. Pour the caramel on to the marble slab or into the tins. Leave it to set before marking it into 2.5 cm (1 inch) squares. When the caramel is cold, cut it into the marked squares with a sharp knife and wrap each square in wax paper.

SKUSE'S COMPLETE CONFECTIONER

Honey-Almond Sweets

Sohan Asali

The quantity of saffron specified in this recipe will colour the sweets bright orange-yellow. If a paler colour is desired, use only 1 teaspoon of saffron; the technique of using saffron as a colouring is shown on page 15. Although the mixture is stirred, the honey will help to prevent crystallization of this soft toffee.

To make about 500 g (1 lb)

250 g	granulated sugar	8 oz
2 tbsp	honey	2 tbsp
45 g	butter	1½ oz
175 g	blanched almonds, slivered	6 oz
1 tbsp	powdered saffron, dissolved in 2 tablespoons hot water	1 tbsp
About 60 g	pistachio nuts, coarsely chopped, or blanched almonds, slivered	About 2 oz

Butter a baking sheet. Place the granulated sugar, honey and butter in a saucepan over a medium heat, stirring occasionally until the sugar dissolves, about 10 minutes. Add the 175 g (6 oz) of slivered almonds and stir occasionally until the almonds turn golden-brown, about 10 minutes. Do not stir too much, or the butter may separate. Add the saffron, and remove the pan from the heat. Allow the mixture to cool to lukewarm, then drop teaspoonfuls of it on to the baking sheet. Sprinkle each sweet with a few slivers of almonds or chopped pistachio nuts. When the sweets are completely cold and firm, use a palette knife to lift them off the baking sheet. Store the sweets in an airtight container.

NESTA RAMAZANI
PERSIAN COOKING

Stick Candy

The technique of making pulled sugar sweets is shown on pages 26-29. Alternative flavourings and colourings are discussed on page 14. If corn syrup is not available, use 4 tablespoons of liquid glucose.

To make 500 g (1 lb)

500 g	granulated sugar	1 lb
12.5 cl	white corn syrup	4 fl oz
12.5 cl	water	4 fl oz
1	lemon, rind grated, juice squeezed and strained	1
1 tsp	lemon extract, or 1 tsp peppermint extract and a few drops of red colouring	1 tsp

Butter one large dish for the lemon sticks or two large dishes for the peppermint sticks. In a saucepan, dissolve the sugar with the corn syrup and water over a medium heat. Bring the mixture to the boil and boil the syrup without stirring until a few drops become brittle in cold water [*hard-crack stage, pages 10-11*]. Stir in the lemon rind and juice. Remove the pan from the heat.

For lemon sticks, add the lemon extract and pour the syrup on to a buttered dish. When the syrup is cool enough to handle, after a couple of minutes, pull it until it is opaque, roll it into sticks and cut the sticks into pieces with oiled scissors.

For peppermint sticks, add the peppermint extract instead of the lemon extract and pour half the syrup on to a buttered dish. To the other half of the syrup, add the red colouring. Pour the red syrup on to the other buttered dish. When the syrups are cool enough to handle, pull them separately, then twist one around the other. Form them into canes or sticks.

MRS. SIMON KANDER (EDITOR)
THE SETTLEMENT COOK BOOK

Bull's-Eyes

To make 1 kg (2 lb)

1 kg	soft brown or Demerara sugar	2 lb
$\frac{1}{4}$ litre	water	8 fl oz
	cream of tartar	
$\frac{1}{2}$ tsp	lemon essence	$\frac{1}{2}$ tsp
$\frac{1}{4}$ tsp	tartaric acid	$\frac{1}{4}$ tsp

Butter a large dish or marble slab. Dissolve the brown sugar in the water over a medium heat, add a pinch of cream of tartar and boil the syrup to the soft-crack stage [*page 10*]. Pour the syrup into the buttered dish or on to the marble slab. As the syrup cools and hardens, slice off about one quarter to

one half of it and pull it until it is white and opaque. Pull the white mixture into a rope and cut it into thin lengths. To the remaining syrup, add the lemon essence and tartaric acid and mix well. Lay the lengths of the white mixture on the brown unpulled mixture at about 2.5 cm (1 inch) intervals. Fold the brown mixture in two lengthwise. Pull the folded sweet and break or cut it into strips. Twist the strips, holding them by each end and turning the ends in opposite directions. Then, using buttered scissors, cut the strips into small equal pieces.

MAY BYRON (EDITOR)
PUDDINGS, PASTRIES AND SWEET DISHES

French Pulled Sugar Sweets

Berlingots

Suitable flavourings and colourings are discussed on page 14. The technique for pulling sugar syrup is shown on pages 26-29. These sweets are often flavoured with peppermint.

To make about 1 kg (2 lb)

1 kg	granulated sugar	2 lb
$\frac{1}{2}$ litre	tepid water	16 fl oz
1	lemon, juice strained, rind grated	$\frac{1}{2}$
	flavouring (optional)	
	colouring (optional)	

In a saucepan, put the sugar, warm water and lemon juice. Stir over a medium heat until the sugar has dissolved, then increase the heat and cook the syrup to the soft-ball stage [*pages 10-11*]. Add the lemon rind or whatever flavouring you prefer, and a colouring, if used. Cook the mixture to the hard-crack stage [*pages 10-11*].

Pour the syrup on to an oiled, cold work surface. Use a palette knife to quickly fold the mixture towards the centre as it spreads out. As soon as the sugar is cool enough to handle, pull and knead it in your hands until it becomes opaque. Then roll it between your hands until it forms one long strip the thickness of a finger. Cut it with oiled scissors into small pieces the size of hazelnuts. Store the sweets in a dry place.

MME. ROSALIE BLANQUET
LE PÂTISSIER DES MÉNAGES

Candy Balls

Stroopballetjes

These sweets are soft and sticky. It is advisable to wrap them individually in cellophane before storing them or they will stick to each other.

To make about 500 g (1 lb)

9 tbsp	granulated sugar	9 tbsp
10 g	butter	$\frac{1}{3}$ oz
$\frac{1}{2}$ litre	treacle, warmed	16 fl oz

Oil a stone slab. Dissolve the sugar and the butter in the warmed treacle over a medium heat. Boil the mixture, without stirring, until it has the consistency of a thick syrup [*soft-ball stage, pages 10-11*]. Pour the syrup on to the stone slab. As soon as it begins to set, form it into a ball and pull off a thick strip. Cut this strip into small pieces and roll them into balls.

C. J. WANNÉE (EDITOR)
KOOKBOEK VAN DE AMSTERDAMSE HUISHOUDSCHOOL

Berlingots

The technique of making pulled sugar sweets is shown on pages 26-29. If preferred, you can cook the red and white portions of syrup to the same temperature. Colouring can be added to the syrup in the pan just before it is poured out.

To make 500 g (1 lb)

500 g	granulated sugar or lump sugar	1 lb
1 tbsp	liquid glucose	1 tbsp
15 cl	water	$\frac{1}{4}$ pint
	red colouring	

On a marble slab, oil two areas, each about 30 cm (12 inches) square. Boil the sugar, glucose and water to 121°C (250°F) [*hard-ball stage, pages 10-11*]. Pour half the syrup in a thin stream on to one oiled area of the slab. Add a few drops of red colouring and fold in the edges of the syrup as they spread. Boil the remainder of the syrup to 149°C (300°F) [*hard-crack stage, pages 10-11*] and pour it on to the other oiled area of the slab. When this second portion of the syrup is cool enough, pull it until it is white.

Working rapidly, form the red portion into an egg shape and fold the white part round it, gradually working the ball into a two-coloured stick 1 cm ($\frac{1}{2}$ inch) thick. Use oiled scissors to cut the stick into 2.5 cm (1 inch) long pieces and roll the pieces between your palms to make them round.

BEATRICE MANDERS AND E. M. MILLNER
THE ART OF SWEET-MAKING

Bristol Mints

The technique of making pulled sugar sweets is shown on pages 26-29. The plain and the coloured sugar syrups should be cooked simultaneously so that neither has a chance to harden before it can be pulled or shaped. It is advisable to ask a friend to help you so that the pulling of the plain syrup can be done before the syrups become hard and brittle.

These sweets are smartly striped in black and white like a fine French ribbon.

To make 500 g (1 lb)

250 g	granulated sugar	8 oz
250 g	soft dark brown or Demerara sugar	8 oz
$\frac{1}{4}$ litre	water	8 fl oz
	cream of tartar	
1 tsp	peppermint extract	1 tsp
	brown colouring	

Butter a large marble slab or work surface. Dissolve the granulated sugar in half the water, over a medium heat. Add a pinch of cream of tartar and half the peppermint extract and cook the syrup to 149°C (300°F) [*hard-crack stage, pages 10-11*]. Remove the pan from the heat and pour the syrup on to one area of the marble slab. Leave it to cool until it can be handled—2 to 3 minutes—then pull and work it until it is white and opaque. With an oiled spatula, shape it into a square. Meanwhile, add the brown sugar to the rest of the water, stirring constantly over a medium heat until the sugar has dissolved. Boil the brown sugar syrup to 149°C (300°F) [*hard-crack stage, pages 10-11*] and add the rest of the peppermint extract and the brown colouring. Pour the syrup on to the buttered marble slab. With an oiled spatula, shape the cooled brown syrup into a square. Cut the white and the brown squares in half, pile them on top of each other, brown-white, brown-white, and press them together. Then cut them into strips with a sharp, oiled knife. With oiled scissors, cut the strips into small squares. Leave the mixture to set.

NELL HEATON (EDITOR)
HOME-MADE SWEETS

Striped Candies

Polkagrisar

One tablespoon of liquid glucose can be substituted for the powdered glucose in this recipe.

To make about 500 g (1 lb)

500 g	granulated sugar	1 lb
1 tbsp	powdered glucose	1 tbsp
¼ litre	water	8 fl oz
2 tsp	malt vinegar	2 tsp
	peppermint flavouring	
	red colouring	

Oil a marble slab or baking sheet. In a saucepan, mix the sugar, glucose, water and vinegar. Dissolve the sugar over a medium heat, stirring constantly; then bring to the boil, without stirring. Boil the syrup to a temperature of 135°C (275°F) or until the mixture becomes brittle when dropped in cold water [*soft-crack stage, page 10*]. Remove the pan from the heat and leave it to cool for 3 to 4 minutes. Pour three-quarters of the contents on to the baking sheet. Add 3 drops of peppermint flavouring and, with a spatula, turn the edges of the mixture constantly towards the centre until the mixture is cool enough to handle. Oil your hands and stretch and pull it: folding, stretching and folding until it is opaque and white. Then pull the toffee into one long strip and lay it on the marble slab or baking sheet. Colour the reserved syrup in the pan with a few drops of the red colouring. Pour it on to the slab or baking sheet in two strips on either side of the pulled toffee. Working quickly, twist the strips together. Use oiled scissors to cut them immediately into shapes.

SAM WIDENFELT (EDITOR)
FAVOURITE SWEDISH RECIPES

Vinegar Candy

The technique of making pulled sugar sweets is demonstrated on pages 26-29.

To make about 1 kg (2½ lb)

1 litre	molasses	1¾ pints
¼ litre	cider vinegar	8 fl oz

Add the cider vinegar to the molasses. Over a medium heat, boil the mixture until it reaches the point where a little dropped into cold water becomes very hard and brittle [*hard-crack stage, pages 10-11*]. Pour the mixture into shallow, buttered platters and leave until cool enough to be handled, about 2 to 3 minutes. Then form the sweet into a large roll which may be pulled to any size and cut into sticks.

HOW TO MAKE CANDY

Salt Water Taffy

If white corn syrup is not available, you can substitute 5 tablespoons of liquid glucose. The technique of making pulled sugar sweets is shown on pages 26-29.

This famous candy is sold all along the Boardwalk at Atlantic City and, it is claimed, is made with sea water.

To make about 300 g (10 oz)

250 g	granulated sugar	8 oz
1 tbsp	cornflour	1 tbsp
17.5 cl	white corn syrup	6 fl oz
15 g	butter	½ oz
12.5 cl	water	4 fl oz
¼ tsp	salt	¼ tsp
	colourings and flavourings	

Mix the sugar and cornflour in a saucepan. Stir in the corn syrup, butter, water and salt. Cook the mixture over a moderate heat until it reaches 123°C (254°F), or until a few drops tested in cold water form a ball which holds its shape [*hard-ball stage, pages 10-11*]. Remove the pan from the heat, add a few drops of food colouring and flavouring extract, and pour the mixture on to a buttered dish. Cool it until it can be handled comfortably, about 2 to 3 minutes. Butter your hands and pull the taffy until it is light in colour and firm enough to hold a shape. Stretch it into a roll about 2.5 cm (1 inch) in diameter and snip bits off the roll with oiled kitchen scissors. Wrap each piece separately in wax paper.

THE EDITORS OF AMERICAN HERITAGE
THE AMERICAN HERITAGE COOKBOOK

Dotty Dimple's Vinegar Candy

The technique of making pulled sugar sweets is demonstrated on pages 26-29.

Rebecca Sophia Clarke (Sophie May) of Norridgewock, Maine, wrote more than 40 books for children, including the six-volume series, the *Dotty Dimple Stories*, published from 1867 to 1869. This candy became as popular with children as did the books.

To make 750 g (1½ lb)

750 g	granulated sugar	1½ lb
35 cl	vinegar	12 fl oz

Combine the sugar with the vinegar and cook over a low heat, stirring constantly, until the sugar is dissolved. Continue cooking until the syrup reaches the soft-crack stage—132° to

143°C (270° to 290°F)—or until a few drops tested in cold water separate into threads which are hard but not brittle [*page 10*]. Pour the syrup on to a large buttered dish and let it cool until the candy can be handled comfortably. Butter your hands and pull the syrup until it is white and almost firm. Stretch it into a rope about 2.5 cm (1 inch) in diameter and snip off pieces with oiled scissors.

THE EDITORS OF AMERICAN HERITAGE
THE AMERICAN HERITAGE COOKBOOK

Honey Taffy

For a change of taste, add 1 teaspoon of instant coffee crystals to the boiling syrup. Or melt 90 g (3 oz) of semi-sweet chocolate pieces with 15 g (½ oz) of butter and leave to cool; after cutting the taffy into pieces, dip one end of each piece into the cooled melted chocolate, covering about half the piece. Let the chocolate dry on wax paper before wrapping the taffy.

To make 1 kg (2 lb)

500 g	granulated sugar	1 lb
600 g	honey	1¼ lb
¼ litre	water	8 fl oz
¼ tsp	salt	¼ tsp
2 tsp	vanilla extract	-2 tsp

Thoroughly oil a 23 by 30 cm (9 by 12 inch) Swiss roll tin and place it on a wire rack. Lightly oil the inside of a 3 litre (5 pint) saucepan. Combine the sugar, honey, water and salt in the pan. Cook the mixture over a medium heat, stirring constantly, until the sugar is completely dissolved. Wipe down sugar crystals above the liquid line, using a clean pastry brush dipped in cold water, until the syrup comes to the boil. Boil it, without stirring, until the thermometer registers 138°C (280°F) [*soft-crack stage, page 10*]. Stir in the vanilla extract. Pour the syrup into the tin.

Leave the taffy to cool until it can be handled comfortably, about 3 minutes, then start working it. Shape the taffy into a ball, then start pulling. Form a long rope; double it. Redouble the rope; pull it out again. When the taffy feels light and pliable, shape it into a long rope about 1 cm (½ inch) in diameter. Using well-oiled scissors, cut the ropes into 2.5 cm (1 inch) pieces. Wrap each piece individually in cellophane or wax paper. Store in a cool place in an airtight container.

MIRIAM LOWENBERG
CREATIVE CANDY MAKING

Edinburgh Rock

The original Edinburgh rock, made in Edinburgh and sold in boxes printed with the Ferguson or Royal Stewart tartan, is shipped all over the world. The rock should be pastel coloured and lightly flavoured. Traditionally, plain white rock is flavoured with lemon, vanilla or peppermint, pink rock is flavoured with raspberry extract or rose-water, pale brown rock is flavoured with 1 teaspoon of ground ginger, and yellow rock is flavoured with orange-flower water, orange or tangerine flavouring. If you do not have a dough hook, the rock can also be pulled by hand.

To make 750 g (1½ lb)

750 g	granulated sugar	1½ lb
1 tbsp	liquid glucose	1 tbsp
30 cl	water	½ pint
¼ tsp	cream of tartar	¼ tsp
	flavouring and colouring	

Butter a marble slab. In a heavy saucepan, dissolve the sugar in the glucose and water over a medium heat. Add the cream of tartar and boil the syrup to 135°C (275°F) [*soft-crack stage, page 10*]. Pour the syrup on to the marble slab. Add the flavouring and colouring. Fold the edges of the mixture to the centre as they cool. As soon as the sweet is cool enough, pull it over an oiled hook—such as the dough hook of a food mixer—for about 15 minutes. Then pull the rock into sticks, being careful not to twist it, and, when cold, break it into pieces. Leave it exposed to the air for at least 24 hours in a warm place, until the process of granulation is complete and the rock is powdery and soft. Store it in tins.

BEATRICE MANDERS AND E. M. MILLNER
THE ART OF SWEET-MAKING

Molasses Taffy

To make about 500 g (1 lb)

200 g	soft brown sugar	7 oz
1 litre	molasses	1¾ pints
12.5 cl	water	4 fl oz
45 g	butter	1½ oz
½ tsp	bicarbonate of soda	½ tsp

Thoroughly butter a shallow 20 cm (8 inch) square tin. Combine the molasses, sugar and water. Cook the mixture over a low heat until it reaches the soft-crack stage—133°C (272°F) [*page 10*]. Remove the pan from the heat; add the butter and bicarbonate of soda. Turn the mixture into the tin and let it stand until cool enough to handle. Gather the mixture into a ball and pull it until it is opaque. With oiled scissors, cut the taffy into about forty-eight 2.5 cm (1 inch) pieces.

· MARY MARGARET MCBRIDE
HARVEST OF AMERICAN COOKING

Toffee and Fanny

Taffi a Ffani

Taffi *and* Ffani *are two names that are given to pulled toffee in* South Wales.

To make about 350 g (12 oz)

500 g	soft brown sugar	1 lb
¼ litre	cold water	8 fl oz
2 tsp	vinegar	2 tsp
30 g	butter	1 oz
	peppermint flavouring	

Butter or oil a marble slab or large dish. Put the sugar, water, vinegar and butter into a cast-iron saucepan and cook them over a moderate heat, stirring continuously until the sugar has dissolved. Bring the mixture to the boil and boil it for 15 minutes. Test a teaspoonful of the boiling mixture in cold water, and if it hardens immediately [*soft-crack stage, page 10*] remove the mixture from the heat.

Pour the bulk of the mixture on to the slab or dish, but retain a little in the saucepan and keep the saucepan in a warm place to prevent the toffee from hardening.

Grease both your hands with butter and, as quickly as possible, pull the toffee while it is hot, adding a few drops of peppermint flavouring while pulling. Continue pulling until the toffee turns a creamy colour and forms long strips about 2.5 cm (1 inch) wide.

Butter or oil the slab or dish again. Lay the toffee in strips on the slab or dish. Pour the reserved toffee in a thin stream on to the toffee to form a thin brown line along the centre of each strip. Cut the toffee into smaller pieces before it hardens.

S. MINWEL TIBBOTT
WELSH FARE

Molasses Candy

The technique of making pulled sugar sweets is shown on pages 26-29. Flavourings are discussed on page 14. As the molasses and brown sugar will themselves impart a strong flavour, orange or peppermint would be suitable flavourings.

To make about 1 kg (2 lb)

175 g	soft dark brown sugar	6 oz
1 litre	molasses	1¾ pints
60 g	butter	2 oz
½ tsp	bicarbonate of soda	½ tsp
	flavouring (optional)	

Butter two 20 cm (8 inch) square tins. Into a large heavy pan, put the sugar, molasses and butter. Cook them over a low heat, stirring frequently to dissolve the sugar and prevent burning. Boil until the mixture thickens. Test the mixture by taking some out and dropping a few drops in a cup of cold water. If the drops harden quickly and break short between the teeth [*soft-crack stage, page 10*], the mixture is boiled enough. Remove the pan from the heat.

Now put in the bicarbonate of soda and stir the mixture well. Pour the mixture in a long thin stream in strips into the buttered tins. If you are using flavouring, put a couple of drops on each strip of candy. After about 2 to 3 minutes, when the candy is cool enough to handle, butter your hands thoroughly. Pull and fold the candy strips in half, then pull again until the candy turns whitish yellow. It may then quickly be cut into pieces and rolled or twisted.

MRS. F. L. GILLETTE AND HUGO ZIEMANN
THE WHITE HOUSE COOKBOOK

Welsh Toffee

Cyflaith

Noson Gyflaith (the Toffee Evening) was a traditional part of Christmas or New Year festivities in some areas of North Wales earlier this century. Families would invite friends to their homes for supper and the meal would be followed by merriment, playing games, making toffee and story telling. When the required ingredients for the toffee had boiled to a certain degree, the toffee was poured on to a well-greased slate or stone slab. The hearthstone itself was used for this purpose in some houses. Members of the gathering would then cover their hands with butter and attempt to pull the toffee while it was warm, until it became golden-yellow.

To make about 1.5 kg (3 lb)

1.5 kg	soft brown sugar	3 lb
15 cl	boiling water	¼ pint
1	lemon, juice strained	1
250 g	salted butter, softened	8 oz

Butter a marble slab or a large flat dish. Using an enamelled or steel pan over a low heat, gradually dissolve the sugar in the boiling water. Stir it continuously with a wooden spoon until the sugar is thoroughly melted. This usually takes from 20 to 30 minutes. Remove the saucepan from the heat, add the lemon juice and the softened butter, and stir them into the sugar. Boil this mixture fairly briskly, without stirring it, for a further 15 minutes.

Gently drop a teaspoonful of the mixture into a cupful of cold water; if it hardens at once, it has reached the required consistency [*soft-crack stage, page 10*]. Pour the mixture slowly on to the slab or dish. Do not scrape the pan clean as the scrapings might turn the toffee back into sugar.

Use extra butter to butter your hands. Pull the toffee into long, golden strands while it is still hot. Cut the strands of toffee into smaller pieces.

S. MINWEL TIBBOTT
WELSH FARE

Lellie Ishmael's Cream Candy

The technique of making pulled sugar sweets is demonstrated on pages 26-29.

After the candy has been allowed to stand 3 to 4 hours in a warm room, it becomes creamy, but at first it is chewy.

To make about 1 kg (2 lb)

1 kg	granulated sugar	2 lb
¼ litre	water	8 fl oz
½ tsp	salt	½ tsp
⅛ tsp	bicarbonate of soda	⅛ tsp
¼ litre	single cream	8 fl oz

Butter a marble slab or enamel work surface. In a heavy metal pan, combine the sugar, water, salt and bicarbonate of soda. Do not stir these ingredients. Put the pan on a high heat. When the mixture begins to form large, clear bubbles, and will spin a hair thread 7.5 to 15 cm (3 to 6 inches) long [*soft-crack stage, page 10*], add the cream, drop by drop, as if you were making a mayonnaise. The syrup must never stop boiling and this process of adding the cream cannot be rushed. After the last drop of cream has been added, lower the heat and simmer until the mixture turns pale brown and will once more spin a thread 7.5 to 15 cm (3 to 6 inches) long. The whole cooking process does not take more than 15 to 20 minutes.

In a warm place, such as near the open door of a heated oven or by a fire, pour the syrup in a thin, narrow stream about 15 to 20 cm (6 to 8 inches) long on to the buttered slab or work surface. Leave a space and pour out another narrow stream of syrup next to it, and so on until the syrup is used up. Do not scrape the pan, as the scrapings will crystallize.

Begin to pull the candy immediately. Beginning with the first thin strip of syrup, start pulling, then add the next and incorporate that, and so on until all the syrup is used up. Continue to pull until the mixture turns white or the palest ivory colour and is too stiff to continue pulling. When pulling the candy, it will be found that two people can handle the stiff candy better than one. When the candy becomes too stiff to pull any longer, twist it into a rope about 4 cm (1½ inches) thick and cut it with kitchen scissors into pieces 2.5 to 4 cm (1 to 1½ inches) wide; then spread it out on the buttered work surface. It is necessary to work quickly as the candy gets hard very suddenly and, again, two pairs of hands are better than one. One person can cut from one end of the rope, another from the other end. Either leave the candy to soften to a creamy consistency on the work surface or pack it into tin boxes, putting a sheet of wax paper or tin foil between each layer.

MARION FLEXNER
OUT OF KENTUCKY KITCHENS

Yum Yum

The technique of making pulled sugar sweets is demonstrated on pages 26-29.

To make 500 g (1 lb)		
500 g	soft brown sugar	1 lb
90 g	butter	3 oz
15 cl	water	¼ pint

Oil a marble slab or work surface. Over a low heat, stir the sugar with the butter and the water until the sugar has completely dissolved. Increase the heat and bring the mixture to the boil. Boil it until it is brittle when dropped into cold water [*soft-crack stage, page 10*].

Pour the syrup on to the marble slab or work surface. When the mixture is cool enough to handle, in about 2 to 3 minutes, pull it until it is creamy white. Shape it into sticks or bars and cut it into pieces with oiled scissors.

GRACE E. DENISON (EDITOR)
THE NEW COOK BOOK BY THE LADIES OF TORONTO
AND OTHER CITIES AND TOWNS

Plain Milk Fudge

To make about 1 kg (2 lb)		
850 g	granulated sugar	1¾ lb
30 cl	milk	½ pint
120 g	butter	4 oz
2 tsp	vanilla extract	2 tsp

Butter an 18 cm (7 inch) square tin. Pour the milk into a pan. Bring it slowly to the boil. Add the sugar and the butter and heat them slowly, stirring all the time, until the sugar dissolves and the butter melts. Bring the mixture to the boil and cover the pan with a lid. Boil the mixture for 2 minutes, then uncover the pan and continue to boil the mixture steadily,

stirring occasionally, until a little of the mixture dropped into a cup of cold water forms a soft ball when rolled gently between the finger and thumb. The temperature on the sugar thermometer should read 115° to 116°C (238° to 240°F) [*soft-ball stage, pages 10-11*].

Remove the pan from the heat and stir in the vanilla extract. Leave the mixture to cool for 5 minutes. Beat the fudge until it just begins to lose its gloss and is thick and creamy. Transfer the fudge to the tin. When it has cooled, mark it into squares. When it has set firm, cut it into about 50 squares with a sharp knife. Store it in an airtight tin.

SONIA ALLISON
THE DAIRY BOOK OF HOME COOKERY

Banana/Chocolate Fudge

If corn syrup is not available, 1 tablespoon of liquid glucose can be used instead.

To make 600 g (1¼ lb)		
90 g	soft brown sugar	3 oz
350 g	granulated sugar	12 oz
1	medium-ripe banana, mashed	1
60 g	plain chocolate, broken into pieces	2 oz
17.5 cl	milk	6 fl oz
⅛ tsp	salt	⅛ tsp
2 tbsp	white corn syrup	2 tbsp
45 g	butter	1½ oz
½ tsp	vanilla extract	½ tsp
60 g	walnuts, chopped (optional)	2 oz

Lightly butter a 22 by 11 by 6 cm (8½ by 4½ by 2½ inch) tin. In a saucepan, combine the banana, chocolate, brown and granulated sugars, milk, salt and corn syrup. Stirring constantly, cook the mixture over a medium heat, until the sugars dissolve. If sugar crystals form on the sides of the pan, wipe them off with a pastry brush dipped in water. Continue cooking over a medium heat, stirring occasionally to prevent the mixture from sticking, until it reaches the soft-ball stage—113°C (236°F) [*pages 10-11*]. Remove the pan from the heat. Add the butter without stirring; cool the mixture to lukewarm—43°C (110°F).

Add the vanilla extract; beat the mixture until it loses its gloss and starts to thicken. Pour it into the tin. Sprinkle it with the walnuts, if used, gently pressing them into the fudge with a spoon. When it is cool and firm, cut it into 32 pieces.

NELL B. NICHOLS (EDITOR)
HOMEMADE CANDY

Chocolate Fudge

To make about 750 g (1½ lb)

500 g	granulated sugar	1 lb
6 tbsp	milk	6 tbsp
30 g	butter	1 oz
175 g	plain chocolate, grated or chopped	6 oz

Put the sugar into a saucepan and mix it with the milk to form a thick paste. Add the butter and stir in the grated or chopped chocolate. Put the pan on a gentle heat and cook, stirring constantly. Do not let the contents of the saucepan come to the boil until the sugar is dissolved and the chocolate has melted. Increase the heat slightly and let the mixture boil for about 5 minutes or until it reaches the soft-ball stage [*pages 10-11*]. Take the fudge off the heat, beat it until it is thick and pour it on to buttered soup plates or dishes, or into a buttered 20 cm (8 inch) square tin. Cut it into squares before it gets cold.

MRS. C. F. LEYEL AND MISS OLGA HARTLEY
THE GENTLE ART OF COOKERY

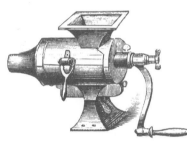

Milk Fudge

The technique of making fudge is shown on page 38. The author suggests this recipe can be varied by substituting a further 3 tablespoons of desiccated coconut or 125 g (4 oz) of grated chocolate for the glacé cherries. Vanilla sugar (page 15) can be used instead of sugar and vanilla extract.

To make about 1 kg (2 lb)

850 g	granulated sugar	1¾ lb
30 cl	milk	½ pint
125 g	butter	4 oz
2 tsp	vanilla extract	2 tsp
60 g	glacé cherries, chopped, or 30 g (1 oz) currants and 30 g (1 oz) chopped, blanched almonds (optional)	2 oz

Put the milk into a heavy saucepan. Add the sugar and the butter and heat the mixture slowly, stirring all the time, until the sugar dissolves and the butter melts. Bring the mixture to the boil and cover the pan with a lid. Boil it for 2 minutes and

then uncover it. Without stirring, boil the mixture steadily for 10 to 15 minutes or until it reaches the soft-ball stage [*pages 10-11*]. Remove the mixture from the heat, dip the base of the pan briefly in cold water, stir in the vanilla extract and leave it to cool to lukewarm. Beat the fudge until it loses its glossy appearance and is thick and creamy. Pour it into a greased 20 cm (8 inch) square tin. Leave it to cool completely before marking it into 2.5 cm (1 inch) squares.

If you like, add chopped glacé cherries or currants and almonds to the mixture just before it is poured into the tin.

MARY NORWAK
TOFFEES, FUDGES, CHOCOLATES AND SWEETS

Maple Cream Candy

This candy is short-lived when cut in pieces and exposed to the air, but if left in the tin with wax paper cover, it may be kept for a few weeks in good condition.

To make about 750 g (1½ lb)

500 g	granulated sugar	1 lb
¼ litre	maple syrup	8 fl oz
12.5 cl	single cream	4 fl oz
12.5 cl	water	4 fl oz
30 g	butter	1 oz
30 g	nuts, finely chopped (optional)	1 oz

In a saucepan, mix the sugar, the maple syrup, the cream and the water. Stir until the sugar has dissolved over a moderate heat, and then boil without stirring to approximately 110°C (230°F). Add the butter and lower the heat; boil the mixture to 113°C (236°F), or to a soft ball by the water test [*pages 10-11*]. With a damp cloth, wipe away the crystals from the pouring side of the pan and pour the hot syrup into a shallow bowl. Allow it to cool undisturbed to a temperature of 43° to 46°C (110° to 115°F). Stir the cooled syrup with a heavy spoon or spatula until it is well creamed, then add the nuts, if using.

Continue to stir until the mixture has a soft dough-like consistency. Knead it in your hands or on a moulding board until it is soft and plastic. Mould the mixture into a 20 cm (8 inch) square tin that has been lightly buttered or lined with wax paper. Press the mixture down to form a sheet of uniform thickness and smooth off the top by gently patting it with your fingers. Cover it with wax paper.

After standing a few minutes, the candy may be removed from the tin and cut into pieces suitable for serving.

WALTER W. CHENOWETH
HOW TO MAKE CANDY

Maple Fudge

If corn syrup is not available, 1 tablespoon of liquid glucose can be used instead.

This fudge is particularly good when made with walnuts. Add 125 g (4 oz) of broken walnuts to the fudge just before turning it out into the tin to cool.

To make 500 g (1 lb)		
500 g	granulated sugar	1 lb
12.5 cl	maple syrup	4 fl oz
¼ litre	milk	8 fl oz
2 tbsp	white corn syrup	2 tbsp
	salt	
30 g	butter	1 oz
1 tsp	vanilla extract	1 tsp

Thoroughly oil a 20 by 20 by 5 cm (8 by 8 by 2 inch) tin. Lightly oil the inside of a 1.5 to 2 litre (2½ to 3½ pint) saucepan. Combine the sugar, maple syrup, milk, corn syrup and a pinch of salt in the pan. Cook the mixture over a low heat until the sugar is dissolved completely and the mixture boils. Wipe down the sugar crystals above the liquid line with a clean pastry brush dipped in cold water. Cook, without stirring, until the soft-ball stage is reached—114°C (238°F) [*pages 10-11*]. Remove the pan from the heat immediately. Add the butter, *but do not stir.* Cool the mixture to 43°C (110°F) or until the bottom of the pan feels barely warm to the touch. Add the vanilla extract. Beat the mixture vigorously until it is thick and has just lost its glossy look. Turn out the mixture into the tin and spread it evenly to cool. When it is cold, cut it into squares.

MIRIAM LOWENBERG
CREATIVE CANDY MAKING

Buttermilk Candy

This fudge can also be made with yogurt in place of butter-milk. If corn syrup is not available, 1 tablespoon of liquid glucose can be used instead.

To make about 750 g (1½ lb)		
500 g	granulated sugar	1 lb
¼ litre	cultured buttermilk	8 fl oz
1 tsp	bicarbonate of soda	1 tsp
2 tbsp	white corn syrup	2 tbsp
60 g	butter	2 oz
125 g	pecan nuts, chopped	4 oz

Butter a 20 cm (8 inch) square tin. In a heavy 3 litre (5 pint) saucepan, combine the buttermilk and the bicarbonate of soda. Let the mixture stand for 20 minutes.

Add the sugar and the corn syrup to the buttermilk. Bring the mixture to the boil, stirring until the sugar has dissolved. When the mixture boils, add the butter and cook, stirring occasionally if necessary, to the soft-ball stage—113° to 114°C (236° to 238°F) [*pages 10-11*]. The mixture should turn a medium-brown colour.

Remove the pan from the heat and cool the mixture to lukewarm—43°C (110°F). Beat the mixture until it loses its gloss and starts to thicken. Stir in the nuts. Turn the candy into the tin. Cool it until it is firm; then cut it into 36 pieces.

NELL B. NICHOLS (EDITOR)
HOMEMADE CANDY

Orange Caramel Fudge

To make about 500 g (1 lb)		
350 g	soft dark brown sugar	12 oz
12.5 cl	cream	4 fl oz
½ tsp	bicarbonate of soda	½ tsp
7.5 g	butter	¼ oz
1	orange, rind grated	1
125 g	nuts, coarsely chopped	4 oz
	salt	

In a saucepan, dissolve the sugar with the cream and bicarbonate of soda over a medium heat, stirring constantly, and bring it to the boil. Stop stirring and boil the mixture until it makes a thick syrup which forms a medium-soft ball in cold water [*firm-ball stage, pages 10-11*]. Remove the pan from the heat and add the butter, orange rind, nuts and a pinch of salt. Beat the mixture well until it becomes quite thick. Turn it out into a buttered 20 cm (8 inch) square tin and, when cold, cut it into 2.5 cm (1 inch) squares; or drop teaspoons of the fudge on to a large buttered dish.

MARION FLEXNER
OUT OF KENTUCKY KITCHENS

Mexican Orange Candy

To give this caramel a more pronounced orange flavour, use the grated rind of two oranges. The technique of cooking sugar without water to make caramel is shown on page 9.

	To make 1 kg (2 lb)	
750 g	granulated sugar	1½ lb
35 cl	milk, scalded	12 fl oz
1	orange, rind grated	1
⅛ tsp	salt	⅛ tsp
125 g	butter	4 oz
125 g	chopped nuts	4 oz

Lightly butter a 23 cm (9 inch) square tin. In a deep, heavy 4 litre (7 pint) saucepan, melt 250 g (8 oz) of the sugar, stirring constantly. When the sugar has melted to a light golden-brown, take it off the heat and pour the milk into it all at one time. Stir the mixture quickly; it will foam up.

Return the saucepan to the heat, add the rest of the sugar and cook, stirring constantly, until the sugar dissolves. Continue cooking, without stirring, to the soft-ball stage—114°C (238°F) [*pages 10-11*]. Remove the pan from the heat; add the orange rind, salt and butter but do not stir. Let the mixture stand until it is lukewarm—43°C (110°F). Beat the mixture until it loses its gloss and starts to thicken. Add the nuts; stir to mix, then pour it into the tin. Mark the sweet into 49 pieces while it is still warm; cut it when it is cool and firm.

NELL B. NICHOLS (EDITOR)
HOMEMADE CANDY

Pineapple Penochi

Penochi or penuche is an American sweet with a fudge-like consistency. The technique of making crystallized pineapple is shown on page 46. The lemon extract can be replaced with 1 teaspoon of finely grated lemon rind.

	To make about 1 kg (2 lb)	
250 g	crystallized pineapple, chopped	8 oz
750 g	granulated sugar	1½ lb
¼ litre	milk	8 fl oz
30 g	butter, softened and cut into small pieces	1 oz
	lemon extract	

Melt the sugar in the milk over a gentle heat, stirring until the sugar dissolves. Add the butter gradually and stir constantly until the mixture begins to boil. Reduce the heat,

cover the mixture and let it simmer for 3 minutes. Remove the lid and boil the mixture rapidly until it reaches 114°C (238°F)—the soft-ball stage [*pages 10-11*].

Lift the saucepan from the heat. Add a few drops of lemon extract and the pineapple. Beat the mixture with a wooden spoon until thick and creamy. Butter a 30 by 20 by 3 cm (12 by 8 by 1¼ inch) baking tin and pour the mixture into it. Leave it until it has set and cut it into 1 cm (½ inch) squares.

ESMÉ GRAY BOOKER
SWEETS THAT HAVE TEMPTED ME

Smith College Fudge

Fudge was popular in the late 19th century in American women's colleges. Sometimes cooked over the gaslight which hung from the centre of the ceiling, it was used as the excuse for parties after "lights out". This fudge recipe was given by a well-known cookery writer, Maria Parloa, in a booklet distributed in 1905 by a chocolate manufacturer.

	To make about 600 g (1¼ lb)	
250 g	granulated sugar	8 oz
200 g	soft brown sugar	7 oz
2 tbsp	molasses	2 tbsp
12.5 cl	single cream	4 fl oz
60 g	plain chocolate, coarsely chopped	2 oz
60 g	butter	2 oz
1½ tsp	vanilla extract	1½ tsp

In a saucepan, combine the two sugars, the molasses, cream and the chocolate. Cook them over a medium heat, stirring until the sugar and the chocolate have melted. Continue cooking, without stirring, until the mixture reaches 114°C (238°F) or until a few drops tested in cold water form a soft ball [*pages 10-11*]. Remove the pan from the heat, stir in the butter and vanilla and cool slightly, until the mixture is tepid. Then beat it until the fudge begins to harden. Pour it out on to a buttered dish and cut it into squares before the fudge is completely hard.

THE EDITORS OF AMERICAN HERITAGE
THE AMERICAN HERITAGE COOKBOOK

Coconut Penuche Patties

Originally from Mexico, penuche is a type of fudge very popular in the United States. If corn syrup is not available, use 1½ tablespoons of liquid glucose. The technique of opening a coconut and grating the flesh is shown on page 13.

To make about 750 g (1½ lb)

350 g	granulated sugar	12 oz
200 g	soft light brown sugar	7 oz
3 tbsp	white corn syrup	3 tbsp
¼ litre	single cream	8 fl oz
75 g	coconut, finely grated	2½ oz
1 tsp	vanilla extract	1 tsp
60 g	butter	2 oz
About 18	pecan nuts, halved	About 18

In a heavy saucepan, combine the sugars, the corn syrup and the cream. Bring the mixture to the boil over a low heat, stirring constantly. Continue to boil gently, without stirring, until a small amount of the mixture forms a soft ball in cold water—or to a temperature of 112°C (234°F) [*pages 10-11*]. Remove the pan from the heat.

Add the coconut, the vanilla extract and the butter. Do not blend. Cool the mixture to lukewarm—49°C (120°F)—without stirring. Then stir to blend the ingredients. Quickly drop the mixture in about 36 tablespoonfuls on to wax paper. Press a pecan nut half on to each pattie and allow the patties to stand until they are firm, about 3 hours. Wrap the patties in wax paper to store them.

JASPER GUY WOODROOF, Ph.D.
COCONUTS: PRODUCTION PROCESSING PRODUCTS

Penuchi

If desired, 125 g (4 oz) of chopped candied cherries may be substituted for 125 g (4 oz) of the nuts, and the mixture dropped by teaspoons on to wax paper.

To make about 750 g (1½ lb)

560 g	soft light brown sugar	1 lb 2 oz
¼ litre	single cream	8 fl oz
20 g	butter	¾ oz
1½ tsp	vanilla extract	1½ tsp
125 g	walnuts, broken into pieces	4 oz

Butter a 20 cm (8 inch) square tin. Cook and stir the soft light brown sugar and the cream until the mixture boils. Cook without stirring until the soft-ball stage is reached—113°C (236°F) [*pages 10-11*]. Remove the pan from the heat and add the butter. Cool the mixture until it is lukewarm and add the vanilla extract. Beat the mixture until it is creamy and thick; add the walnuts. Pour the mixture into the tin, and leave it to cool until it is firm. Cut it into 2.5 cm (1 inch) squares.

MILDRED GROSBERG BELLIN
THE JEWISH COOK BOOK

Mexican Panocha

Soft dark brown sugar takes a long time to dissolve; ensure that it has completely dissolved before allowing the mixture to boil. The technique for melting chocolate is shown on page 65.

To make about 750 g (1½ lb)

525 g	soft dark brown sugar	1 lb 2 oz
¼ litre	milk	8 fl oz
15 g	plain chocolate, melted	½ oz
15 g	butter	½ oz
2.5 cm	vanilla pod, split lengthwise	1 inch
175 g	nuts, coarsely chopped	6 oz

In a saucepan over a medium heat, dissolve the sugar in the milk and add the chocolate, stirring constantly. Reduce the heat and add the butter and the vanilla pod. Bring the mixture slowly to the boil. Stir until the mixture reaches the soft-ball stage [*pages 10-11*] and remove the pan from the heat. Add the nuts, mixing them in thoroughly and beating until the mixture begins to harden. Turn it out into a buttered 20 cm (8 inch) square tin. When it is completely cold, cut it into 2.5 cm (1 inch) squares.

CORA, ROSE AND BOB BROWN
THE SOUTH AMERICAN COOK BOOK

Milk Peppermint Lozenges

To make 500 g (1 lb)

500 g	castor sugar	1 lb
15 cl	milk or single cream	¼ pint
About 1 tsp	peppermint flavouring or peppermint liqueur	About 1 tsp

Have ready several sheets of wax paper. Dissolve the castor sugar in the milk or single cream over a medium heat and boil the syrup for about 10 minutes [*firm-ball stage, pages 10-11*]. Take the pan off the fire and stir in the peppermint flavouring or liqueur. Beat the mixture until it is cool and firm enough to be dropped a teaspoonful at a time without running. Drop the mixture on to the wax paper as quickly as possible, as soon as the mixture begins to set. If it sets too firmly to drop, warm the mixture again for a moment.

MRS. M. E. RATTRAY
SWEETMEAT-MAKING AT HOME

Walnut Roll

If corn syrup is not available, 2 tablespoons of liquid glucose can be used instead.

To make about 1 kg (2 lb)

500 g	granulated sugar	1 lb
200 g	soft brown sugar	7 oz
12.5 cl	white corn syrup	4 fl oz
¼ litre	single cream	8 fl oz
1 tsp	vanilla extract	1 tsp
150 g	walnuts, chopped	5 oz

Combine the sugars, corn syrup and cream. In a heavy saucepan, cook the mixture over a low heat, stirring constantly until the sugars dissolve. Bring the mixture to the boil and continue cooking it over a low heat, without stirring, to the soft-ball stage—113°C (236°F)—[*pages 10-11*]. Remove the pan from the heat and leave the mixture to cool to 43°C (110°F). Add the vanilla extract. Beat the mixture until it stiffens and a spoon leaves a trail in it. Then cool it and knead it until it is firm. Shape it into rolls 3 cm (1½ inches) in diameter. Coat the rolls in the chopped walnuts. Wrap the rolls in wax paper and chill them until they are firm. Slice the rolls into about 24 pieces 1 cm (½ inch) thick.

MARY MARGARET MCBRIDE
HARVEST OF AMERICAN COOKING

Bordeaux Chocolate Squares

Niniches Bordelaises

To make about 400 g (14 oz)

125 g	castor sugar	4 oz
80 g	semi-sweet chocolate, grated	3 oz
40 g	butter	1½ oz
100 g	honey	3½ oz
20 cl	milk	7 fl oz

Oil a marble slab or large dish. Place a bowl of ice-cold water at hand. In a saucepan, combine the grated chocolate and all the other ingredients. Set the pan over a medium heat and stir the mixture constantly. When the mixture begins to thicken, let a drop fall from a spoon into the bowl of water. If the drop dissolves in the water, continue to cook the mixture, still stirring it constantly. Repeat the process until the drop of mixture falls to the bottom of the bowl like a little pearl—103° to 105°C (217° to 221°F). Then remove the pan from the heat.

Pour the mixture on to the oiled marble slab or dish and spread out the mixture with a palette knife. Mark the sweet into 2 cm (¾ inch) squares with an oiled knife. Leave the sweet to cool. When cold, cut it out along the marked lines.

CÉLINE VENCE
ENCYCLOPÉDIE HACHETTE DE LA CUISINE RÉGIONALE

Cream Bonbons

Nidelzeltli

To make about 1 kg (2 lb)

560 g	granulated sugar	1 lb 2 oz
1 litre	milk and cream in equal quantities or 1 litre (1¾ pints) milk and 30 g (1 oz) butter	1¾ pints

In a 4 litre (7 pint) saucepan, bring the sugar and the milk and cream, or the milk and butter, to the boil. Stir constantly until the mixture is reduced to a thick, yellowish-brown paste which comes away easily from the bottom of the saucepan. Pour the paste into a buttered 30 by 20 by 3 cm (12 by 8 by 1¼ inch) shallow tin, spread it out to a thickness of about 1 cm (½ inch) and leave it to cool for 10 minutes. Dip the tip of a knife in oil and cut the mixture into 2.5 cm (1 inch) squares. Allow the mixture to get cold before breaking up and serving it.

EVA MARIA BORER
TANTE HEIDI'S SWISS KITCHEN

Coconut Sanduskys

The techniques for the extraction of milk and grating of fresh coconut are shown on page 13.

To make about 375 g (13 oz)

200 g	granulated sugar	7 oz
150 g	soft brown sugar	5 oz
90 g	coconut, freshly grated	3 oz
12.5 cl	coconut milk	4 fl oz
4 tbsp	water	4 tbsp
1 tsp	vanilla extract	1 tsp

Cook the grated coconut, coconut milk, sugars, water and vanilla extract together, stirring occasionally to prevent burning. Cook the mixture to a temperature of 113°C (236°F), the soft-ball stage; cold water test the syrup [*pages 10-11*].

Remove the pan from the heat and cool the mixture to 49°C (120°F). Beat it until it is thick and creamy. This requires a long beating, about 5 to 10 minutes. Turn the mixture into a greased 20 cm (8 inch) square tin. When the mixture has set, cut it into about 12 squares.

This is rather a soft sweet. If you wish a firmer sweet which can be cut and served soon after making, cook the mixture to a slightly higher temperature.

MAY B. VAN ARSDALE AND RUTH PARRISH CASA EMELLOS
CANDY RECIPES AND OTHER CONFECTIONS

White or Pink Pralines

Pralines Blanches ou Roses de Coco

These dainty white or pink pralines are peculiar to Creole confections and are much sought after by strangers visiting New Orleans. Never boil the coconut for longer than a few minutes in the sugar.

To make about 750 g (1½ lb)

500 g	granulated sugar	1 lb
4 tbsp	water	4 tbsp
350 g	fresh coconut, grated	12 oz
½ tsp	cochineal (optional)	½ tsp

Use a copper or other heavy saucepan. Put the sugar into the saucepan with the water and let it boil well. When it begins to form a syrup, take it from the heat and stir in the grated coconut. Mix thoroughly and return the pan to the heat. Be careful to stir the mixture constantly from the time you add the coconut. Cook it for 2 to 3 minutes when it will begin to bubble; it should have reached the thread stage [*page 10*].

This will be sufficient cooking if you wish the pralines to be light and flaky. Add the cochineal, if using, just before taking the mixture from the heat.

Have ready a wet marble slab or buttered dish. Take a kitchen spoon and use it to drop spoonfuls of the mixture on to the slab or dish, spreading them out with a fork until they form neat round cakes about 5 mm (¼ inch) thick and 10 or 12.5 cm (4 or 5 inches) in diameter. Let them dry, then take a knife and gently raise them from the slab or dish.

THE PICAYUNE'S CREOLE COOK BOOK

Chocolate Log Cabin Rolls

To make about 750 g (1½ lb)

250 g	Demerara sugar	8 oz
175 g	granulated sugar	6 oz
12.5 cl	maple syrup	4 fl oz
¼ litre	single cream	8 fl oz
30 g	butter	1 oz
	salt	
45 g	plain chocolate, broken into small pieces	1½ oz
1	egg white, lightly beaten	1
125 g	pecan nuts, broken	4 oz

Butter a work surface. In a heavy 3 litre (5 pint) saucepan combine the sugars, the maple syrup, the cream, the butter, a pinch of salt and the chocolate. Bring the mixture to boiling point over a low heat, stirring constantly. Cover the pan and cook the mixture for 5 minutes. Remove the lid and, stirring occasionally, cook until the mixture forms a soft ball in cold water—113°C (236°F) [*pages 10-11*].

Remove the pan from the heat and leave the contents to cool until the bottom of the pan feels lukewarm—43°C (110°F). Beat the fudge vigorously until it begins to lose its gloss and holds its shape. Turn it out on to a buttered work surface. Knead the fudge until it can be shaped, keeping your hands well buttered. Shape the fudge into two 23 cm (9 inch) rolls. Brush the rolls with the lightly beaten egg white and roll them in the broken nuts, pressing the nuts into the roll to make them adhere. Wrap the rolls in plastic film or grease-proof or wax paper and chill them. To serve, cut each roll of fudge into about 18 slices.

JOSH GASPERO (EDITOR)
HERSHEY'S 1934 COOKBOOK

Toasted Almond Bark

If corn syrup is not available, you can substitute ½ tablespoon of liquid glucose.

To make about 750 g (1½ lb)

500 g	granulated sugar	1 lb
15 cl	milk	¼ pint
1 tbsp	corn syrup	1 tbsp
¼ tsp	salt	¼ tsp
30 g	butter	1 oz
1 tsp	vanilla extract	1 tsp
150 g	unblanched almonds, toasted	5 oz

Spread a baking sheet with wax paper. In a heavy 2 litre (3½ pint) saucepan, combine the sugar, the milk, the corn syrup and the salt. Stirring constantly, cook the mixture until the sugar dissolves and the syrup comes to the boil. Then cook the mixture without stirring to the soft-ball stage—112°C (234°F) [*pages 10-11*].

Remove the pan from the heat; add the butter, but do not stir. Let the mixture cool to lukewarm—43°C (110°F). Then add the vanilla. Beat until the mixture thickens and is creamy. Add the toasted almonds. Then spread the mixture on the wax paper in a layer about 1 cm (½ inch) thick. Leave the sweet to cool, then break it into pieces.

NELL B. NICHOLS (EDITOR)
HOMEMADE CANDY

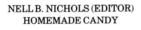

Pralines

The technique of cooking sugar to a caramel without water is shown on page 9. Although these sweets are called pralines, they have a soft, fudge-like consistency.

To make about 1 kg (2 lb)

600 g	granulated sugar	1¼ lb
¼ litre	single cream	8 fl oz
15 g	butter	½ oz
250 g	pecan nut halves	8 oz

In a heavy iron pan, combine 500 g (1 lb) of the sugar with the cream and butter and bring to the boil over medium heat. In a separate heavy saucepan, melt the rest of the sugar and cook it until it is caramel-coloured. Add the cream, butter and sugar syrup to the caramel mixture. Add the pecan halves and cook the mixture to the soft-ball stage, 113°C (236°F) on the sugar thermometer [*pages 10-11*]. Remove the pan from the heat and beat the mixture until it thickens. Drop spoonfuls of the mixture about 5 to 7.5 cm (2 to 3 inches) in diameter on to wax paper. Leave the pralines to harden.

THE JUNIOR LEAGUE OF NEW ORLEANS
THE PLANTATION COOKBOOK

Gold Nuggets

To make about 600 g (1¼ lb)

350 g	granulated sugar	12 oz
3 tbsp	orange juice	3 tbsp
4 tbsp	tepid water	4 tbsp
¼ tsp	ground cinnamon	¼ tsp
4 tbsp	grated orange rind	4 tbsp
300 g	walnuts or other nuts	10 oz

Have ready a sheet of wax paper or lightly butter a baking sheet. In a saucepan, mix the sugar and orange juice with the water. Over a medium heat, dissolve the sugar, stirring constantly. Bring to the boil, cover the pan and let the syrup boil for 1 minute covered, to steam down sugar crystals from the sides of the pan. Remove the lid and cook the mixture without stirring until a small amount forms a soft ball when dropped in very cold water—116°C (240°F) on a sugar thermometer [*pages 10-11*]. Remove the pan from the heat. Add the remaining ingredients. Stir with a fork until the mixture becomes creamy. Turn it out on to the wax paper or the baking sheet. Separate the nuts with a fork. Cool the nuggets and store them in an airtight container.

WOMAN'S DAY COLLECTOR'S COOK BOOK

Spiced English Walnuts

To make about 600 g (1¼ lb)

250 g	granulated sugar	8 oz
¼ tsp	salt	¼ tsp
1 tsp	ground cinnamon	1 tsp
12.5 cl	milk	4 fl oz
350 g	walnuts	12 oz
1 tsp	vanilla extract	1 tsp

In a heavy saucepan, combine the sugar, salt, cinnamon and milk. Cook over a medium heat, stirring constantly, until the sugar dissolves, then boil without stirring until the syrup forms a soft ball in cold water [*pages 10-11*]. Remove the pan from the heat and add the nuts and vanilla extract. Spread the mixture out on wax paper and leave it until it is cool before storing it. When cold, cut it into squares.

LOUIS SZATHMÁRY (EDITOR)
FIFTY YEARS OF PRAIRIE COOKING

Curd Toffee

To make about 750 g (1½ lb)

500 g	granulated sugar	1 lb
500 g	yogurt	1 lb
2 tbsp	blanched, slivered almonds	2 tbsp
2 tbsp	slivered cashew nuts	2 tbsp
¼ tsp	saffron, dissolved in 2 teaspoons of hot milk	¼ tsp
1 tbsp	blanched pistachio nuts	1 tbsp
10	cardamom pods, seeds extracted	10

Hang the yogurt in a muslin cloth or bag and leave it to drip overnight. The next day, butter a dish or 20 cm (8 inch) square tin. Gently heat the thickened yogurt in a pan with the sugar, the almonds and cashew nuts. Stir continuously until the mixture thickens and comes away from the sides of the pan, about 15 minutes. Stir in the saffron and mix well. Turn the mixture out into the buttered dish or tin, and flatten it out.

Grind the pistachio nuts and the cardamom seeds together, then sprinkle them over the toffee. Leave the mixture to cool. Store it in an airtight container.

JACK SANTA MARIA
INDIAN SWEET COOKERY

Coconut and Almond Candy

The technique of preparing and grating a fresh coconut is demonstrated on page 13.

To make about 1 kg (2 lb)

500 g	granulated sugar	1 lb
¼ litre	hot milk	8 fl oz
125 g	almonds, blanched and chopped	4 oz
350 g	coconut, grated	12 oz
6	egg yolks, lightly beaten	6

Mix the sugar and the hot milk and stir them over a low heat until the sugar dissolves. Bring the syrup to boiling point, then add the almonds and stir constantly until the mixture thickens and reaches the thread stage [*page 10*]. Add the grated coconut and the egg yolks.

Stir the mixture constantly over a low heat until it begins to thicken into a cream, about 5 to 10 minutes. Remove the pan from the heat and leave it until the mixture is cool enough to handle. Then shape the mixture into small balls. Leave the balls on wax paper overnight to dry out and harden.

CORA, ROSE AND BOB BROWN
THE SOUTH AMERICAN COOK BOOK

Catalan Sweets

Bombones Nuria

To make about 1.5 kg (3 lb)

400 g	granulated sugar	14 oz
400 g	almonds, blanched, toasted and chopped	14 oz
200 g	hazelnuts, skinned, toasted and chopped	7 oz
400 g	chocolate, grated	14 oz
2	egg yolks	2
15 cl	milk	¼ pint
	icing sugar	

In a saucepan, combine the granulated sugar, chopped almonds and hazelnuts, grated chocolate and egg yolks. Stir thoroughly over a low heat. Gradually add the milk, stirring constantly, until the mixture forms a thick paste. Remove the pan from the heat and leave the mixture to cool. When it is cold, form it into small balls of more or less the same size. Roll the balls in the icing sugar.

ANA MARIA CALERA
COCINA CATALANA

Alice's Pecan Pâtés

To make about 750 g (1½ lb)

250 g	granulated sugar	8 oz
350 g	dark brown sugar	12 oz
15 g	butter	½ oz
⅛ tsp	salt	⅛ tsp
¼ litre	single cream	8 fl oz
2 tsp	vanilla extract	2 tsp
125 g	pecan nuts, coarsely chopped	4 oz
¼ tsp	cream of tartar	¼ tsp

Butter a large dish or cold work surface. In a saucepan, combine the sugars with the butter, the salt and the cream. Stir to dissolve over a medium heat and boil, stirring occasionally, until a little of the mixture dropped into iced water makes a firm ball [*pages 10-11*].

Remove the pan from the heat. Add the vanilla, the pecan nuts and the cream of tartar to the mixture and beat it hard until it becomes stiff and creamy. Drop tablespoons of the mixture on to the buttered dish or work surface. If the mixture hardens too quickly, pour it into a buttered dish and cut it into 2.5 cm (1 inch) squares when it is cold. Wrap each piece in wax paper. They will keep for a long time in an airtight tin box.

MARION FLEXNER
OUT OF KENTUCKY KITCHENS

Pecan Caramel

The technique of cooking sugar without water to make a caramel is shown on page 9. If pecan nuts are not available, you can use walnuts.

To make about 1.25 kg (2¾ lb)

1 kg	granulated sugar	2¼ lb
¼ litre	milk	8 fl oz
250 g	pecan nuts, chopped	8 oz
30 g	butter	1 oz

Boil 750 g (1½ lb) of the sugar with the milk. In an iron frying pan over a very low heat, melt the rest of the sugar until it becomes caramel coloured. When a little of the sugar and milk mixture forms a soft ball when dropped into cold water [*pages 10-11*], add the caramel, nuts and butter. Take the mixture off the heat and beat it until it is creamy.

Pour the mixture into a buttered dish. When the mixture is cold, cut it into squares.

A BOOK OF FAMOUS OLD NEW ORLEANS RECIPES

Pine-Nut Candy

Pour Faire le Pignolat en Roche

Michel de Nostredame, or Nostradamus as he is better known, was a physician who lived in Provence in the early 16th century. He is famous for his book of prophecies, couched in rather obscure language. This recipe is from his book of beauty preparations and confections published in 1552.

If shelled and skinned pine-nuts are used, they should be roasted for only 15 minutes or until they are light brown. An electuary, a term used in this recipe to describe a stage of cooking, is a medicinal thick syrup. The sugar boiling equivalent is the firm-ball stage, about 118°C (244°F), shown on pages 10-11. Nostradamus suggests decorating some of these sweets with gold leaf. He also says that almonds can be candied in the same way.

To make about 1.5 kg (3 lb)

500 g	granulated sugar	1 lb
1.25 kg	pine-nuts, shelled	2½ lb
2 to 3 tbsp	rose-water	2 to 3 tbsp
1	egg white, lightly beaten	1

Roast the pine-nuts in their skins in a preheated 130°C (250°F or Mark ½) oven for about 30 minutes or until lightly coloured. Then skin the nuts.

In a saucepan, dissolve the sugar and the rose-water and bring them to the boil. Cook the syrup until it is as thick as an electuary. In the winter or in wet weather you will have to boil the syrup for a little longer; in summer, you will find it is ready as soon as it boils without foaming and making a noise, for the noise is a sign that there is still some moisture left in it.

Remove the syrup from the heat, dip the pan briefly in cold water to stop the cooking and rest the base of the pan on a barrel top or other surface which will hold it well.

Use a wooden spoon or spatula to beat the mixture briskly until it turns white. When the mixture begins to cool, add the egg white. Beat the mixture again and return it to a low heat. Cook it for 2 to 3 minutes, until the moisture from the egg white has evaporated and the mixture is as thick as it was before the white was added.

Add the pine-nuts to the thick syrup. Mix them in well. While keeping the pan on the low heat, so that the mixture does not cool, use a palette knife to remove portions of the mixture, each weighing about 45 to 60 g (1½ to 2 oz). Spread these pieces on greaseproof paper and leave them to cool.

MICHEL DE NOSTREDAME
EXCELLENT ET MOULT UTILE OPUSCULE

Benné Candy

Sesame seeds were first brought to the United States via Charleston, South Carolina, by African slaves in about 1600. The African word for sesame—benné—has persisted as the local name for the seeds. To toast sesame seeds, spread them evenly in a dry frying pan and cook them, stirring frequently, over a medium heat, until they darken and give off their characteristic nut-like aroma.

To make about 850 g (1¾ lb)

500 g	soft brown sugar	1 lb
15 g	butter	½ oz
12.5 cl	milk	4 fl oz
1 tbsp	vinegar	1 tbsp
275 g	sesame seeds, toasted	9 oz
1 tsp	vanilla extract	1 tsp

In a saucepan, mix the brown sugar, the butter, the milk and the vinegar. Cook over a medium heat, stirring, until the sugar has dissolved. Boil the mixture until it begins to thread [*firm-ball stage, pages 10-11*]. Remove the pan from the heat and beat in the sesame seeds. Add the vanilla and beat the mixture until it is creamy. Drop a teaspoon at a time on to a buttered dish or paper and leave the candies to cool.

HARRIET ROSS COLQUITT (EDITOR)
THE SAVANNAH COOK BOOK

Chocolate Pecan Pralines

Although these sweets are called pralines, they have a fudge-like consistency.

To make about 750 g (1½ lb)

250 g	granulated sugar	8 oz
250 g	soft light brown or maple sugar	8 oz
12.5 cl	single cream	4 fl oz
¼ tsp	salt	¼ tsp
60 g	plain chocolate, broken into small pieces	2 oz
125 g	pecan nuts, coarsely chopped	4 oz
15 g	butter	½ oz
1 tsp	vanilla extract	1 tsp

Butter some flat dishes or two sheets of wax paper. In a heavy saucepan, combine the sugars, cream and the salt. Cook the mixture over a medium heat, stirring constantly, until it reaches a temperature of 109°C (228°F) on a sugar thermometer. Remove the pan from the heat and add the chocolate, the butter and the pecan nuts. Return the pan to the heat and, stirring constantly, cook the mixture to 112°C (234°F)—the soft-ball stage [*pages 10-11*].

Remove the pan from the heat and add the vanilla extract; leave to cool for 5 minutes. Beat the mixture for 10 to 15 seconds or until it has slightly thickened. Use a large spoon to quickly drop the mixture in about 24 spoonfuls on to the buttered dishes or wax paper. If the mixture becomes too thick to drop, stir in a tablespoon of hot water.

JOSH GASPERO (EDITOR)
HERSHEY'S 1934 COOKBOOK

New Orleans Pralines

To make about 850 g (1¾ lb)

175 g	soft dark brown sugar	6 oz
500 g	granulated sugar	1 lb
¼ litre	milk	8 fl oz
½ tsp	bicarbonate of soda	½ tsp
125 g	pecan nuts	4 oz

Butter two baking sheets. Melt the brown sugar in a frying pan, stirring constantly. Bring the milk to the boil and add the bicarbonate of soda to it. Stir the milk mixture into the melted sugar. Add the granulated sugar and cook until a drop of the mixture forms a soft ball in cold water—115°C (238°F) [*pages 10-11*]. Cool the mixture to lukewarm and add the pecan nuts. Beat the mixture until it is creamy and drop it on the baking sheets in spoonfuls about 5 cm (2 inches) in diameter.

MILDRED GROSBERG BELLIN
THE JEWISH COOK BOOK

Orange Pralines

If light corn syrup is not available, use half the quantity of liquid glucose. If pecan nuts are not available, walnuts can be substituted. The technique of using saffron as a food colouring is shown on page 15.

To make about 750 g (1½ lb)

500 g	granulated sugar	1 lb
17.5 cl	single cream	6 fl oz
¼ tsp	salt	¼ tsp
2½ tbsp	white corn syrup	2½ tbsp
1	orange, rind grated, juice strained	1
60 g	butter	2 oz
1 tsp	vanilla extract	1 tsp
¼ tsp	powdered saffron (optional)	¼ tsp
250 g	pecan nuts, chopped	8 oz

Place the sugar, cream, salt and corn syrup in a saucepan and stir constantly until the mixture boils. Add the orange juice slowly and continue cooking until the mixture reaches the soft-ball stage—116°C (240°F) on the sugar thermometer [*pages 10-11*]. Add the grated orange rind and cook until the thermometer again shows 116°C (240°F). Add the butter, vanilla extract and the saffron, if using. Cool the mixture, then beat it until it holds its shape. Add the pecan nuts. Drop bite-sized pieces of the mixture on to wax paper to dry. Store the pralines in a tin or plastic container.

JUNIOR LEAGUE OF JACKSON, MISSISSIPPI
SOUTHERN SIDEBOARDS

Sesame Pralines

Although these sweets are called pralines, their consistency more resembles that of fudge.

To make about 750 g (1½ lb)

250 g	granulated sugar	8 oz
200 g	soft dark brown sugar	7 oz
40 g	sesame seeds	1½ oz
¼ litre	double cream	8 fl oz
30 g	butter	1 oz
250 g	pecan nut halves	8 oz

Butter a sheet of wax paper or aluminium foil or a marble slab. Toast the sesame seeds in a preheated 180°C (350°F or Mark 4) oven, stirring occasionally, for 10 to 15 minutes or until they are golden-brown. In a 3 litre (5 pint) saucepan, combine the sugars and the cream. Cook the mixture over a medium heat, stirring until the sugar dissolves. Wash the crystals from the side of the pan with a damp pastry brush until the syrup boils. Cook the mixture to 110°C (230°F), then add the butter, pecan nuts and sesame seeds; stirring occasionally, continue cooking until the mixture reaches 112°C (234°F), the soft-ball stage [*pages 10-11*]. Remove the pan from the heat. Cool the mixture for 2 to 3 minutes, then stir it for 2 minutes or until it thickens slightly. Working quickly, drop the mixture from a spoon on to the buttered surface, spacing each praline slightly apart.

McCORMICK
SPICES OF THE WORLD COOKBOOK

Maylie's Restaurant New Orleans Pralines

If light molasses is not available, use golden syrup.

To make about 1 kg (2½ lb)

350 g	soft brown sugar	12 oz
¼ litre	light molasses	8 fl oz
½ litre	double cream	16 fl oz
60 g	butter	2 oz
1 tsp	vanilla extract	1 tsp
500 g	pecan nuts	1 lb

Butter two baking sheets. Boil the brown sugar, molasses, cream and butter, stirring all the time, until a soft ball is formed when a drop is placed in cold water [*soft-ball stage, pages 10-11*]. Add the vanilla and the nuts and stir the mixture until it begins to crystallize. Drop spoonfuls of the mixture in small heaps on the baking sheets, leaving enough room between them for the mixture to spread slightly.

MARY LAND
NEW ORLEANS CUISINE

Wagner's Pralines

Although these sweets are called pralines, the result will be more like a fudge.

To make about 1 kg (2 lb)

500 g	granulated sugar	1 lb
¾ tsp	bicarbonate of soda	¾ tsp
¼ litre	single cream	8 fl oz
7 g	butter	¼ oz
250 g	pecan nuts, halved	8 oz

Combine the sugar and the bicarbonate of soda in a deep 3 litre (5 pint) saucepan. Mix well. Add the single cream and stir well. Bring the mixture to the boil over a medium heat, stirring to prevent scorching. Cook the mixture until it forms a soft ball when tested in water [*pages 10-11*]. Remove the pan from the heat and add the butter. Add the pecan nut halves and beat the mixture until it is thick enough to drop from a spoon. Drop spoonfuls of the mixture on to wax paper.

MARY LAND
NEW ORLEANS CUISINE

Peanut Confection

Erdnusskonfekt

Walnuts or grated coconut can be used instead of peanuts, in which case the salt should be omitted. If using coconut, add ½ teaspoon of vanilla extract.

To make about 550 g (1 lb 2 oz)

350 g	Demerara sugar	12 oz
15 g	butter	½ oz
10 cl	milk or single cream	3½ fl oz
175 g	peanuts, roasted and chopped	6 oz
¼ tsp	salt	¼ tsp

Melt the butter in a saucepan. Add the sugar and milk or cream. Bring the mixture to the boil and simmer until it forms a soft ball when dropped into cold water [*pages 10-11*]. Remove the pan from the heat and beat the mixture until it is thick and creamy. Sprinkle the nuts with the salt and stir them into the mixture. Turn the mixture out on to a buttered baking sheet. Leave it until it is warm to the touch before cutting it into 2.5 cm (1 inch) squares.

ELIZABETH SCHULER
MEIN KOCHBUCH

Ginger Fondant

Gemberborstplaat

If no suitable ring moulds are available, small, plain, circular biscuit cutters can be used instead.

To make about 500 g (1 lb)

500 g	granulated sugar	1 lb
1 tsp	ground ginger	1 tsp
10 cl	water	3½ fl oz
50 g	crystallized ginger, finely shredded	2 oz

Put some small ring moulds into cold water. In a saucepan, stir the ground ginger into the sugar. Add the water and cook, stirring constantly, over a medium heat until the sugar has dissolved. Boil the syrup for 10 minutes [*soft-ball stage, pages 10-11*]. Then add the shredded crystallized ginger and let the mixture boil for 1 to 2 minutes more. Remove the pan from the heat. Let it thicken whilst stirring continuously. The fondant should be thick, but not too thick to pour.

Remove the ring moulds from the water and put them on a sheet of greaseproof or non-stick baking paper. Pour the fondant into the ring moulds and leave it to set. As soon as the top surface of the fondant is firm, turn the moulds over and leave the fondant to firm on the opposite surface. Do not leave the fondant rings too long on one side or the bottom surface of the fondant will stick to the paper.

C. J. WANNÉE (EDITOR)
KOOKBOEK VAN DE AMSTERDAMSE HUISHOUDSCHOOL

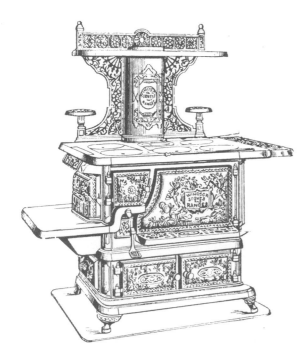

Preserved Ginger Fondant

Ingwer-Fondant

To make about 750 g (1½ lb)

550 g	soft light brown sugar	1 lb 2 oz
¼ litre	milk	8 fl oz
2 tbsp	butter	2 tbsp
2 tbsp	finely chopped, preserved ginger	2 tbsp

In a large pan, bring the sugar and the milk to the boil, stirring constantly. Stir until the syrup reaches a temperature of 112° to 115°C (234° to 239°F) [*soft-ball stage, pages 10-11*]. Remove the pan from the heat, stir in the butter, and allow the mixture to cool to lukewarm. Then beat it until it is creamy. Finally, stir in the chopped ginger.

Warm and butter a baking sheet. Spread it with the mixture to a thickness of 2 cm (¾ inch). Leave the fondant to cool completely. When it is cold, cut it into cubes with a knife dipped in hot water between each cut.

MARGRET UHLE AND ANNE BRAKEMEIER
KONFEKT ZUM SELBERMACHEN

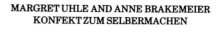

Maple-Flavoured Fondant

It is important to use real maple syrup for this recipe and not maple-flavoured syrup.

To make about 750 g (1½ lb)

600 g	granulated sugar	1¼ lb
¼ litre	maple syrup	8 fl oz
12.5 cl	water	4 fl oz
⅛ tsp	cream of tartar	⅛ tsp

In a saucepan, mix the ingredients and dissolve the sugar over a moderate heat, stirring constantly. Boil the mixture, without stirring, to a temperature of approximately 110°C (230°F); lower the heat and cook the syrup until it reaches a temperature of 112° to 113°C (234° to 236°F), or to a very soft ball by the water test [*pages 10-11*]. Wipe the crystals from the pouring side of the saucepan and pour the hot syrup into a shallow bowl. Allow it to cool undisturbed to a temperature of 43°C (110°F); stir it with a heavy spoon or spatula until the mixture is thoroughly creamed and the whole mass has a cheese-like consistency. Knead it until it is soft and plastic. Store it in a covered container.

WALTER W. CHENOWETH
HOW TO MAKE CANDY

Fondant Discs

Borstplaat

These fondant sweets can be dipped in chocolate. The method of dipping fondant in chocolate is shown on page 74. If small ring moulds are not available, use small circular biscuit cutters about 2.5 cm (1 inch) in diameter.

To make 500 g (1 lb)

500 g	granulated sugar	1 lb
15 cl	water	¼ pint
	flavouring or 20 g (½ oz) cocoa powder or 1 tbsp powdered instant coffee	

Put some small ring moulds into cold water. Put the sugar into a pan and pour the water on to it. Dissolve the sugar completely, stirring over a medium heat, and boil the syrup until a drop of it falling from the spoon leaves a thin thread [*soft-ball stage, pages 10-11*]. Remove the pan from the heat. Continue to stir until the mixture becomes opaque, then add the flavouring, cocoa powder or coffee. Wait until the fondant becomes a thick, but still liquid, mass—about 10 minutes.

Remove the ring moulds from the water, shaking off any excess moisture, and put them on to a sheet of greaseproof or cartridge paper. Pour the fondant into the ring moulds and leave it to harden. After a few minutes, when it is hard on top, turn the rings over and leave the fondant to set on the other side. Then remove the rings. Do not leave the fondant for too long on one side or the mixture may stick to the paper.

C. J. WANNÉE
KOOKBOEK VAN DE AMSTERDAMSE HUISHOUDSCHOOL

Italian Cream

To make about 500 g (1 lb)

60 g	soft moist brown sugar	2 oz
250 g	castor sugar	8 oz
2 tbsp	tepid water	2 tbsp
17.5 cl	liquid glucose	6 fl oz
15 cl	double cream	¼ pint
	vanilla extract	
60 g	fondant (*page 166*), cut into small pieces	2 oz
90 g	walnuts, chopped	3 oz

Line a 17.5 to 20 cm (7 to 8 inch) square tin with wax paper. Put the sugars, the water, the glucose and the cream into a saucepan. Over low heat dissolve the sugars carefully, stirring all the time. Boil the mixture to 113°C (236°F) [*soft-ball stage, pages 10-11*], stirring it constantly. Remove the pan from the heat and leave the mixture to cool for 2 to 3 minutes. Add the vanilla, fondant and the walnuts. Stir the mixture with a wooden spoon or spatula until it is just beginning to grain. Do not overstir, or it will grain too much and the smooth texture will be spoilt.

Pour the mixture into the tin. When it has set, cut it into cubes. It should cut smoothly like cheese. Wrap it in wax paper and aluminium foil. It keeps well for months.

D. F. HUTTON AND E. M. BODE
SIMPLE SWEETMAKING

Grand Operas

If white corn syrup is not available, use 1 tablespoon of liquid glucose. To coat the sweets with chocolate, use 250 g (8 oz) of plain dipping chocolate; the technique is shown on page 74.

To make 750 g (1½ lb)

500 g	granulated sugar	1 lb
3 tbsp	white corn syrup	3 tbsp
12.5 cl	double cream	4 fl oz
35 cl	milk	12 fl oz
¼ tsp	salt	¼ tsp
1 tsp	vanilla extract	1 tsp

Put all of the ingredients except the vanilla into a saucepan and cook them on a low heat, stirring constantly, until the temperature of 115°C (238°F) is reached [*soft-ball stage, pages 10-11*]. It is better to cook the mixture rather slowly so that some of the milk sugar may caramelize.

Turn the mixture into a bowl. Cool the mixture until it is tepid—about 43°C (110°F). Beat it with a spatula until it becomes thick and creamy and has lost its shiny appearance—about 3 to 4 minutes. Press the mixture into a lightly oiled 20 cm (8 inch) square tin. When it is completely cold, cut it into 2.5 cm (1 inch) squares.

MAY B. VAN ARSDALE AND RUTH PARRISH CASA EMELLOS
CANDY RECIPES AND OTHER CONFECTIONS

Marshmallows

The technique of making marshmallows is shown on page 40. Colourings and flavourings are discussed on page 14. Marshmallows can be dusted with a mixture of equal quantities of icing sugar and cornflour to give them a smooth, firm crust. The technique of preparing a tin by dusting it with icing sugar and cornflour is shown on page 18.

A few chopped fruits or nuts or some desiccated coconut may be added if preferred while the mixture is still stiff but not set.

To make about 600 g (1¼ lb)

500 g	granulated sugar	1 lb
35 cl	water	12 fl oz
1 tbsp	liquid glucose	1 tbsp
30 g	powdered gelatine	1 oz
2 tbsp	orange-flower water	2 tbsp
	colourings and flavourings (optional)	
2	egg whites, stiffly beaten	2
	icing sugar, sieved	
	cornflour	

Over a medium heat, combine the sugar and the glucose in 20 cl (7 fl oz) of the water. Stir constantly until the sugar is completely dissolved. Bring the syrup to the boil without stirring. Increase the heat and boil until the syrup reaches 127°C (260°F), the hard-ball stage [*pages 10-11*].

Soak the gelatine in the rest of the water and the orange-flower water for 5 to 10 minutes and then dissolve it very gently over boiling water. Add the colourings and flavourings, if you are using them.

Combine the syrup and the melted gelatine. Whisking continuously, gradually pour this mixture on to the stiffly beaten egg whites. Continue whisking until the mixture is a thick, white opaque mass which will hold its shape.

Lightly oil a 30 by 20 by 3 cm (12 by 8 by 1¼ inch) tin and dust it with a mixture of equal quantities of icing sugar and cornflour. Turn the marshmallow mixture out into the tin, smooth it flat with a palette knife and leave it to set for several hours. Loosen the mixture at the edges of the tin with a knife blade. Dust a work surface with icing sugar and turn the marshmallow out on to it. Dust the marshmallow thickly with icing sugar and leave it for 1 hour to allow the mixture to dry out and the icing sugar to form a crust. Then cut it into squares or rounds. Alternatively, the marshmallow can be cut into shapes before being dusted with icing sugar and then left to dry out for about 1 hour.

HELEN JEROME
SWEET-MAKING FOR ALL

Yellow Divinity

Divinity is an American confection with a texture resembling that of soft nougat. If corn syrup is not available, use 2 tablespoons of liquid glucose.

To make about 750 g (1½ lb)

500 g	granulated sugar	1 lb
12.5 cl	white corn syrup	4 fl oz
12.5 cl	milk	4 fl oz
2	egg yolks	2
125 g	nuts, coarsely chopped	4 oz
1 tsp	vanilla extract	1 tsp

Combine the sugar, corn syrup and milk and cook them until the mixture reaches 120°C (248°F) on a sugar thermometer [*firm-ball stage, pages 10-11*]. While the syrup is cooking, whisk the egg yolks until they are thick and creamy. Slowly add the hot syrup to the egg yolks, whisking the mixture until it cools slightly. Add the chopped nuts and the vanilla extract. Drop the mixture in tablespoonfuls on to wax paper.

JUNIOR LEAGUE OF JACKSON, MISSISSIPPI
SOUTHERN SIDEBOARDS

Divinity

If corn syrup is not available, use 1½ tablespoons of liquid glucose. To make sea foam, a variation of this recipe, the author suggests substituting soft light brown sugar for the granulated sugar and using only 1 tablespoon of corn syrup or half a tablespoon of liquid glucose.

To make about 375 g (13 oz)

315 g	granulated sugar	10½ oz
5 tbsp	white corn syrup	5 tbsp
4 tbsp	water	4 tbsp
1	egg white	1
1 tsp	vanilla extract	1 tsp
60 g	nuts, chopped	2 oz

Put the sugar, corn syrup and water in a saucepan. Heat them, stirring, until the sugar has completely dissolved and the mixture starts to boil. Without stirring, cook the syrup to 124°C (256°F) [*hard-ball stage, pages 10-11*].

While the syrup is boiling, beat the egg white in a large bowl until it is very stiff. Slowly pour the hot syrup into the egg white in a thin stream, beating all the time you are pouring. Keep beating until the mixture is no longer shiny; by then it will be very stiff. Mix in the vanilla and chopped nuts and drop the divinity in about 18 spoonfuls on to wax paper.

CAROLYN MEYER
LOTS AND LOTS OF CANDY

Oklahoma Cherry Divinity

If corn syrup is not available, 4 tablespoons of liquid glucose can be used instead.

To make about 600 g (1¼ lb)

500 g	granulated sugar	1 lb
12.5 cl	white corn syrup	4 fl oz
¼ tsp	salt	¼ tsp
12.5 cl	water	4 fl oz
2	egg whites, stiffly beaten	2
1 tsp	vanilla extract	1 tsp
125 g	candied cherries, chopped	4 oz

Mix the sugar, syrup, salt and water in a saucepan and place it over a low heat, stirring until the sugar has dissolved. Cook, without stirring, to 120°C (248°F) on the sugar thermometer [*firm-ball stage, pages 10-11*]. Wipe off sugar crystals with a damp cloth during cooking. Remove the pan from the heat and gradually pour the mixture into the egg whites, beating constantly. Add the vanilla and beat until the mixture will hold its shape when dropped from a spoon. Add the cherries, mix well and drop the mixture in spoonfuls on to wax paper.

THE EDITORS OF SOUTHERN LIVING
THE COOKIES AND CANDY COOKBOOK

Divinity That Never Fails

If corn syrup is not available, use 3 tablespoons of liquid glucose. Suitable flavourings are discussed on page 14.

To make about 600 g (1¼ lb)

600 g	granulated sugar	1¼ lb
17.5 cl	white corn syrup	6 fl oz
4 tbsp	water	4 tbsp
2	egg whites, stiffly beaten	2
	flavouring	

Butter or oil a 20 cm (8 inch) square tin. Dissolve the sugar in the corn syrup and water over a medium heat, stirring constantly. Bring the syrup to the boil and boil it to the thread stage [*page 10*]. Pour two-thirds of the syrup in a thin stream over the beaten egg whites, whisking all the time. Put the rest of the syrup back on the heat and cook it to the soft-ball stage. Pour the syrup into the egg white mixture, whisking constantly. Add the flavouring and continue whisking until the mixture forms stiff peaks. Then pour it into the tin. Leave the divinity until it is set, then cut it into squares.

LOUIS SZATHMÁRY (EDITOR)
FIFTY YEARS OF PRAIRIE COOKING

Divinity Drops

If white corn syrup is not available, use 4 tablespoons of liquid glucose. About 125 g (4 oz) of chopped candied fruit can be added when adding the chopped nuts. To make chocolate-flavoured drops, add 175 g (6 oz) of semi-sweet chocolate, broken into small pieces, when adding the vanilla and nuts. To make ginger divinity drops, replace the vanilla extract with 1 teaspoon of powdered ginger and add 125 g (4 oz) of very finely chopped candied ginger when adding the nuts.

To make about 750 g (1½ lb)

625 g	granulated sugar	1¼ lb
12.5 cl	white corn syrup	4 fl oz
¼ tsp	salt	¼ tsp
12.5 cl	water	4 fl oz
2	egg whites, beaten until stiff but not dry	2
1 tsp	vanilla extract	1 tsp
125 g	nuts, coarsely chopped	4 oz
About 18	red glacé cherries, halved	About 18
60 g	green glacé cherries or angelica, chopped	2 oz

In a saucepan, mix the sugar, corn syrup, salt and water. Cook, stirring, until the sugar is dissolved. Continue cooking, without stirring, until a small amount of the mixture forms a firm ball when dropped in cold water—120° C (248°F) on a sugar thermometer [*pages 10-11*].

Pour about half the syrup over the egg whites, beating constantly. Cook the remainder of the syrup until a small amount forms hard threads in cold water—133°C (272°F) [*soft-crack stage, page 10*]. Add the cooked syrup to the egg white syrup, beating until the mixture holds its shape. Add the vanilla extract and the nuts. Drop tablespoonfuls of the mixture on to sheets of wax paper. Decorate the divinity with the red cherry halves and the green cherries or angelica. Let the divinity stand until it is firm.

WOMAN'S DAY COLLECTOR'S COOK BOOK

Honey Almond Divinity

If white corn syrup is not available, 2 tablespoons of liquid glucose can be used instead. The technique of blanching almonds is shown on page 12.

To make about 750 g (1½ lb)

625 g	granulated sugar	1¼ lb
150 g	almonds, blanched and coarsely shredded	5 oz
¼ litre	water	8 fl oz
4 tbsp	white corn syrup	4 tbsp
4 tbsp	strained honey	4 tbsp
2	egg whites, stiffly beaten	2
½ tsp	vanilla extract	½ tsp

Toast the shredded almonds in a 130°C (250°F or Mark ½) oven for about 20 minutes or until they are light brown.

In a saucepan, combine 375 g (12 oz) of the sugar, half the water, the corn syrup and the honey, stirring over a medium heat until the sugar is dissolved; then cook the mixture without stirring until a temperature of 119°C (246°F) is reached [*firm-ball stage, pages 10-11*].

While the mixture is cooking, combine the rest of the sugar and the water in another saucepan, stirring over a medium heat until the sugar is dissolved. Boil it while you remove the sugar and honey syrup from the heat and pour it slowly over the beaten egg whites, beating constantly during the addition. Continue beating until the sugar and water syrup in the second saucepan has reached a temperature of 124°C (255°F) [*hard-ball stage, pages 10-11*]. Pour this hot syrup into the first mixture and beat it until the confection will not adhere to your finger when you gently touch the surface. Add the vanilla and almonds, and pour the mixture into a lightly buttered 30 by 20 by 3 cm (12 by 8 by 1¼ inch) tin. Cut it into 2.5 cm (1 inch) squares when it is cold; it will yield about 36 pieces.

MAY B. VAN ARSDALE AND RUTH PARRISH CASA EMELLOS
CANDY RECIPES AND OTHER CONFECTIONS

Cremona Nougat

Torrone di Cremona

To make about 850 g (1¾ lb)

250 g	granulated sugar	8 oz
500 g	blanched almonds, toasted and chopped	1 lb
1 tsp	finely chopped candied orange peel	1 tsp
½ tsp	ground cinnamon	½ tsp
12.5 cl	thin honey	4 fl oz
2	egg whites, stiffly beaten	2
	rice paper	

Line a shallow tin, approximately 25 by 20 by 6 cm (10 by 8 by 2½ inches), with rice paper. Pound the almonds in a mortar with the sugar, then add the candied peel and cinnamon. Put the honey in a heavy pan, add the almond mixture and stir and cook until the mixture begins to brown [*soft-crack stage, page 10*]. Remove the pan from the heat and quickly fold in the egg whites. Pour the mixture into the tin; let it cool, then cut it into small, rectangular pieces.

BERYL GOULD-MARKS
THE HOME BOOK OF ITALIAN COOKERY

Nougat

Hylam

The cooked mixture is spread between plate-sized sheets of thin wafers somewhat similar to those used for ice cream sandwiches. These wafers may be replaced with rice paper.

To make about 500 g (1 lb)

250 g	granulated sugar	8 oz
125 g	walnuts, coarsely chopped	4 oz
150 g	honey	5 oz
2 tbsp	water	2 tbsp
2	egg whites, stiffly beaten	2
1 tsp	vanilla extract	1 tsp
	wafers or rice paper	

Bake the nuts in a preheated 130°C (250°F or Mark ½) oven for 15 to 20 minutes until they are dried out but not toasted. Mix the sugar, honey and water in a saucepan and cook over a low heat, stirring constantly, until the sugar has dissolved. Then cook, stirring occasionally, until a firm ball is formed when a little of the syrup is dropped into cold water [*pages 10-11*].

Pour half the syrup in a slow stream over the beaten egg whites, beating constantly. Return the remaining syrup to the heat and cook it to a temperature of 143°C (290°F) or until a cracking sound is heard when a little of it is dropped into cold water and knocked against the side of a cup [*soft-crack stage, page 10*]. Pour the syrup gradually over the rest of the mixture, beating constantly. Place the bowl with this nougat mixture in it over hot water and beat the mixture constantly until it begins to harden. Beat in the nuts and the vanilla extract. Line a 20 cm (8 inch) square tin with wafers or rice paper and spread it with the nougat mixture. Cover the mixture with wafers or rice paper and press down firmly. When the mixture is cold, invert the tin and cut the nougat into bars. Wrap the bars separately in wax paper and store them in an airtight tin.

SAVELLA STECHISHIN
TRADITIONAL UKRAINIAN COOKERY

Almond Nougat

If corn syrup is not available, 17.5 cl (6 fl oz) of liquid glucose can be substituted.

To make about 750 g (1½ lb)

500 g	granulated sugar	1 lb
35 cl	white corn syrup	12 fl oz
¼ tsp	salt	¼ tsp
4 tbsp	water	4 tbsp
2	egg whites, stiffly beaten but not dry	2
½ tsp	almond extract	½ tsp
	green colouring	
60 g	butter, softened	2 oz
125 g	unblanched almonds, toasted	4 oz

Butter a 20 cm (8 inch) square tin. In a heavy saucepan, mix the sugar, corn syrup and salt with the water. Cook, stirring, until the sugar is dissolved. Continue to cook, without stirring, until a small amount of the mixture forms a hard ball when dropped in very cold water—121°C (250°F) on a sugar thermometer [*pages 10-11*].

Gradually beat about one quarter—not more—of the syrup into the beaten egg whites and continue beating until the mixture holds it shape. Cook the remaining syrup until a small amount separates in hard brittle threads when dropped in very cold water—149°C (300°F) [*hard-crack stage, pages 10-11*]. Gradually beat this syrup into the egg white and syrup

mixture and continue beating until the mixture holds its shape. Add the almond flavouring and a few drops of colouring to tint the mixture to a delicate green. Beat in the butter and continue beating until the mixture is very thick and satiny. Stir in the nuts and press the mixture into the tin, smoothing the surface.

Let the nougat stand until it is firm, then turn it out of the tin and cut it into 2.5 cm (1 inch) squares. Wrap each piece in wax paper or plastic film. For the best flavour, store the nougat in an airtight container in a cool place for several days.

WOMAN'S DAY COLLECTOR'S COOK BOOK

Raspberry Noyeau

Other kinds of jam may be used, such as apricot or strawberry. Honey noyeau is made in the same way as raspberry noyeau, using 60 g (2 oz) honey and a little yellow colouring, in place of raspberry jam and pink colouring. Melt the honey in a small pan before adding it to the cooled mixture.

To make about 600 g (1¼ lb)

400 g	granulated sugar	14 oz
15 cl	water	¼ pint
90 g	liquid glucose	3 oz
60 g	raspberry jam, pressed through a fine-meshed sieve	2 oz
	pink colouring	
90 g	almonds, blanched and roughly chopped	3 oz
	rice paper	

Line a 15 by 10 by 2.5 cm (6 by 4 by 1 inch) tin or box with rice paper. Dissolve the sugar in the water. Add the glucose and boil the syrup to 118°C (244°F) [*firm-ball stage, pages 10-11*].

Remove the pan from the heat. Rinse out a bowl with cold water and pour the syrup into it. Leave the syrup until it is slightly cooled but still hot. Add the sieved jam and the colouring. Stir the mixture until it forms a soft, creamy paste. Work it with your fingers, then work in the chopped almonds. If the mixture is too stiff, add a few extra drops of tepid water.

Put the paste into the box or tin and flatten the surface. Dampen the surface with cold water and cover it with more rice paper. Place a piece of stiff cardboard or a thin piece of wood on the top and then a 500 g to 1 kg (1 to 2 lb) weight on top of that. Leave the mixture overnight. Then turn it out, cut it into bars and wrap these in wax paper.

D. F. HUTTON AND E. M. BODE
SIMPLE SWEETMAKING

Italian Chocolate Nougat

Torrone di Cioccolato

This is a very hard, brittle nougat, cooked to a caramel. Most nougats are cooked to the hard-ball stage.

To make 1 kg (2½ lb)

250 g	granulated sugar	8 oz
175 g	cocoa powder	6 oz
2 tbsp	water	2 tbsp
125 g	honey	4 oz
2	egg whites, stiffly beaten	2
500 g	skinned, finely chopped and toasted hazelnuts	1 lb
	rice paper	

Line a 25 by 20 cm (10 by 8 inch) tin with rice paper. Mix the cocoa powder and the water and cook them together until they form a smooth cream, stirring all the time. Set aside.

In a heavy saucepan, heat the sugar and honey together until they begin to brown. Gradually add the beaten egg whites; mix them in well. Off the heat, add the cocoa and the hazelnuts to the honey mixture. Pour the mixture into the tin; the mixture should be about 5 cm (2 inches) deep. Let it cool, then cut it into small rectangles.

BERYL GOULD-MARKS
THE HOME BOOK OF ITALIAN COOKERY

Chocolate Honey Nougat

Schokoladen-Nougat

The syrup for this nougat is cooked to a stage between the hard-ball and the soft-crack. Most nougats are cooked to the hard-ball stage, but nougats containing a large amount of honey are cooked to a higher temperature.

To make about 600 g (1¼ lb)

250 g	castor sugar	8 oz
210 g	honey	7 oz
2½ tbsp	liquid glucose	2½ tbsp
2 tbsp	water	2 tbsp
1	large egg white, stiffly beaten	1
100 g	plain chocolate, melted	3½ oz
75 g	skinned and chopped hazelnuts	2½ oz
100 g	blanched and chopped almonds	3½ oz

Line a baking sheet with buttered aluminium foil. In a small pan, melt the honey over a low heat, stirring constantly. Put the pan into a bowl of hot water to keep the honey warm.

In a second pan, dissolve the sugar and the glucose in the water over a low heat, stirring constantly. Boil the syrup without stirring to 131°C (268°F). Stir in the beaten egg white, then add the warm honey. Over a low heat, stirring constantly, cook the mixture until it becomes a stiff paste.

Remove the pan from the heat and stir in the melted chocolate, hazelnuts and almonds. Turn the hot nougat mixture on to the lined baking sheet and, with a knife dipped in boiling water, spread the mixture out evenly. Leave the nougat to cool and harden before cutting it into squares, diamonds or bars.

MARGARET UHLE AND ANNE BRAKEMEIER
KONFEKT ZUM SELBERMACHEN

Nougats

The flavour of the honey may be impaired by lengthy boiling; it can therefore be warmed separately and added to the syrup only when the syrup reaches a temperature of 138°C (280°F). The corn syrup can be replaced by 1½ tablespoons of liquid glucose. To prevent the syrup from cooling and setting prematurely, warm the nuts in a moderate oven for 5 minutes before adding them to the syrup and egg white mixture.

To make about 850 g (1¾ lb)

250 g	granulated sugar	8 oz
150 g	clear honey	5 oz
3 tbsp	corn syrup	3 tbsp
12.5 cl	water	4 fl oz
2	egg whites, stiffly beaten	2
1 tsp	vanilla extract	1 tsp
300 g	blanched and toasted almonds, chopped	10 oz
125 g	skinned pistachio nuts, chopped	4 oz
	rice paper	

Line a 20 cm (8 inch) square tin with rice paper. Put the sugar, honey, corn syrup and water into a saucepan and stir them over a medium heat until the sugar has dissolved. Without stirring, cook the syrup until it reaches a temperature of 143°C (290°F) [*soft-crack stage, page 10*].

Remove the pan from the heat and gradually pour the hot syrup on to the beaten egg whites, beating constantly. Beat the mixture thoroughly. Add the vanilla extract and the nuts. The mixture should be stiff. If it has not stiffened, put it in the top of a double boiler or in a pan over hot water, and stir it constantly until it dries out a little and becomes firm.

Turn the mixture into the tin lined with rice paper. Cover the mixture with a layer of rice paper. Place a board on top of the nougat and place a heavy weight on the board. Leave the nougat to set for 15 hours. Remove the weight and cut the nougat into rectangular pieces.

MARY B. BOOKMEYER
CANDY AND CANDY-MAKING

Honey Nougat

To dry the almonds, spread them out on a baking sheet and bake them in a preheated 130°C (250°F or Mark ½) oven for about 20 minutes. As this nougat is very sticky, it may be preferable to replace the greaseproof paper with rice paper, so that the paper does not have to be removed before eating. The rice paper should not be oiled.

	To make about 2 kg (4 lb)	
750 g	granulated sugar	1½ lb
750 g	clear honey	1½ lb
3	egg whites, stiffly beaten	3
	orange flavouring	
750 g	almonds, blanched and dried	1½ lb

Oil four sheets of greaseproof paper. Put the granulated sugar and the honey in a saucepan over a very gentle heat and stir them until the sugar dissolves. Cook the syrup until it becomes quite brittle [*soft-crack stage, page 10*]. Add the beaten egg whites and stir them in. Stir in the orange flavouring and the almonds and remove the pan from the heat. Spread the mixture on two of the pieces of greaseproof paper in a layer 5 cm (2 inches) thick. Lay the other sheets of greaseproof paper on top of the mixture. Lay two boards on top of the nougat and lay heavy weights on top of the boards. Leave the nougat until completely cold, then cut it into strips.

OSCAR TSCHIRKY
"OSCAR" OF THE WALDORF'S COOK BOOK

Catalan Nougat

Turrón de Agramunt

When making nougat, the nuts should always be warmed before use. Instead of sandwiching squares of nougat between sheets of rice paper when cold, you can pour the mixture from the pan on to a sheet of rice paper, put a second sheet of rice paper on top and weight it down. Leave the nougat to set until cold, then cut it into squares.

	To make about 500 g (1 lb)	
250 g	blanched almonds, warmed	8 oz
100 g	hazelnuts, roasted, skinned and kept warm	3½ oz
500 g	thick white honey	1 lb
2	egg whites, stiffly beaten	2
	rice paper	

Put the honey in a heavy saucepan and place over a medium heat. Stir it with a wooden spoon and when the honey begins to boil, remove the pan from the heat. Continue stirring until the honey thins to a syrupy consistency. Stir in the egg whites and return the mixture to the heat; continue cooking until it reaches a toffee-like consistency [*hard-ball stage, pages 10-11*]. Stir in the nuts and mix well.

Spread the mixture out in a thin sheet on buttered or oiled marble or a cold work surface. Leave it to cool, then cut it into 2.5 cm (1 inch) squares and sandwich each square between pieces of rice paper cut to fit.

ANA MARIA CALERA
COCINA CATALANA

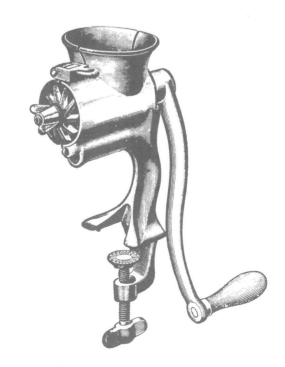

Halva

Irmik Helvasi

To make about 600 g (1¼ lb)

250 g	granulated sugar	8 oz
¼ litre	milk	8 fl oz
¼ litre	water	8 fl oz
30 g	butter	1 oz
250 g	fine semolina	8 oz
60 g	pine-nuts or blanched almonds	2 oz
1 tsp	ground cinnamon (optional)	1 tsp
¼ litre	double cream, whipped (optional)	8 fl oz

Make a syrup by cooking the sugar in the milk and water over a medium heat, stirring until the sugar dissolves. Boil the syrup, stirring frequently, for 15 minutes. Remove the pan from the heat and leave it to cool.

In a large saucepan, over a low heat, melt the butter and fry the semolina and the nuts, stirring frequently, while the nuts brown. Keep scraping the bottom of the pot so that the semolina does not burn. Brown the mixture for 30 minutes, then add the milk syrup, stirring until it is mixed. Cover the pan and simmer the mixture until the syrup is absorbed. Remove the pan from the heat and place a napkin or a smooth towel between the cover and the halva mixture. Leave the pan in a warm place for about 30 minutes. Stir the contents again and turn them into a serving dish, forming the halva into a mound. Shape and cut the halva into squares or ovals. Serve it topped with cinnamon or whipped cream if desired.

OZEL TURKBAS
THE TURKISH COOKBOOK

Turkish Halva

Türkische Halva

To make about 600 g (1¼ lb)

300 g	granulated sugar	10 oz
5	egg whites, stiffly beaten	5
130 g	honey, warmed	4½ oz
150 g	almonds, blanched and coarsely chopped	5 oz
100 g	mixed crystallized fruit, finely chopped	3½ oz
	rice paper	

Beat the sugar into the egg whites, and continue to beat until the sugar has dissolved. Add the honey and put the mixture over a saucepan of hot water. Cook for 25 minutes, stirring constantly. When the mixture has thickened to a paste, stir in the almonds and crystallized fruit. Use a wet knife to spread it on to rice paper. Cover the mixture with another piece of rice paper and press it down evenly. Leave it to set in a cool place for a day. Cut the halva into narrow bars before serving.

MARIA HORVATH
BALKAN-KÜCHE

Macedonian Halva

Mazedonische Halva

The technique for making brittle is shown on page 30. Instead of crushing it in a mortar, you can crush it in a plastic bag as for praline powder (page 167). In the Balkans, special rice paper wafers are sold for making halva, but ordinary rice paper can be substituted.

To make about 1 kg (2 lb)

500 g	granulated sugar	1 lb
6	egg yolks	6
150 g	hazelnuts, toasted, skinned and ground	5 oz
100 g	almonds, blanched and ground	3½ oz
250 g	butter, cut into small pieces	8 oz
1 tsp	vanilla extract	1 tsp
30 g	cocoa powder	1 oz
	rice paper	

Cook half the sugar without water to a caramel [*page 9*], allow it to cool on a marble slab or dish sprinkled with water and then pound it to a powder in a mortar.

Whisk the rest of the sugar with the egg yolks until the mixture is frothy. Add the nuts and the butter. Put the mixture into a bowl over a saucepan of hot water and beat it until it forms a thick paste. Add the vanilla extract and cocoa powder. Remove the bowl from the hot water, stir until the mixture has cooled and then mix it thoroughly with the pounded caramelized sugar.

Spread the mixture over a piece of rice paper, place another piece of rice paper on top and press the mixture down with a heavy weight. Leave it in a cool place for a few hours. Cut the halva into long, narrow bars to serve.

MARIA HORVATH
BALKAN-KÜCHE

Pecan Pralines

Pralines aux Pacanes

To make 750 g (1½ lb)

500 g	soft dark brown sugar	1 lb
500 g	pecan nuts	1 lb
4 tbsp	water	4 tbsp

Have ready a wet marble slab or a large buttered dish. Divest the pecan nuts of their shells and cut some into fine pieces, others into halves and others again into demi-halves. Thoroughly dissolve the sugar in the water, then bring it to the boil. Add the pecan nuts. Let all boil, stirring constantly, until the mixture begins to bubble and then take it off the stove.

Drop the mixture on to the slab or dish by spoonfuls, spreading them out with a fork until each forms a neat, round cake about 1 cm (½ inch) thick and 10 to 12.5 cm (4 to 5 inches) in diameter. Let them dry, then prise them off the marble slab or dish with a palette knife.

THE PICAYUNE'S CREOLE COOK BOOK

Pecan Pralines New Orleans-Style

If pecan nuts are not available, you can use walnuts instead.

To make about 1 kg (2 lb)

500 g	granulated sugar	1 lb
17.5 cl	water	6 fl oz
½ tbsp	vinegar	½ tbsp
500 g	pecan nuts, halved	1 lb

Put to boil the sugar, water and vinegar until the syrup makes a soft ball when dropped into a cup of cold water [*pages 10-11*]. Put in the pecan nuts and cook until the syrup forms a hard ball in a cup of cold water.

Have ready large buttered platters or tins, drop on to them tablespoons of the mixture about 15 cm (6 inches) apart. Let the pralines cool. When they are cold and hard, run a knife under each of the pralines and put them on a plate.

A BOOK OF FAMOUS OLD NEW ORLEANS RECIPES

Sugared Almonds

The author recommends cooking the sugar coating mixture in a copper bowl, but an untinned copper or other heavy saucepan can be substituted.

To make 1.5 kg (3 lb)

1 kg	lump sugar	2 lb
¼ litre	water	8 fl oz
500 g	almonds, blanched	1 lb

In a copper bowl, dissolve 750 g (1½ lb) of the sugar in about 15 cl (¼ pint) of the water over a medium heat. Bring the syrup to the boil; boil to the soft-ball stage, 116°C (240°F) [*pages 10-11*]. Off the heat, add the almonds and, with a wooden spoon, stir until the syrup sets. Continue stirring until the sugar grains and looks like powder. Turn the mixture out on to a marble slab and pick out all the almonds, or put the mixture into a coarse sieve so that the sugar passes through the sieve and the almonds remain.

Return this almond sugar to the copper bowl, add half of the remaining water and wash down the sides of the bowl with a wet pastry brush while boiling the syrup until it reaches the soft-ball stage. Add the almonds, stir the mixture until the sugar separates and crystallizes again and remove the almonds from the sugar as before.

Put the reserved 250 g (8 oz) of lump sugar into the pan, add the sieved cooked sugar and the remaining water, wash down the sides of the pan as before while cooking, and cook the syrup to the soft-ball stage. Add the almonds. Stir as before, and continue stirring until the syrup sets and looks a little powdery, as before. Continue stirring over the heat until you notice that the crystallized sugar on the sides of the pan is starting to melt and that the almonds look shiny. Now, without delay, turn all the contents of the pan on to a marble slab and separate the almonds to prevent them from sticking to each other. Within a few minutes, the sugared almonds will be ready to serve.

E. J. KOLLIST
FRENCH PASTRY, CONFECTIONERY AND SWEETS

Burnt Sugared Almonds

Gebrannte Mandeln

To make about 1 kg (2 lb)

500 g	granulated sugar	1 lb
2 to 3 tbsp	water	2 to 3 tbsp
500 g	unblanched almonds	1 lb
1 tsp	ground cinnamon (optional)	1 tsp

Butter a flat dish. Rub the almonds in a cloth to remove dust and loose skin. In a saucepan over a medium heat, dissolve the sugar in the water and boil the syrup to the thread stage [*page 10*]. Tip in the almonds, and use a wooden spatula to stir them constantly until they have absorbed the syrup. Remove the pan from the heat and stir the almonds continuously until they are dry; return the pan to the heat and stir until the almonds are glazed and their sugar coating has browned lightly. Remove the pan from the heat. Stir in the cinnamon, if used. Tip the glazed almonds on to the buttered dish and separate the almonds from each other.

HENRIETTE DAVIDIS
PRAKTISCHES KOCHBUCH

Candied Almonds

Amandes à la Siamoise

This recipe for candied almonds is from a book written in 1698 by the chef to King Louis XIV of France. It is not clear why they are referred to as Siamese-style almonds.

To make about 1 kg (2½ lb)

500 g	granulated sugar	1 lb
12.5 cl	water	4 fl oz
500 g	almonds, blanched, split and lightly toasted	1 lb
About 125 g	icing sugar or hundreds-and-thousands (optional)	About 4 oz

Dissolve the sugar in the water over a medium heat and cook the syrup to the hard-ball stage [*pages 10-11*]. Remove the pan from the heat and toss the toasted almonds into it.

The mixture may be poured on to a sheet of buttered or oiled greaseproof paper that has been spread out on a rack and then left to harden. Alternatively, you may remove the almonds one by one from the syrup with a spoon and roll them in icing sugar or hundreds-and-thousands before leaving them to dry on greaseproof paper.

NOUVELLE INSTRUCTION POUR LES CONFITURES,
LES LIQUEURS ET LES FRUITS

Pine-Nut Sweets

Pinocchiate

Pinocchiate are confections from the Umbria region of Italy and are made for Christmas in Assisi, Gubbio and Perugia. The method of preparation, shape and ingredients vary, but they are usually diamond-shaped and wrapped in pairs, one plain and one chocolate-flavoured. To flavour *pinocchiate*, add 75 g (2½ oz) cocoa powder to the basic mixture.

To make about 2 kg (4 lb)

1 kg	granulated sugar	2 lb
30 cl	water	½ pint
	cream of tartar	
800 g	pine-nuts	1¾ lb
1 tbsp	flour	1 tbsp

Butter or oil a marble slab. In a large pan, dissolve the sugar in the water then add a pinch of cream of tartar. Boil the syrup to the soft-crack stage [*page 10*]. Remove the pan from the heat and add the pine-nuts and the flour. Mix well with a wooden spoon and, when the ingredients are thoroughly blended, turn the mixture on to the marble slab. Use a spatula to flatten it out until it is 1.5 cm (about ½ inch) thick and cut it into 4 cm (1½ inch) diamonds.

PIERO LUIGI MENICHETTI E LUCIANA MENICHETTI PANFILI
VECCHIA CUCINA EUGUBINA

Almond Pralines

Amandes Pralinées

These sugared almonds may turn pale brown during cooking—it is very difficult to get them coloured snowy white—but this will not impair their flavour.

Peanuts, which have been dubbed "pistaches" by the Creoles, may be made into delightful confections by following the same mode of procedure as outlined for Almond Pralines.

To make about 1 kg (2 lb)

500 g	almonds, blanched	1 lb
500 g	castor sugar	1 lb
	red colouring (optional)	

Rub the almonds with a linen cloth to take off any dust. Put them into a frying pan with the sugar and a dash of red colouring, if you wish to tinge them to a beautiful rose. But they are very beautiful when a snowy white. Place the frying pan on a very low heat, stirring all the time until the almonds make a loud crackling sound. Then take the pan off the heat and stir until the sugar becomes sandy and well detached from the almonds. Put the almonds in a colander with large holes and shake off the loose sugar. Reserve the sugar. Again put the almonds on the heat, stirring them lightly with a spoon as they again pick up the sugar. Pay strict attention to the heat, that it be not too high. When the almonds have taken up this part of the sugar, put in the reserved sugar and continue to cook the almonds, stirring lightly until they have taken up all that sugar. Then take a piece of paper and put it in the colander and throw the almonds upon it, shaking around so as to separate those which still cling together. Each almond must be separate and encrusted with sugar.

THE PICAYUNE'S CREOLE COOK BOOK

Candied Orange Pecans

To make 1 kg (2¼ lb)

750 g	granulated sugar	1½ lb
¼ litre	orange juice	8 fl oz
20 g	butter	¾ oz
1 tsp	grated orange rind	1 tsp
350 g	pecan nuts	12 oz

Grease a marble slab or baking sheet with oil or butter. In a saucepan, combine the sugar and the orange juice. Using a sugar thermometer, cook the mixture to the soft-ball stage, 113°C (236°F) [*pages 10-11*].

Remove the saucepan from the heat and immediately add the butter and orange rind. Beat with a wooden spoon until the mixture is just ready to set. Quickly add the pecan nuts and continue to beat the mixture until it becomes sugary. Turn the mixture out at once on to the buttered or oiled surface and separate the nuts before the mixture cools.

JEAN HEWITT
THE NEW YORK TIMES SOUTHERN HERITAGE COOKBOOK

Crystallized Confections and Jellies

Crystallized Flowers

The technique of crystallizing flowers is shown on page 49. The gum arabic may be dissolved in the rose-water in a bowl, stirring occasionally. The colouring may be omitted, and the flowers may be dried on wire racks without the netting. The crystallizing mixture should be enough to coat about 12 to 14 freesias, 50 rose petals or a mixture of four freesias, one geranium and one to two roses, petals separated. Whole flowers can also be crystallized; a little green colouring may be needed for the stems and leaves.

Though not "sweets", crystallized flowers are edible and form a pleasing decoration for iced cakes, sweet dishes and so on. The process is not difficult, but needs care and patience.

	flower petals	
250 g	castor sugar	8 oz
1 tsp	gum arabic	1 tsp
2 tsp	rose-water	2 tsp
	colouring	

Pick the flowers, which should be fresh and dry but not faded and separate into petals. Dissolve the gum arabic in the rose-water in a small bottle with a cork or screw top, shaking the bottle occasionally. Pour half a teaspoon of the solution into a saucer. As the colours of the flowers are likely to fade, add a few drops of edible colouring to the solution. The colouring should match the flower petals as nearly as possible.

With a soft brush, lightly paint the front and back of each petal, making sure the whole petal is coated. Sprinkle all the petals with the castor sugar.

Place the petals on a wire rack covered with a piece of coarse netting to dry in a warm place at a temperature not exceeding 49°C (120°F)—in an unlit oven with a pilot light or in an airing cupboard. Dry the petals for 1 to 2 hours, then move them to a different place on the netting and dry them for a further 1 to 2 hours.

When crisp, take the petals out and leave them for about 6 hours to dry completely. Store them in an airtight container on tissue or greaseproof paper. They will keep for months.

D. F. HUTTON AND E. M. BODE
SIMPLE SWEETMAKING

Crystallized Violets

Violettes Pralinées

To make about 150 g (5 oz)

About 150 g	Parma violets, stems removed	About 5 oz
500 g	granulated sugar	1 lb
10 cl	water	3½ fl oz

In a copper pan, cook the granulated sugar and water to the hard-crack stage [*pages 10-11*]. Throw in the violets and stir over a high heat until the sugar dries around the flowers. Do not allow the sugar to turn yellow. Remove the pan from the heat. The sugar that does not cling to the violets will be as perfumed as the flowers.

MME. JEANNE SAVARIN (EDITOR)
LA CUISINE DES FAMILLES

Candied Vegetables

To crystallize coconut in the same way as the vegetables in this recipe, drill the eyes of a coconut and drain off the liquid. Bake the coconut in a preheated 180° C (350° F or Mark 4) oven for 20 minutes. With a hammer or the back of a cleaver, tap the coconut about a third of the way from the end opposite the eyes. The coconut will fracture along a natural seam. Continue tapping until the nut cracks open along this line. Remove the flesh from the shells. With a sharp knife, peel off the brown skin, then slice the coconut flesh into strips and proceed as in the following recipe.

To make about 750 g (1½ lb)

500 g	pumpkin, carrots, sweet potatoes or other firm-fleshed vegetables, peeled and thinly sliced	1 lb
250 g	granulated sugar	8 oz
12.5 cl	water	4 fl oz
	castor sugar	

Put the granulated sugar and water into a saucepan. Stirring, heat them until the mixture starts to boil. Lower the heat and cook the syrup gently for 15 minutes [*thread stage, page 10*]. Add the vegetable slices to the syrup and cook gently for about 15 minutes or until they are tender when you poke them with the point of a sharp knife.

With a slotted spoon, lift the slices out of the syrup and spread them out to dry on a wire rack. Put a piece of wax paper underneath the rack to catch the drips.

After the vegetable slices have been drying for several hours, sprinkle another sheet of wax paper with castor sugar and roll the vegetable slices in it. Put the slices back on the rack to dry thoroughly.

CAROLYN MEYER
LOTS AND LOTS OF CANDY

Candied Orange Peel

Skórka Pomarańczowa

Instead of rolling the orange peel in sugar, it can be dipped in melted chocolate or fondant. The peel must be allowed to dry out thoroughly before dipping.

To make about 850 g (1¾ lb)

2	oranges, peel pared	2
500 g	castor sugar	1 lb
12.5 cl	water	4 fl oz
	granulated sugar (optional)	

Cut the orange peel into very thin strips and simmer it in water for 2 to 3 hours or until tender, changing the water several times. Or soak it in cold water for several days, changing the water every day; this will shorten the cooking time to 30 to 40 minutes. Drain the peel and dry it.

In a large saucepan over a medium heat, dissolve the castor sugar in the water and cook them to a syrup. Cook the syrup for 5 minutes, then lower the heat and add the orange peel; simmer for 15 minutes more, or until the liquid is thick. Drain the orange peel and allow it to dry overnight, reserving the syrup. Reboil the syrup the following day and cook it to the hard-crack stage [*pages 10-11*]. Dip each piece of peel separately in the syrup and dry it on a rack in a preheated 130°C (250°F or Mark ½) oven for 7 to 10 minutes. When the peel is dry and the glaze has hardened, it can be stored. It can also be rolled in granulated sugar while still warm from the oven.

MARJA OCHOROWICZ-MONATOWA
POLISH COOKERY

Candied Fruit Peel

Peel keeps almost indefinitely and may be used diced in baking or served as a confection. Orange and grapefruit peel should not be combined as the distinctive flavour of each would be spoiled.

To make about 1 kg (2 lb)

3	large grapefruits or 5 large navel oranges	3
675 g	granulated sugar	1 lb 6 oz
¼ litre	water	8 fl oz
1½ tsp	ground ginger	1½ tsp

Cut the fruit in half crosswise. Scrape out and discard the fruit pulp and membranes, but leave the white pith attached to the rind. Cut the peel into long strips 5 mm to 1 cm (¼ to ½ inch) wide. Put the peel into a pan, cover it with boiling water and simmer it for 5 minutes. Drain the peel well. Repeat the process four more times, using fresh boiling water each time and draining well between boilings. This will remove the bitter oils from the peel.

In a heavy-bottomed saucepan, combine 500 g (1 lb) of the sugar with the water, add the ginger and cook until the sugar dissolves. Add the peel and mix it with the syrup. Cook the mixture slowly, partially covered, for about 30 to 45 minutes or until the peel is soft. Turn the peel out on to a large sheet of aluminium foil or wax paper, spreading it out in a single layer. Allow the peel to cool thoroughly, then sprinkle it liberally with the remaining sugar. Leave to stand uncovered until it is completely dry, about 5 to 7 hours or overnight. Store the peel in a tightly closed jar.

WILLIAM HARLAN HALE AND THE EDITORS OF HORIZON MAGAZINE
THE HORIZON COOKBOOK

Crystallized Chestnuts

Marrons Glacés

In this recipe, the crystallizing process is achieved by increasing the concentration of the sugar in the syrup at each successive boiling, without adding additional sugar. Each time the syrup is boiled, it is cooked to a slightly higher temperature; do not let the syrup cook as high as the soft-ball stage, however, or the syrup will not penetrate the chestnuts, but will merely glaze them. Both this method and the method shown on page 48 can be used for crystallizing fruit.

The technique of peeling chestnuts is described on page 56.

To make about 750 g (1½ lb)

500 g	peeled chestnuts	1 lb
500 g	granulated sugar	1 lb
2 tbsp	liquid glucose	2 tbsp
10 cl	water	3½ fl oz

Cook the peeled chestnuts in water to cover until a needle inserted in the base of a chestnut enters without difficulty, about 40 minutes. Dissolve the sugar and glucose in the water and cook it until the syrup boils and becomes smooth, about 101°C (215°F). Pour the syrup into a heatproof bowl and leave it to cool; when the syrup is completely cold, immerse the chestnuts in it and leave them for 24 hours.

Put the bowl containing the syrup and chestnuts into a bain-marie and gradually heat the syrup. Remove the chestnuts when the syrup reaches boiling point. Cook the syrup to 102°C (216°F). Remove the bowl from the bain-marie. Return the chestnuts to the syrup and leave them for 12 hours.

Remove the chestnuts from the syrup, drain them and put the syrup back in the bain-marie. Cook the syrup to 104°C (220°F). Remove the bowl from the bain-marie, return the chestnuts to the syrup and leave them for a further 12 hours.

Remove the chestnuts from the syrup, return the syrup to the bain-marie and cook the syrup to 106°C (223°F). Remove the bowl from the heat, immerse the chestnuts in the syrup and leave them for 12 hours. Finally, remove the chestnuts from the syrup, put the bowl of syrup into the bain-marie and cook the syrup to 108°C (227°F). Immerse the chestnuts in the syrup and leave them for 12 hours. Drain the chestnuts and leave them to dry in a wire basket or on wire racks. Dry them first in a dry room for 12 hours, then for a further 12 hours in a warm, dry place such as an airing cupboard or an unlit oven with a pilot light.

GINETTE MATHIOT
LA PÂTISSERIE POUR TOUS

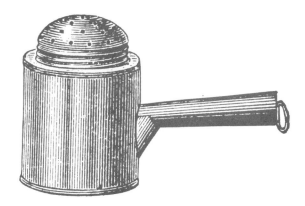

Candied Sweet Potato Balls

To make 1.5 kg (3 lb)

1 kg	sweet potatoes	2 lb
500 g	granulated sugar	1 lb
12.5 cl	water	4 fl oz
1 tsp	vanilla extract	1 tsp

Scoop out little balls from the sweet potatoes with a vegetable scoop. Put the balls into slightly salted boiling water to cover and cook them until they are tender enough to pierce with a toothpick—about 10 to 15 minutes. Remove the pan from the heat and drain.

Dissolve the sugar in the water and cook the syrup to the hard-crack stage [pages 10-11]. Add the vanilla extract. Drop in the potato balls, a few at a time, simmering them in the syrup until they are thickly coated and are transparent, about 5 minutes. Remove the balls one at a time with a skimmer or a fork and drop them on to wax paper. They should harden up on the outside and make a delicious confection.

MARY M. WRIGHT
CANDY-MAKING AT HOME

Candied Ginger

To make about 500 g (1 lb)

500 g	freshly dried ginger root, peeled and sliced into 5 mm (¼ inch) thick pieces	1 lb
3 tbsp	water	3 tbsp
About 750 g	granulated sugar	About 1½ lb

Put the pieces of ginger root into a saucepan and cover with water. Boil them over a medium heat until tender—about 30 minutes. Drain the ginger in a colander and leave it to cool.

When the ginger is cold, weigh it and put it into a pan with an equal weight of sugar and the 3 tablespoons of water. Boil the ginger and sugar slowly until the sugar dissolves, stirring often, then stir occasionally until the ginger becomes transparent and the liquid has nearly boiled away.

Reduce the heat and stir the crystallized ginger continually. When it is practically dry, remove the pan from the heat and use a slotted spoon to put several pieces of ginger at a time into a paper bag containing 250 g (8 oz) sugar. Shake the bag and remove the pieces of ginger with a slotted spoon; lay them on wax paper. Repeat the process until all the ginger has been sugared. Stored in a glass jar at the back of the cabinet, it will last all winter for nibbles.

GRACE FIRTH
A NATURAL YEAR

Hawaiian Candied Ginger

To make about 250 g (8 oz)

150 g	fresh ginger root, scraped and sliced across the grain into 5 mm (¼ inch) slices	5 oz
125 g	granulated sugar	4 oz
4 tbsp	castor sugar	4 tbsp

Put the ginger slices in a pan with cold water to cover and boil them for 5 minutes. Drain them. Cover them with cold water again and boil them for 5 minutes. Drain them, then spread the ginger slices on a clean dry towel.

In a pan, combine the granulated sugar with 4 tablespoons of water. Stir over a medium heat until the sugar dissolves. Cook the syrup without stirring over a low heat for 15 minutes or until it thickens [*thread stage, page 10*]. Add the ginger and cook over a low heat until the syrup is absorbed by the ginger, about 10 minutes. Shake the pan occasionally so that the ginger will not burn. Place the ginger slices on a wire rack to dry for at least an hour. Roll the ginger slices in the castor sugar. Leave them to stand until the sugar crystallizes. Store the ginger in an airtight jar.

ELIZABETH AHN TOUPIN
HAWAII COOKBOOK AND BACKYARD LUAU

Candied Carrots

To make about 1 kg (2 lb)

600 g	carrots, cut into slices 3 mm (⅛ inch) thick	1¼ lb
250 g	granulated sugar	8 oz
12.5 cl	water	4 fl oz
175 g	castor sugar	6 oz

In the pan, combine the granulated sugar and water over a medium heat, stirring until the sugar dissolves. Simmer the syrup over a low heat for 15 minutes [*threadstage, page 10*]. Add the carrots and raise the heat to medium. Cook the mixture for about 15 minutes until the carrots are glazed and all the syrup has been absorbed. Dry the carrot slices on wire racks for several hours. Roll the carrots in the castor sugar. Leave them until the castor sugar has crystallized. Then store the candied carrots in an airtight jar.

ELIZABETH AHN TOUPIN
HAWAII COOKBOOK AND BACKYARD LUAU

Fig Jellies

To make about 350 g (12 oz)

60 g	preserved figs, chopped	2 oz
30 g	powdered gelatine	1 oz
15 cl	water	¼ pint
125 g	granulated sugar	4 oz
½	orange, juice squeezed, rind grated	½
2 tbsp	lemon juice	2 tbsp
30 g	pistachio nuts or almonds, chopped	1 oz
125 g	angelica	4 oz
125 g	icing sugar and cornflour in equal quantities or 175 g (6 oz) castor sugar	4 oz

Soften the gelatine in half of the water. Boil the rest of the water with the sugar, orange juice and lemon juice for 10 minutes. Remove the pan from the heat and add the figs, nuts and grated orange rind. Boil the mixture for 10 minutes. Add the softened gelatine, stirring the mixture in one direction only. Boil the mixture for a further 10 minutes, making 30 minutes cooking time in all.

Pour the jelly mixture into a wet 30 by 20 by 3 cm (12 by 8 by 1¼ inch) tin and leave it to set for 24 hours. Cut the jelly into small oval shapes, cut the angelica into narrow strips to resemble fruit stalks and add them to the jelly shapes. Roll the jellies in the mixture of icing sugar and cornflour or dust them liberally on each side with the castor sugar. Allow the sweets to dry thoroughly before packing them away.

ESMÉ GRAY BOOKER
SWEETS THAT HAVE TEMPTED ME

Fresh Fruit Jellies

The technique of making fresh fruit jellies is shown on page 52.
The quantities may be doubled to make two flavours of jelly,
which can be set one on top of the other to make a striped sweet.

To make about 500 g (1 lb)		
15 cl	fruit juice (lemon, orange, raspberry or blackcurrant)	¼ pint
90 g	granulated sugar	3 oz
3 to 6 tbsp	liquid glucose	3 to 6 tbsp
30 g	powdered gelatine, softened in 4 tbsp water	1 oz
	colouring (optional)	
	castor sugar	

Put the fruit juice, sugar and glucose in a pan and heat them
slowly, stirring until the sugar dissolves. Add the gelatine
and continue heating the mixture until the gelatine dissolves. If the mixture is too pale, a suitable colouring can be
added. Pour the mixture into a wetted tin about 15 cm (6
inches) square and about 5 mm (¼ inch) deep. Leave the jelly to
set for at least 6 hours in a cool place, or overnight.

When firm, turn the tin out on to a work surface and cut the
jelly into cubes or use a cutter to cut it into crescent shapes to
resemble orange or lemon segments. If you have no cutter of
that shape, use a small round one and cut some of the shapes
again to make crescents. Roll the jelly shapes in castor sugar.

WINIFRED GRAHAM
CHOCOLATES AND CANDIES FOR PLEASURE AND PROFIT

Turkish Delight

To make about 500 g (1 lb)		
1	lemon, rind thinly pared and cut into strips, juice strained	1
1	orange, rind thinly pared and cut into strips, juice strained	1
500 g	lump sugar	1 lb
30 cl	water	½ pint
30 g	powdered gelatine	1 oz
2 tbsp	icing sugar	2 tbsp
1 tbsp	cornflour	1 tbsp

Dissolve the lump sugar in half the water over a medium heat.
Add the strips of lemon and orange rind and the juices. Bring
the mixture to the boil and simmer for 15 minutes. Soften the
gelatine by soaking it for 5 to 10 minutes in the rest of the
water. Add the gelatine to the sugar syrup and boil, stirring
well, for 20 minutes. Strain the mixture into wetted shallow
tins or plates and leave it for 24 hours to set. Cut the sweets
into 2.5 cm (1 inch) cubes. Sieve the icing sugar and the
cornflour together into a shallow dish. Roll the pieces of
Turkish delight in the mixture. Store the sweets in boxes with
more icing sugar and cornflour in between them.

THE KING'S COLLEGE HOSPITAL BOOK OF COOKING RECIPES

Lemon Turkish Delight

To make orange-flavoured Turkish delight, the author su-
gests replacing the juice and rind of the lemons with the juice
and rind of 3 oranges and the juice of 3 lemons, and adding a
little orange colouring. To make crème de menthe *Turkish*
delight, add 1 tablespoon of peppermint extract or crème de
menthe *and a few drops of green colouring.*

To make 3 kg (6 lb)		
6	lemons, rind grated, juice strained	6
3 kg	granulated sugar	6 lb
60 cl	water	1 pint
350 g	cornflour, sieved	12 oz
135 g	gelatine, softened in 30 cl (½ pint) water	4½ oz
	icing sugar, sieved	

Place the sugar, juice and rind of the lemons and the water
into a copper pan and bring the syrup to the thread stage [*page*
10]. Gradually whisk in the cornflour, mix well and bring the
mixture to the boil again; gradually add the softened gelatine
and allow the mixture to boil for about 7 minutes, stirring
occasionally—otherwise the mixture might burn. Strain the
mixture through a sieve into three wetted 20 cm (8 inch)
square tins and allow the mixture to cool overnight. Cut into
squares, roll them in icing sugar and they are ready to serve.

E. J. KOLLIST
FRENCH PASTRY, CONFECTIONERY AND SWEETS

Confectionery Pastes

Boiled Marzipan

If more than one flavouring is used, these should be added, with the appropriate colourings, to separate portions of the marzipan during the kneading stage. Flavourings and colourings for marzipan are discussed on page 14. The technique for making marzipan is shown on page 58.

If, after storage, the marzipan becomes hard and inclined to crack, add two or three drops of tepid water and knead the mixture thoroughly until it becomes pliable again.

To make about 1 kg (2 lb)

350 g	ground almonds	12 oz
500 g	granulated sugar	1 lb
17.5 cl	water	6 fl oz
2	egg whites, lightly beaten	2
1 tsp	orange-flower water (optional)	1 tsp
	icing sugar	

In a pan, gently heat the granulated sugar and water together, stirring constantly, until the sugar has completely dissolved. Stop stirring as soon as the liquid comes to the boil. Increase the heat and boil the syrup until it reaches a temperature of 116°C (240°F) [*soft-ball stage, pages 10-11*]. Remove the pan from the heat and stir the syrup lightly until you observe a faint cloudiness. This means the syrup has begun to grain. Stir in the ground almonds. Add the beaten egg whites and return the pan to a low heat. Cook very gently for a minute or two until the marzipan mixture firms up slightly. Add the orange-flower water, if using, and mix well.

Dust a work surface with icing sugar and turn out the marzipan on to it. Allow the marzipan to cool until it can be handled easily. Then knead it until it is smooth and pliable; if the mixture is too moist, work in 2 to 4 tablespoons of icing sugar. Divide the marzipan into portions as required, and flavour and colour it while it is still warm.

To store the marzipan, wrap each coloured piece separately in wax paper or plastic film. Store the marzipan in a plastic bag in a tin or in the refrigerator.

HELEN JEROME
SWEET-MAKING FOR ALL

Koenigsberg Marzipan

Königsberger Marzipan

Marzipan is traditionally eaten at Christmas in Germany and it is moulded into fruit and vegetable shapes which are hung on the Christmas tree. Koenigsberg marzipan is a marzipan moulded into tiny cup shapes, filled with fondant or, as in this case, crystallized fruits or fruit jellies. In Germany, special moulds are sold to make the shapes, but they can also be fashioned by hand. If bitter almonds are not available, use 25 g (1 oz) more of sweet almonds and add a few drops of almond extract. In the German method of making marzipan, the ground almonds are added with the sugar and water at the beginning of the cooking process. The marzipan must be taken off the heat as soon as it loses its stickiness, indicating that the almonds are giving up their oil. If the marzipan is overcooked, it will foam in the pan.

To make about 1.5 kg (3 lb)

500 g	almonds, blanched and very finely ground	1 lb
25 g	bitter almonds, blanched and very finely ground	1 oz
175 g	granulated sugar	6 oz
6 tbsp	water	6 tbsp
500 g	icing sugar	1 lb
1 tsp	rose-water	1 tsp
125 g	crystallized fruits or fruit jellies, cut into decorative shapes	4 oz

Put the almonds, granulated sugar and water into a saucepan on a medium heat and stir the mixture with a wooden spoon for about 5 to 8 minutes, until the mixture is smooth and comes away cleanly from the sides of the pan and a kitchen towel pressed against the mixture does not stick to it. Leave the marzipan to cool; then put it in a closed tin and leave it until the following day.

The next day, gradually work in 350 g (12 oz) of the icing sugar and the rose-water until the mixture is smooth. The marzipan is now ready for use.

Shape the marzipan with moulds or with your fingers into cylinders about 2.5 cm (1 inch) high and 2.5 cm (1 inch) in diameter and make a deep depression in the middle of each cylinder with your thumb. Arrange the marzipan shapes on a baking sheet covered with greaseproof paper. In a bowl, mix the rest of the icing sugar with enough tepid water to make a thick syrup. Use this syrup to paint the tops and sides of the marzipan shapes.

Bake the marzipan on the top shelf of a preheated 200°C (400°F or Mark 6) oven for 4 to 5 minutes. Remove from the oven and leave to cool. When cold, fill the depressions in the shapes with the crystallized fruit or jellies.

FRITZ BECKER
DAS KOCHBUCH AUS MECKLENBURG, POMMERN UND OSTPREUSSEN

Lübeck Marzipan
Lübecker Marzipan

Make sure you do not cook the marzipan for too long; it must be removed from the heat as soon as it loses its stickiness, otherwise it will release all its oil and will no longer be a smooth paste. The method of crystallizing flowers is on page 49.

To make 1 kg (2 lb)		
500 g	almonds, blanched and finely ground	1 lb
2 to 3 tbsp	orange-flower water	2 to 3 tbsp
600 g	icing sugar, sieved	1¼ lb
	crystallized flowers	
	crystallized orange peel	

In a small saucepan over a gentle heat, stir the almonds with the orange-flower water and 500 g (1 lb) of the icing sugar. The mixture is ready when it no longer sticks to your fingers, about 5 to 8 minutes, but it should not get any drier than that.

Turn the mixture out on to a board sprinkled with some of the remaining icing sugar and roll it out, sprinkling more icing sugar, both on top and underneath, as you work. The marzipan can either be formed into a large cake, or cut into small shapes with a biscuit cutter.

Put the marzipan into a preheated 130°C (250°F or Mark ½) oven for about 15 minutes to dry. It must not become hard, but remain soft and snow-white. Decorate the marzipan with crystallized flowers and crystallized peel cut into leaf shapes.

HENRIETTE DAVIDIS
PRAKTISCHES KOCHBUCH

Almond Sticks

To make about 1 kg (2 lb)		
250 g	almond paste (*page 167*)	8 oz
500 g	icing sugar	1 lb
2 tsp	lime juice	2 tsp
3 or 4	egg whites, lightly beaten	3 or 4
250 g	almonds, blanched, toasted and coarsely chopped	8 oz

Mix the almond paste with the icing sugar and lime juice. Add enough beaten egg white to make the mixture into a smooth, stiff paste. Roll out the paste and cut it into sticks. Roll the sticks in the chopped almonds. Set out the sticks in a preheated 130°C (250°F or Mark ½) oven with the door open and let them dry out for about 1 to 1½ hours.

MARY LAND
NEW ORLEANS CUISINE

Marzipan Sweets
Massepains

*Menon, whose first name is unknown, was a chef at the court of Louis XV. He wrote several cookery books; the one in which this recipe appears—*La Cuisinière Bourgeoise, *published in 1746—was the most popular French cookery book for more than a hundred years.*

The almonds can also be ground in a food processor. If crystallized orange flowers are not available, use a few drops of orange-flower water. The technique for making a cooked fruit paste is shown on page 50.

To make about 1.5 kg (3 lb)		
500 g	almonds, blanched	1 lb
3	egg whites	3
About 150 g	thick apricot jam or cooked fruit paste	About 5 oz
1 tbsp	crystallized orange flowers, pounded	1 tbsp
About 500 g	icing sugar	About 1 lb
Marzipan icing		
1	lime, seeded and finely chopped	1
6	egg whites, lightly beaten	6
About 350 g	icing sugar, sieved	About 12 oz

Pound the almonds in a mortar, adding the egg whites a little at a time during the pounding. Mix the almonds with the apricot jam or a cooked fruit paste that must not be liquid, and the orange flowers. When everything is well mixed, put the almond mixture into a saucepan with half the icing sugar and dry it out on the heat, stirring constantly, until it is stiff.

Turn the paste out on to the table and knead it, adding icing sugar to stop it sticking to your fingers, until it is smooth. Then roll it out and shape it as you want.

To make the icing, add the lime to the lightly beaten egg whites. Dip the marzipan shapes into the mixture, then roll them in the icing sugar, as much as they will take. Arrange them on baking sheets covered with greaseproof paper. Bake them in a preheated 130°C (250°F or Mark ½) oven for about 20 minutes, or until the icing is dry but not browned.

MENON
LA CUISINIÈRE BOURGEOISE

White Sugar Lowzina

Lowzina b'Shakar

This delectable confection is usually made for weddings; decorated with gold-leaf paper, it is sent to relatives and friends by the bride's family.

To make about 400 g (12 oz)

150 g	ground blanched almonds	5 oz
250 g	granulated sugar	8 oz
12.5 cl	water	4 fl oz
½ tsp	strained lemon juice	½ tsp
1 tsp	rose-water	1 tsp
2 or 3	cardamom seeds	2 or 3
⅛ tsp	ground cardamom	⅛ tsp

Combine the sugar and the water and cook them over a medium heat for 7 to 8 minutes or until the syrup spins a long thread when dropped from a spoon [*thread stage, page 10*]. Add the lemon juice and cook for 1 to 2 minutes. Add the rose-water and let the syrup return to the boil. Remove the pan from the heat and stir with a wooden spoon until the syrup is almost cold. Add 100 g (3½ oz) of the almonds and the whole cardamom seeds. Stir until the mixture turns white.

Mix the ground cardamom with the rest of the ground almonds and sprinkle about half the mixture in a thin layer on a tray. Empty the sugar and almond mixture on top of this layer. Gradually sprinkle over the rest of the ground almonds and cardamom while flattening the mixture evenly until it forms a layer about 1 cm (½ inch) thick. Leave the sweet to cool and set for about 5 minutes, then cut it into diamond shapes about 2.5 cm (1 inch) long, or larger if desired. Place the sweets in an airtight tin box and refrigerate them to preserve their softness and flavour.

DAISY INY
THE BEST OF BAGHDAD COOKING

Almond Sweets

Mandelkonfekt

To make the cocoa icing, sieve 250 g (8 oz) icing sugar and 15 g (½ oz) cocoa into a bowl. Mix with a little warm water to make an icing thick enough to coat a metal spoon.

To make about 350 g (12 oz)

180 g	granulated sugar	6 oz
3 tbsp	water	3 tbsp
130 g	almonds, blanched, 75 g (2½ oz) finely chopped and lightly toasted, the rest finely ground	4½ oz
30 g	cocoa powder, sieved	1 oz
60 g	vanilla sugar	2 oz
	icing sugar	
	cocoa icing (optional)	

Cook the granulated sugar in the water over a medium heat, stirring until the sugar dissolves. Bring this syrup to the boil and cook it to the soft-ball stage [*pages 10-11*].

Remove the pan from the heat, add the chopped and the ground almonds, the cocoa powder and the vanilla sugar, and stir the resulting paste well.

Sprinkle a work surface with icing sugar and turn the mixture out on to it. When the paste is cool enough to handle, roll it out and cut it into shapes. When dry, the shapes can be coated with cocoa icing if desired.

MÁRIA HAJKOVÁ
MÚČNIKY

Pistachio Marzipan

Les Massepains Ordinaires de Pistaches

The techniques of skinning and grinding pistachio nuts are demonstrated on page 12.

To make about 850 g (1¾ lb)

500 g	shelled pistachio nuts, blanched and finely ground	1 lb
375 g	sugar	13 oz
2 to 3 tbsp	water	2 to 3 tbsp
About 275 g icing sugar		About 9 oz
1	egg white	1
	orange-flower water	

Dissolve the sugar in the water and cook it to the soft-ball stage [*pages 10-11*]; stir in the pistachio nuts. Without stirring, cook this paste on a low heat for 3 to 4 minutes, until it begins to dry out. Sprinkle a work surface with icing sugar. Pour the paste from the pan and spread it out on the work surface to cool.

When the paste is cold, roll it with a pin to a thickness of about 1 cm (½ inch). Cut it into decorative shapes with sharp-edged cutters. Lay the marzipan shapes on baking sheets covered with greaseproof paper. Bake them in a preheated 130°C (250°F or Mark ½) oven for about 20 minutes or until the tops of the shapes are dry to the touch. Remove them from the oven and leave them to cool on the sheets. Turn them over.

Prepare a royal icing by beating the egg white with 250 g (8 oz) icing sugar and a few drops of orange-flower water. The mixture should be stiff, but should spread easily. Use this icing to coat the soft top and sides of the marzipan shapes. Return the shapes to the oven at the same temperature to dry out for about 10 minutes.

PIERRE JOSEPH BUC'HOZ
L'ART DE PRÉPARER LES ALIMENTS

Iced Marzipan

Massepain Glacé

This recipe first appeared in an anonymous book published in 1732. The almonds can be ground in a food processor; in this case, add the egg whites after the almonds are combined with the syrup. The technique for making iced marzipan is shown on page 62. Colourings and flavourings for marzipan are discussed on page 58. If you prefer a snow-white marzipan and icing, bake the marzipan in a preheated 130°C (250°F or Mark ½) oven for 15 minutes, both before and after icing it.

To make about 3 kg (6 lb)		
1.5 kg	almonds, blanched and dried	3 lb
750 g	granulated sugar	1½ lb
15 cl	water	¼ pint
4 to 5	egg whites	4 to 5
	icing sugar	
	Glacé icing	
750 g	icing sugar	1½ lb
6 tbsp	water	6 tbsp
	orange-flower water (optional)	

Pound the almonds in a mortar, adding some of the egg white from time to time to prevent them from becoming too oily.

Dissolve the sugar in the water over a medium heat and

cook the syrup to the soft-ball stage [*pages 10-11*]. Remove the pan from the heat. Add your almonds and blend all the ingredients with a spatula, carefully scraping the sides of the pan to prevent sticking. You will know that your paste is ready if none sticks to the back of your hand when you touch it.

Sprinkle a board with icing sugar. Take the paste out of the pan and put it on the board. Sprinkle the marzipan with more sugar and leave it to cool. Roll out the marzipan to a thickness of about 5mm (¼ inch) and cut your shapes out of it with biscuit cutters. Lay the shapes out on greaseproof paper and press them down slightly with the tip of your finger. Bake the marzipan in a preheated 200°C (400°F or Mark 6) oven for 5 minutes or until it is dry.

To make the icing, mix the water and a few drops of orange-flower water or other flavouring with the icing sugar, stirring the mixture until it is as thick as porridge.

Remove the marzipans from the oven, gently lift them off the paper and turn them over. Use a palette knife to spread a little icing on the unbaked sides. Return the marzipans iced side up to the paper and put them back in the preheated 200°C (400°F or Mark 6) oven for a further 5 to 10 minutes, or until the icing is dry and lightly browned at the edges. Store the marzipan in an airtight tin for use when required.

PROSPER MONTAGNÉ
NEW LAROUSSE GASTRONOMIQUE

Iced Chestnut Balls

Kastanienkugeln

The technique of peeling and cooking chestnuts is described on page 56. To make a purée, sieve the chestnuts or put them through a food mill. To make the chocolate icing for this recipe, sieve 250 g (8 oz) icing sugar and 15 g (½ oz) cocoa powder into a bowl. Mix in a tablespoon or two of warm water to make an icing thick enough to coat the back of a spoon.

To make about 750 g (1½ lb)		
600 g	chestnuts, peeled and puréed	1¼ lb
300 g	sugar	10 oz
2 to 3 tbsp	water	2 to 3 tbsp
125 g	icing sugar	4 oz
	chocolate icing	

In a pan over a medium heat, dissolve the sugar in the water and boil the syrup to the thread stage [*page 10*]. Stir in the peeled and puréed chestnuts. Form the mixture into small balls, roll the balls in icing sugar and leave them to dry overnight. The next day, dip them in the chocolate icing.

ELEK MAGYAR
KOCHBUCH FÜR FEINSCHMECKER

Sugared Chestnut Balls

To make about 1.25 kg (2½ lb)

1 kg	chestnuts	2 lb
150 g	honey	5 oz
175 g	icing sugar	6 oz
1 tsp	ground cinnamon	1 tsp

Cut a cross in the flat side of each chestnut. Plunge the chestnuts into boiling water and cook them until the skins split, at least 20 to 25 minutes. Drain and cool them and peel off the skins with a sharp knife. Mince the chestnuts or force them through a ricer. Blend them with the honey and shape the mixture into small balls.

Combine the sugar and cinnamon and spread the mixture out on a flat plate. Roll the chestnut balls in this mixture.

GLORIA BLEY MILLER
THE THOUSAND RECIPE CHINESE COOKBOOK

Chestnut Balls

Boules aux Marrons

The technique of peeling and cooking chestnuts is described on page 56. To make the purée, sieve the chestnuts or put them through a food mill.

To make about 350 g (12 oz)

150 g	chestnut purée	5 oz
100 g	chocolate	3½ oz
2 tbsp	double cream	2 tbsp
30 g	butter	1 oz
75 g	icing sugar	2½ oz
	vanilla extract	
60 g	chocolate vermicelli	2 oz

In a small saucepan immersed in hot water, melt the chocolate with the cream and the butter. When the mixture has melted, stir it to obtain a smooth paste.

Remove the bowl from the hot water and stir in the icing sugar, a few drops of vanilla extract and the chestnut purée. Chill the mixture in the refrigerator for 24 hours.

Shape the mixture into small balls and roll them in the chocolate vermicelli. Serve the sweets very cold in individual paper cases. They will keep for one day.

JACQUELINE GÉRARD
BONNES RECETTES D'AUTREFOIS

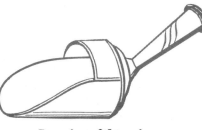

Persian Marzipan

Toot

The Iranian cook will enhance the aroma of her almonds by immersing them in narcissus blossoms for several days. If desired, you may place your almonds in an airtight container with one vanilla pod. These sweets will not keep for very long because they tend to dry out quickly.

To make about 350 g (12 oz)

200 g	ground almonds	7 oz
75 g	icing sugar	2½ oz
4 tbsp	rose-water or 2 tsp vanilla extract	4 tbsp
250 g	castor sugar	8 oz
About 45 g	pistachio nuts, slivered	About 1½ oz

Mix the ground almonds and icing sugar. Add the rose-water or vanilla extract and stir until the mixture forms a stiff smooth paste. Shape the paste into small balls, then roll the balls between the palms of your hands to lengthen them somewhat into the shape of a white mulberry, which this confection is supposed to resemble. Roll each piece in the castor sugar and stick a slivered pistachio nut in one end, to represent the stem. Store the sweets in a tightly covered tin.

NESTA RAMAZANI
PERSIAN COOKING

Spanish Royal Marzipan

Pasta Real

As an alternative to shaping the paste with your fingers, you can cut it into shapes with biscuit cutters.

To make 750 g (1½ lb)

400 g	blanched almonds, finely ground	14 oz
400 g	castor sugar	14 oz
15 cl	water	¼ pint
10	egg yolks	10
	icing sugar	

Over a medium heat, dissolve the castor sugar with the water and bring the syrup to the boil. Add the ground almonds, stirring with a wooden spoon. Cook, stirring constantly, for about 5 minutes. Remove the pan from the heat.

When the mixture has cooled to lukewarm, stir in the egg yolks and return the pan to the heat. Stirring constantly, cook the mixture until it comes away from the sides of the pan, about 5 to 10 minutes.

Turn the paste out on to a wooden surface and leave it to cool. When cold, dust your fingers with icing sugar and mould the paste into decorative shapes such as stars, hearts, books or loaves. Leave the marzipan shapes to dry for at least 12 hours or overnight. On the following day, arrange the dried shapes between sheets of greaseproof paper.

LUIS RIPOLL
NUESTRA COCINA

Indian Coconut Paste

Coconut Barfi

The techniques of opening a coconut and grating the flesh are shown on page 13.

To make about 350 g (12 oz)

125 g	grated or desiccated coconut	4 oz
60 cl	full-cream milk	1 pint
90 g	castor sugar	3 oz
	cochineal	
	vanilla extract	
4	cardamom pods, seeds extracted and crushed	4

Butter a 20 cm (8 inch) square tin. In a heavy pan, heat the milk to the boil. Reduce the heat and simmer the milk for 10 to 12 minutes, stirring occasionally to prevent it boiling over. Add the coconut and stir and scrape the sides of the pan. Add the sugar and continue to stir and scrape until the mixture comes away from the sides and forms a compact mass.

Remove the pan from the heat. Add a few drops of cochineal, 3 or 4 drops of vanilla extract and the cardamom seeds. Spread the mixture evenly over the buttered tin. Smooth the surface with a knife and leave to cool. When the mixture is cold and set, cut it into cubes and store them in an airtight jar.

KAILASH PURI
RASOI KALA (COOKERY BOOK)

Coconut Conserves

Raskara

The technique of opening a coconut is shown on page 13. Treacle or soft dark brown sugar can be substituted for the granulated sugar. The weight of sugar or treacle used should always be half that of the coconut scrapings. Raskara prepared with granulated sugar is often used as a stuffing or filling for other sweets, in the same way as marzipan.

To make about 1.5 kg (3 lb)

4	coconuts, weighing about 500 g (1 lb) each	4
About 500 g	granulated sugar	About 1 lb
4	cardamom pods, seeds extracted	4

Lightly oil a marble slab or flat dish. Break each coconut in half and scrape out the flesh. There should be about 1 kg (2 lb) of coconut scrapings. Mix the sugar with the scrapings. Cook the mass over a gentle heat, stirring constantly, until the mixture forms a soft paste—about 30 minutes. Sprinkle the cardamom seeds into the mixture. Turn the mixture out on to the oiled surface and, when it is cool enough to handle, mould it into balls with the hands.

MRS. J. HALDAR
BENGAL SWEETS

Walnut Balls

Bouchées aux Noix

These walnut balls can be dipped in melted chocolate instead of being rolled in sugar.

To make about 200 g (7 oz)

100 g	walnuts, ground	3½ oz
100 g	icing sugar	3½ oz
15 g	butter, softened	½ oz
2 tbsp	strong black coffee	2 tbsp
	granulated sugar	

Mix the ground walnuts with the icing sugar, the softened butter and the coffee. This paste should be firm enough to be kneaded by hand.

Shape the paste into little balls and roll the balls in the granulated sugar. Chill in the refrigerator for several hours before eating. They will keep for two to three days.

JACQUELINE GÉRARD
BONNES RECETTES D'AUTREFOIS

Coconut Tablets

Tablettes Coco

The technique of extracting the liquid from a coconut, and opening and grating it is shown on page 13.

To make about 300 g (10 oz)

250 g	grated fresh coconut (about half a coconut)	8 oz
150 g	castor sugar	5 oz
1 tsp	ground cinnamon	1 tsp
1	lime, rind grated	1
	vanilla extract	
	bitter almond extract	
3 to 4 tbsp	coconut liquid	3 to 4 tbsp

Mix the grated coconut, sugar, cinnamon, grated lime rind and a few drops each of the vanilla and almond extracts. Put the mixture into a saucepan with the coconut liquid and cook it over a low heat, stirring constantly with a wooden spoon, until the mixture has the colour and consistency of caramel [*pages 10-11*]. Remove from the heat. Pour the mixture out, taking care not to burn yourself, in small pools on to an oiled marble slab or oiled greaseproof paper.

CHRISTIANE ROY-CAMILLE AND ANNICK MARIE
LES MEILLEURES RECETTES DE LA CUISINE ANTILLAISE

Little Praline Balls

Petits Pains au Pralin

The technique of making vanilla sugar is shown on page 15.

To make about 2 kg (4 lb)

1.25 kg	almonds, blanched and dried for about 5 minutes in a cool oven	2½ lb
3	egg whites	3
250 g	castor sugar	8 oz
25 g	flour, sieved	1 oz
150 g	praline powder (*page 167*)	5 oz
1 tbsp	vanilla sugar	1 tbsp

Glacé icing		
3	egg whites, lightly beaten	3
	icing sugar, sieved	

Pound the almonds in a mortar, gradually adding the egg whites. Add the castor sugar, flour and praline powder. Mix well and add the vanilla sugar. Gather the paste into a ball and put it on a marble slab sprinkled with icing sugar.

Roll the paste into a sausage shape and cut off pieces about the size of a walnut. Roll the pieces into balls. To ice the balls, dip them in the beaten egg whites and roll them in icing sugar. Place them on a buttered and floured baking sheet. Arrange the balls so that there is a distance of 3 cm (1¼ inches) between each. Bake in a preheated 130°C (250°F or Mark ½) oven for about 15 minutes, or until cracks begin to appear in them. Remove the sweets from the oven, leave them to cool and arrange them in individual paper cases.

MME. JEANNE SAVARIN (EDITOR)
LA CUISINE DES FAMILLES

Polish Walnut Roll

Rolada Orzechowa

To make about 850 g (1¾ lb)

500 g	walnuts, ground	1 lb
200 g	chocolate, grated	7 oz
2 tbsp	honey	2 tbsp
125 g	almonds, blanched and chopped	4 oz
1	lemon, rind grated, juice strained	1
	icing sugar	

Oil a marble slab or wooden board. Cook the honey, walnuts and chocolate, stirring continuously, until they form a smooth, thick paste. Add the almonds, lemon rind and juice.

Turn the mixture on to the slab or board and shape it into a long sausage-shape about 2.5 cm (1 inch) thick. Coat the roll with icing sugar, wrap it in greaseproof paper and chill it. When it has set, slice the roll diagonally into small ovals about 1 cm (½ inch) thick.

JAN CZERNIKOWSKI
CIASTA, CIASTKA, CIASTECZKA

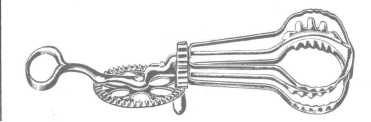

Mallorcan Pine-Nut Sweets

Pinyonat

To make about 560 g (1 lb 2 oz)

100 g	pine-nuts	3½ oz
400 g	granulated sugar	14 oz
4	egg whites, stiffly beaten	4

Cover the pine-nuts with hot water and soak for about 1 hour or until they turn white. Drain them and dry them thoroughly on a kitchen towel. Cover four baking sheets with greaseproof or non-stick baking paper.

In a heavy saucepan, dissolve the sugar in 6 tablespoons of water over a medium heat and, stirring, bring the syrup to the boil. Remove from the heat and leave the syrup to cool until tepid. Gradually add the beaten egg whites, folding them in very carefully to prevent curdling. Stir in the pine-nuts.

Drop teaspoonfuls of the mixture on to the baking sheets. Bake the sweets in a preheated 150°C (300°F or Mark 2) oven for about 50 minutes to 1 hour, or until the sweets are golden.

LUIS RIPOLL
NUESTRA COCINA

Peppermint Cushions

Pepermuntkussentjes

To make 150 g (5 oz)

150 g	icing sugar, sieved	5 oz
	peppermint flavouring	
½	egg white, lightly beaten	½

Stir one or two drops of the peppermint flavouring into 125g (4 oz) of the icing sugar. Add the egg white and continue stirring until the mixture forms a stiff paste.

Dust a board with the rest of the icing sugar, turn the paste out on to it and roll out the paste. Cut it into bars about 2.5 cm (1 inch) thick. Using scissors, cut the bars into small cushion shapes. Leave the cushions to harden in a cool place.

H. H. F. HENDERSON
HET NIEUWE KOOKBOEK

Cinnamon Fingers

Paluszki Cynamonowe

To make about 500 g (1 lb)

140 g	walnuts, ground	5 oz
140 g	castor sugar	5 oz
1 tsp	ground cinnamon	1 tsp
3	cloves, ground	3
1	egg, beaten	1
	icing sugar	
Rum and lemon icing		
120 g	icing sugar	4 oz
1 tbsp	rum	1 tbsp
½	lemon, juice strained	½

Cover a baking sheet with greaseproof paper. Mix the walnuts, castor sugar, cinnamon and cloves together. Bind the mixture with the egg and, on a board, knead it like dough until it is smooth. Dust a rolling pin with icing sugar and roll out the mixture into a rectangle about 1 cm (½ inch) thick. Slice the rectangle into narrow strips the width and length of a finger.

Lay the cinnamon fingers on the baking sheet and bake them in a preheated 130°C (250°F or Mark ½) oven for about 10 minutes or until they are dried out.

To make the icing, mix the icing sugar, rum and lemon juice together in a bowl. Remove the cinnamon fingers from the oven and ice them with the mixture.

MARJA DISSLOWA
JAK GOTOWAĆ

Pepper Cakes

This recipe is from a book published anonymously in 1747, but known to have been written by the English cookery writer, Hannah Glasse.

To make 300 g (10 oz)

300 to 330 g	icing sugar	10 to 11 oz
6 tbsp	sweet sherry	6 tbsp
1 tsp	white peppercorns, tied in a bag	1 tsp

Take the sherry and whole white pepper and put them in a small saucepan. Simmer together covered for 15 minutes. Remove the pan from the heat, then take the pepper out and put in as much icing sugar as will make it like a paste. Mix well, then drop the mixture in what shape you please on plates covered with greaseproof paper and let it dry.

THE ART OF COOKERY, MADE PLAIN AND EASY

Cinnamon Stars

Zimtsterne

To make about 300 g (10 oz)

125 g	icing sugar, sieved	4 oz
2	egg whites, stiffly beaten	2
1 tsp	ground cinnamon	1 tsp
125 g	ground almonds	4 oz
30 g	granulated sugar	1 oz

Add the icing sugar to the egg whites and stir the mixture together until it thickens slightly but is still frothy. Remove and reserve 3 tablespoons of the mixture.

Into the remaining mixture, mix the cinnamon and ground almonds. Knead the ingredients together. Sprinkle a work surface with granulated sugar and roll the mixture out on it until it is the thickness of a finger. With a biscuit cutter, cut it into star shapes and place the shapes on a baking sheet covered with greaseproof or wax paper. Leave the stars to dry for at least 3 hours before icing them with the reserved sugar and egg white mixture. Bake the stars in a preheated 170°C (325°F or Mark 3) oven for 20 to 25 minutes or until the icing is thoroughly dried out but not browned.

ELIZABETH SCHULER
MEIN KOCHBUCH

Tangerine Creams

To make 175 g (6 oz)

2	tangerines, rind grated, juice strained	2
175 g	icing sugar	6 oz
1 tsp	lemon juice	1 tsp

Mix the grated rind with the sugar and lemon juice, and add sufficient tangerine juice to make the mixture into a stiff paste. Knead the mixture well. Cut it into small pieces and mould it into small balls or nuggets.

THE KING'S COLLEGE HOSPITAL BOOK OF COOKING RECIPES

Coffee Truffles

The technique for making this type of truffle is shown on page 64. If liked, a teaspoon of rum, brandy or liqueur can be added to the mixture. Instead of being shaped into balls, the mixture can be piped on to buttered baking sheets or into foil or paper confectionery cases.

To make 600 g (1¼ lb)

250 g	plain chocolate, melted	8 oz
125 g	butter	4 oz
175 g	icing sugar	6 oz
	coffee extract	
	chocolate vermicelli or cocoa powder	

Beat the butter and the icing sugar together into a paste. Allow the melted chocolate to cool for about 5 minutes, then beat it with a few drops of coffee extract into the butter mixture. Continue to stir until the paste is thick and has cooled to tepid. Shape this truffle mixture into small balls and roll the balls in the chocolate vermicelli or cocoa powder.

MARY NORWAK
TOFFEES, FUDGES, CHOCOLATES AND SWEETS

Czech Chocolate Truffles

Schokoladentrüffel

To make about 350 g (12 oz)

200 g	plain chocolate, grated	7 oz
60 g	butter	2 oz
2	egg yolks	2
20 g	icing sugar	¾ oz
70 g	cocoa powder	2½ oz

Beat the butter with the egg yolks and sugar until the mixture is light and creamy. Add the cocoa and 175 g (6 oz) of the grated chocolate. Knead the mixture well, form it into small balls and roll the balls in the reserved grated chocolate.

JOZA BŘÍZOVÁ AND MARYNA KLIMENTOVÁ
TSCHECHISCHE KÜCHE

Rum Balls

Rumkugeln

To make about 400 g (14 oz)

50 g	plain chocolate, grated	2 oz
150 g	hazelnuts, roasted, skinned and ground	5 oz
200 g	castor sugar	7 oz
1	egg white	1
2 tbsp	rum	2 tbsp
	coarse sugar	

Mix the ground hazelnuts with the chocolate, castor sugar, egg white and rum. Wet your hands and knead the mixture until it is smooth. Shape the mixture into small balls about 2.5 cm (1 inch) in diameter. Roll the balls in the coarse sugar and leave them in a warm place for two days to dry out.

HEDWIG MARIA STUBER
ICH HELF DIR KOCHEN

Vanilla Truffles

The technique of making this type of truffle is shown on page 66. The chocolate and cream mixture can also be rolled in cocoa powder, grated chocolate, grated coconut, icing sugar, or a mixture of these. Instead of vanilla, the paste may be flavoured with 1 teaspoon of brandy, rum or a liqueur.

To make about 350 g (12 oz)

250 g	milk or plain chocolate, broken into pieces	8 oz
4½ tbsp	double or whipping cream	4½ tbsp
	vanilla extract	
4 tbsp	cocoa powder	4 tbsp
1 tbsp	icing sugar	1 tbsp

Put the chocolate into a heatproof bowl or double boiler. Put the bowl into hand-hot water. If you use a double boiler or a container where the water does not reach the bottom of the bowl or saucepan holding the chocolate, heat the water to boiling point, then remove it from the heat and put the bowl or saucepan of chocolate over the hot water. Stir the chocolate occasionally until it has thoroughly melted.

Put the cream into another saucepan and bring it to the boil. Then leave it to cool until tepid. Add a few drops of vanilla extract, then tip the cream into the melted chocolate and stir until it is all thoroughly mixed.

Leave the mixture to cool to normal room temperature—about 18°C (65°F)—stirring occasionally. The paste will now be quite thick but not hard. Stir it with a wooden spoon or beat it with a whisk or an electric mixer until the mixture is lighter in colour and fluffy. This process is very important to give the right texture. Refrigerate the mixture until it hardens.

Sieve the cocoa powder and icing sugar together and use them to dust a work surface. Use 2 teaspoons to measure out roughly enough paste to make 2 to 2.5 cm (¾ to 1 inch) balls. Drop these lumps of the mixture on to the work surface at regular intervals until you have used up all the paste. Then, dipping your fingers in a little of the sweetened cocoa powder, pick up the pieces and quickly shape them into balls, putting them back on the cocoa-covered board before the paste melts and the balls become sticky.

Refrigerate the truffles again for a short time to chill and firm their surfaces. If the chocolate and cream mixture is very moist, the truffles can be kept a day or so until the outside has dried and a little crust has formed.

ALEC LEAVER
MAKING CHOCOLATES

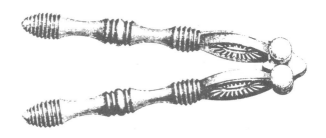

Fernand Point's Chocolate Truffles

Truffes au Chocolat

To make about 250 g (8 oz)

125 g	semi-sweet chocolate	4 oz
1 tbsp	water	1 tbsp
1 tbsp	castor sugar	1 tbsp
90 g	butter	3 oz
1	egg yolk	1
	cocoa powder	

Melt the chocolate in a double boiler with the water, the castor sugar and the butter. Remove the pan from the heat. When the chocolate has cooled a bit, stir in the egg yolk. Leave the mixture to cool at room temperature for 5 hours, then form it into balls and roll them in the cocoa powder.

FERNAND POINT
MA GASTRONOMIE

German Chocolate Truffles

Schokoladetrüffel

To make about 175 g (6 oz)

125 g	plain chocolate, grated	4 oz
60 g	butter	2 oz
1 tbsp	rum	1 tbsp
	chocolate vermicelli	

Beat the butter until it is fluffy; add the grated chocolate and the rum. Stand the mixture in a cold place and leave it to set for 1 to 2 hours. Shape it into small balls and dip the balls in the chocolate vermicelli. Place in individual paper cases and leave to dry for 2 to 3 hours.

ELIZABETH SCHULER
MEIN KOCHBUCH

Bitter Chocolate Truffles

To make brandy or rum truffles, the author suggests using only 10 cl (3½ fl oz) of cream, omitting the vanilla extract and substituting 2 tablespoons of brandy or rum.

To make about 750 g (1½ lb)

90 g	plain chocolate	3 oz
125 g	butter, softened	4 oz
1	egg, well beaten	1
1 tbsp	black coffee	1 tbsp
About 500 g	icing sugar, sieved	About 1 lb
12.5 cl	double cream	4 fl oz
1 tbsp	vanilla extract	1 tbsp
125 g	chocolate vermicelli or grated chocolate	4 oz

Mix the butter and the egg. In the top of a double boiler over hot water, melt the plain chocolate with the coffee.

Put 300 g (10 oz) of the icing sugar into a bowl. Add the butter and egg mixture, the melted chocolate, the double cream and the vanilla. Stir well. If necessary, add more icing sugar to make the mixture into a paste stiff enough to handle. Make the paste into balls the size of butter balls, about 1 cm (½ inch) in diameter. To ensure they are of equal size, use the teaspoon from a set of measuring spoons to measure out the quantity of truffle paste for each ball. While the truffles are still soft, roll them in the chocolate vermicelli or grated chocolate. Put them in the refrigerator until they are firm, about 2 hours. Then remove them and wrap them in wax paper or foil. Store them in tin boxes.

MARION FLEXNER
OUT OF KENTUCKY KITCHENS

Easter Bird's Nest Truffles

Paastruffels

These confections are made for Easter in the Netherlands. The pink and white hundreds-and-thousands should be aniseed-flavoured if possible.

To make about 250 g (8 oz)

30 g	cocoa powder	1 oz
90 g	icing sugar, sieved	3 oz
60 g	butter, softened	2 oz
30 g	chocolate vermicelli	1 oz
25 g	pink and white hundreds-and-thousands	1 oz

Beat the cocoa powder, icing sugar and butter together. Leave it in a cool place for a few hours to stiffen. With cool hands, shape the mixture into about 20 small balls. Slightly flatten the balls and, with the handle of a wooden spoon, make a small indentation in each to give it the shape of a bird's nest. Roll each nest in the chocolate vermicelli and sprinkle the indentation in the middle of the nest with the pink and white hundreds-and-thousands.

H. H. F. HENDERSON
HET NIEUWE KOOKBOEK

Russian Truffles

To make about 350 g (12 oz)

90 g	chocolate, chopped	3 oz
15 cl	double cream, whipped	¼ pint
3 tbsp	icing sugar, sieved	3 tbsp
1 tsp	rum	1 tsp
1 tsp	vanilla extract	1 tsp
175 g	plain dipping chocolate	6 oz
	chocolate vermicelli or grated chocolate	

Melt the chopped chocolate, beat the cream into it and leave the mixture to cool. When cool, mix it into a paste with the icing sugar. Add the rum and vanilla extract and form the mixture into small balls. Melt the plain chocolate and dip the rum-flavoured balls into it. While they are still damp, roll them in the chocolate vermicelli or grated chocolate.

SONIA AGNEW
SWEET-MAKING FOR EVERYWOMAN

Fine Dutch Truffles

Fijne Chocoladetruffels

Creamed coconut is solidified coconut fat. It can be bought at Indian or West Indian grocers.

To make about 300 g (10 oz)

200 g	plain chocolate, broken into small pieces	7 oz
1 tbsp	milk or strong coffee	1 tbsp
40 g	butter or creamed coconut	1½ oz
1	egg, beaten	1
20 g	icing sugar, sieved	¾ oz
20 g	castor sugar mixed with 10 g (⅓ oz) cocoa powder or 30 g (1 oz) chocolate vermicelli	¾ oz

In the top of a double boiler, melt the chocolate with the milk or strong coffee. Add the butter or creamed coconut and allow to melt, stirring constantly. Remove the mixture from the heat and let it cool to lukewarm. Stir the egg into the sieved icing sugar and gradually add the melted chocolate mixture in a thin stream, while beating constantly. Leave the mixture to cool and harden. Shape it into balls and roll each ball immediately in the mixture of castor sugar and cocoa powder or in the chocolate vermicelli.

H. H. F. HENDERSON
HET NIEUWE KOOKBOEK

Chambéry Truffles

Truffes de Chambéry

To make about 200 g (7 oz)

125 g	plain chocolate	4 oz
30 g	butter	1 oz
1½ tbsp	icing sugar	1½ tbsp
2	egg yolks	2
2 tsp	rum	2 tsp
	cocoa powder	

Melt the chocolate in a pan over boiling water and add the butter and icing sugar. Stir until the sugar is melted. Remove the pan from the boiling water and add the egg yolks one at a time, stirring constantly. Add the rum and mix thoroughly. Put the mixture away in a cool place—not the refrigerator—for 12 hours. Then shape it into small balls and roll these in cocoa powder. This makes a very small quantity. Leave the truffles to harden for at least 2 hours. They are exquisite.

ALICE B. TOKLAS
THE ALICE B. TOKLAS COOK BOOK

Chocolate Truffles Duc de Praslin

To make about 1 kg (2½ lb)

200 g	plain chocolate	7 oz
60 g	butter	2 oz
4 tbsp	honey	4 tbsp
800 g	praline powder (*page 167*)	1 lb 10 oz
75 g	cocoa powder	2½ oz
75 g	icing sugar, sieved	2½ oz
2 tbsp	cinnamon	2 tbsp

In the top of a double boiler over boiling water, stir the chocolate with the butter and honey. When the mixture is soft, remove from the heat and stir in the praline powder. Cool the mixture and shape it into balls. Roll the balls in a mixture of the cocoa, icing sugar and cinnamon. Chill the truffles until they are hard. Store them in an airtight container.

JULIETTE ELKON
THE CHOCOLATE COOKBOOK

Michel Oliver's Chocolate Truffles

Truffes au Chocolat

The technique of making vanilla sugar is shown on page 15.

I know that my truffle recipe has a drawback. As the truffles contain quite a lot of cream, they remain soft and must be kept in the refrigerator until they are to be eaten. But, in my opinion, this disadvantage is largely compensated for by their fine flavour. You can replace the rum with any alcohol of your choice or you can leave the alcohol out.

To make about 500 g (1 lb)

300 g	plain chocolate, broken into pieces	10 oz
2 tbsp	water	2 tbsp
15 cl	double cream	$\frac{1}{4}$ pint
125 g	icing sugar, sieved	4 oz
2 tbsp	rum	2 tbsp
1 tbsp	vanilla sugar	1 tbsp
2 tbsp	cocoa powder	2 tbsp

Take a large shallow pan, half fill it with water and put it on a medium heat. Put the chocolate pieces into a large heatproof bowl, add 2 tablespoons of water and put the bowl into the pan when the water in it is lightly boiling. Stir the chocolate with a wooden spoon until it has melted completely, then add the cream, the icing sugar, the rum and the vanilla sugar. Stir the mixture with a wooden spoon to obtain a smooth paste. Then pour the paste into a clean bowl and chill it in the refrigerator for at least 2 hours.

Sprinkle the bottom of a large dish with the cocoa powder. Take the bowl containing the truffle paste out of the refrigerator—it should now be fairly well set. Take a large tablespoonful of the truffle paste and roll the paste in the cocoa powder with the palm of your hand. Do the same with the rest of the truffle paste, making about 12 large truffles, then leave the truffles in the refrigerator until you are ready to eat them.

MICHEL OLIVER
MES RECETTES

Rum Truffles

Bolitas de Ron

To make about 800 g (1 lb 10 oz)

525 g	plain chocolate, broken into pieces	1 lb 2 oz
$\frac{1}{4}$ litre	double cream	8 fl oz
15 cl	rum	$\frac{1}{4}$ pint
200 g	walnuts, chopped	7 oz

Put the cream in a saucepan to boil over a medium heat. Add 500 g (1 lb) of the chocolate. Stir the mixture constantly with a wooden spoon until it forms a smooth, thick cream.

Remove the pan from the heat and leave the mixture to cool. When it is cold, add the rum and the chopped nuts; stir the mixture and leave it until it is firm enough to handle before rolling it into balls about the size of a walnut. Grate the rest of the chocolate and roll the balls in it.

MARIA DEL CARMEN CASCANTE
150 RECETAS DE DULCES DE FÁCIL PREPARACIÓN

Uncooked Chocolate Cream Fudge

Although this sweet is called a fudge, the result more closely resembles a truffle paste. The mixture can also be shaped by putting it through a piping bag.

To make about 600 g (1$\frac{1}{4}$ lb)

100 g	plain chocolate, broken into small pieces	4 oz
50 g	butter	2 oz
3 tbsp	single cream	3 tbsp
1 tsp	vanilla extract	1 tsp
450 g	icing sugar, sieved	1 lb

Put the chocolate pieces and the butter into a bowl standing over a saucepan of hot water. Leave them until they have melted, stirring once or twice.

Remove the bowl from the saucepan of water and stir the cream and vanilla into the chocolate mixture. With a wooden spoon, gradually work in the icing sugar. Mix well. Transfer the mixture to a buttered 20 cm (8 inch) square tin. Leave it in a cool place until it has set, about 3 hours. Cut it into about sixty 2.5 cm (1 inch) squares.

SONIA ALLISON
THE DAIRY BOOK OF HOME COOKERY

Filled Chocolate Balls

Gefüllte Schokoladenkugeln

To make about 350 g (12 oz)

150 g	plain chocolate, grated	5 oz
1	egg white	1
100 g	icing sugar, sieved	3½ oz
2 tsp	rum	2 tsp
60 g	walnuts, ground	2 oz
	Egg yolk filling	
1	hard-boiled egg yolk, sieved	1
1 tsp	icing sugar	1 tsp
½ tsp	butter	½ tsp
	rum	

Mix the egg white with the icing sugar, 100 g (3½ oz) of the chocolate, the rum and the ground walnuts. Knead the mixture into a paste, cut it into small equal-sized pieces and shape each piece into a small ball.

To make the filling, combine the egg yolk, icing sugar, butter and a few drops of rum. Put each ball in the palm of your hand and press it with a finger to make a small indentation. Put in a little of the filling, close the ball up again and roll it in the rest of the grated chocolate.

JOZA BŘÍZOVÁ AND MARYNA KLIMENTOVÁ
TSCHECHISCHE KÜCHE

Finnish Chocolate Drops

Choklad

These sweets can also be cooled on non-stick baking paper, greaseproof paper or wax paper.

To make about 250 g (8 oz)

175 g	plain chocolate	6 oz
40 g	butter	1½ oz
1	small orange, rind grated	1
1	egg, well beaten	1

Heat the chocolate and the butter over a very low heat until the chocolate has melted. Whisk the chocolate mixture and the orange rind into the beaten egg, a little at a time.

Drop teaspoons of the mixture on to a buttered baking sheet or into little paper cases and chill until firm. Remove the chocolate drops from the baking sheet with a knife. This mixture will make 30 to 40 chocolate drops.

GUNNEVI BONEKAMP
SCANDINAVIAN COOKING

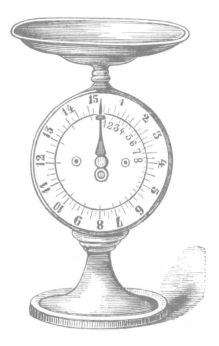

Fruit and Nut Bars

The author suggests varying this recipe by using any combination of the dried fruits given below, or using just one variety of dried fruit or of nuts, in the appropriate quantity.

To make about 750 g (1½ lb)

125 g	dried apricots	4 oz
125 g	dried figs	4 oz
125 g	dates	4 oz
60 g	sultanas	2 oz
30 g	currants	1 oz
30 g	raisins	1 oz
250 g	mixed nuts, coarsely chopped	8 oz
	rice paper	

Put all the fruits and nuts through a meat grinder twice. Then knead the ingredients thoroughly until a compact mass is formed. Roll out the mixture to a thickness of 2 cm (¾ inch), keeping the shape well squared. Cover the top with one sheet of rice paper and pat it down firmly.

Using two spatulas, turn the mixture upside down on to a clean work surface or a piece of greaseproof paper; cover the top of the fruit mixture with rice paper too. Let the sweet stand for at least 3 hours. Then cut it into fingers, each about 10 by 2.5 cm (4 by 1 inch) and wrap each finger in a piece of cellophane, twisting the ends to keep out the air.

ESMÉ GRAY BOOKER
SWEETS THAT HAVE TEMPTED ME

Fruit Paste

The technique of making fruit paste is shown on page 50.

To make about 1 kg (2½ lb)

350 g	prunes, stoned	12 oz
350 g	dried apricots or peaches	12 oz
350 g	dates, stoned	12 oz
About 3 tbsp	honey	About 3 tbsp
About 175 g	granulated sugar or about 125 g (4 oz) flaked or shredded coconut, or a mixture of both	About 6 oz

Pass the fruit through the medium or coarse disc of a food mill. Mix the fruit well with the honey and, if the mixture seems very dry, add a little more honey. Roll equal-sized sections of the mixture between the palms of your hands to form balls about 2 to 2.5 cm (¾ to 1 inch) in diameter. Drop these balls into the granulated sugar or coconut, or drop them into the sugar and then roll them in coconut. Leave the balls to stand on wax paper, foil or cake racks overnight to dry before storing them between wax paper or foil in airtight containers.

JAMES BEARD
JAMES BEARD'S AMERICAN COOKERY

———————◆———————

Apple Balls

Apfelkugeln

To make about 500 g (1 lb)

250 g	apples, peeled, cored and finely chopped	8 oz
250 g	granulated sugar	8 oz
4 tbsp	water	4 tbsp
100 g	almonds, blanched and very finely chopped	3½ oz
1	lemon, rind grated, juice strained	1
	icing sugar, ground almonds or grated coconut	

Dissolve the granulated sugar in the water over a medium heat, stirring constantly. Stop stirring when the sugar has dissolved, increase the heat and boil the syrup until it reaches the soft-ball stage [*pages 10-11*]. Reduce the heat and add the apples. Cook the mixture very slowly over a very gentle heat

for about 10 minutes. Then add the chopped almonds, grated lemon rind and lemon juice. Cook for another 10 to 15 minutes or until you have a thick paste. Turn the paste out on to a work surface thickly dusted with 60 g (2 oz) of icing sugar and leave the paste to cool until it can be handled. Roll it into small balls between the palms of your hands and roll the balls in icing sugar or ground almonds or grated coconut. Serve the balls in individual paper cases.

MÁRIA HAJKOVÁ
MÚČNIKY

———————◆———————

Dried Fruit Candy

Ovochevi Konfeti

The technique of melting chocolate is shown on page 65.

To make about 500 g (1 lb)

125 g	moist prunes, stoned	4 oz
125 g	stoned dates	4 oz
125 g	raisins	4 oz
125 g	walnuts or blanched almonds	4 oz
1 tbsp	honey	1 tbsp
About 90 g	icing sugar or 60 g (2 oz) chocolate	About 3 oz

Put all the fruits and nuts through a food mill, using a coarse disc. Add the honey and mix thoroughly. Shape the mixture into small balls and roll the balls in the icing sugar.

Alternatively, line a 17.5 cm (7 inch) tin with heavy wax paper. Pack the fruit and nut mixture firmly into the tin to a thickness of about 2 cm (¾ inch). Melt the chocolate over warm water and cover the mixture with it. Allow the chocolate to harden, then cut the sweet into 2.5 cm (1 inch) squares.

SAVELLA STECHISHIN
TRADITIONAL UKRAINIAN COOKERY

Apple Candy Squares

To make about 1 kg (2 lb)

600 g	cooking apples, cored and sliced	1¼ lb
4 tbsp	water	4 tbsp
About 500 g	castor sugar	About 1 lb
⅛ tsp	salt	⅛ tsp
3 tbsp	powdered gelatine, soaked in 6 tbsp of cold water	3 tbsp
125 g	walnuts, chopped	4 oz
4 tsp	lemon juice	4 tsp
	icing sugar	

Butter a shallow 20 cm (8 inch) square tin. Cook the apples in the water until soft, about 15 to 20 minutes. Sieve the apples and measure the purée; there should be about ½ litre (16 fl oz). Combine the purée with the same weight of castor sugar and add the salt. Cook the mixture over a medium heat, stirring constantly to prevent scorching, until it thickens, 30 to 40 minutes. Add the softened gelatine, stirring until the gelatine dissolves. Remove the pan from the heat; add the walnuts and lemon juice. Pour the mixture into the tin.

Allow the mixture to cool completely, then refrigerate it. When it has set, cut it into 2.5 cm (1 inch) squares. Cool the squares to room temperature and roll them in the icing sugar.

JUNE ROTH
OLD-FASHIONED CANDYMAKING

———————◆———————

Apple Candy

To make about 1.5 kg (3 lb)

8	medium-sized apples, peeled, cored and cut into small pieces	8
12.5 cl	water	4 fl oz
400 g	soft light brown sugar	14 oz
30 g	powdered gelatine	1 oz
125 g	walnuts, chopped	4 oz
1 tbsp	lemon juice	1 tbsp
75 g	icing sugar	2½ oz
1 tbsp	cornflour	1 tbsp

Have ready a wetted 30 by 20 by 3 cm (12 by 8 by 1¼ inch) tin. In a pan, combine the apples with half the water and cook the fruit until it is tender, about 20 to 25 minutes. Press the cooked apples through a sieve and add the brown sugar. Cook the mixture over a low heat, stirring often, until it is thick, about 30 minutes. Soften the gelatine in the rest of the water.

Add the softened gelatine to the hot apple mixture and stir until the gelatine dissolves. Chill the mixture until it thickens slightly. Stir in the walnuts and the lemon juice.

Pour the mixture into the tin to a depth of about 1 cm (½ inch). Chill the mixture thoroughly, then cut it into 2.5 cm (1 inch) squares. Combine the icing sugar and the cornflour, and roll the squares in this mixture.

DEMETRIA TAYLOR
APPLE KITCHEN COOK BOOK

Apricot and Apple Paste

Pâte Abricots-Pommes

To make about 3 kg (6 lb)

1 kg	ripe apricots, stoned	2 lb
1 kg	apples, cored and chopped but not peeled	2 lb
About 2 kg	castor sugar	About 4 lb
½ litre	water	16 fl oz
	almond oil	
60 g	crystallized sugar	2 oz

Cook the apricots in ¼ litre (8 fl oz) water, stirring frequently, until they are very soft—20 to 30 minutes. Sieve the mixture and weigh the purée. Cook the apples in the same way, crush and sieve them and weigh the purée.

Mix equal weights of apple and apricot purée. Put the mixture into a heavy-based saucepan with castor sugar equal in weight to the combined purées.

Stirring constantly, cook the mixture on a low heat. The moisture will evaporate gradually. The fruit paste will dry out and, when stirred, will come away from the bottom of the saucepan; it will then be cooked.

Oil two 30 by 20 by 3 cm (12 by 8 by 1¼ inch) tins with the almond oil. Sprinkle the oiled surfaces with half the crystallized sugar. Put the paste into the tins in a layer about 1 cm (½ inch) thick. Leave the mixture to cool and dry out in a cool, well-aired place, for four to five days. Then unmould the paste, cut it up and roll it in the rest of the crystallized sugar. Fruit pastes will keep for a long time in tightly closed tins.

JACQUELINE GÉRARD
BONNES RECETTES D'AUTREFOIS

———————◆———————

Apricot Roll

To make 1 kg (2 lb)

350 g	dried apricots, finely chopped	12 oz
500 g	granulated sugar	1 lb
$\frac{1}{4}$ litre	milk	8 fl oz
15 g	butter	$\frac{1}{2}$ oz
250 g	pecan nuts, chopped	8 oz
1 tsp	vanilla extract	1 tsp
	salt	

Dissolve the sugar in the milk, stirring constantly, and boil until the mixture thickens—at about 113°C (236°F) on the sugar thermometer [*soft-ball stage, pages 10-11*]. Add the apricots and boil them, until they melt into the syrup and the mixture reaches about 110°C (230°F) on the sugar thermometer. Remove the pan from the heat and beat the mixture hard. Add the butter, the pecan nuts, vanilla and a pinch of salt. Beat the mixture until it begins to harden.

Pour the mixture out on to a wet, smooth cloth and shape it into a long roll. Leave it to cool; then store it in the refrigerator. Cut it into thin slices to serve.

JUNIOR LEAGUE OF JACKSON, MISSISSIPPI
SOUTHERN SIDEBOARDS

Sugared Apricots

Inkoo Mish-Mush

To make about 750 g (1½ lb)

500 g	dried apricots, minced or finely chopped	1 lb
12.5 cl	water	4 fl oz
250 g	granulated sugar	8 oz
30 g	blanched almonds	1 oz

Put the apricots in a lidded saucepan and add the water. Cover the pan and simmer the apricots until they form a thick paste—about 20 to 30 minutes. Stir in half the sugar and cook 10 minutes longer. Take the pan off the heat and leave the mixture to cool. When it is cold, roll it into small balls and flatten them until they are about 1 cm (½ inch) thick. Press a blanched almond in the centre of each piece of paste. Dip the pieces in the rest of the sugar, coating them all over. Cover the sweets with wax paper until you are ready to serve them.

HELEN COREY
THE ART OF SYRIAN COOKERY

Peach and Apricot Paste

Persicata ed Albicoccata

To make about 7 to 9 kg (15 to 20 lb)

3 to 4 kg	peaches and apricots, stoned	6 to 9 lb
1.5 litres	water	2½ pints
About 5 kg	castor sugar	About 10 lb
3 kg	granulated sugar	6 lb

Put the fruit into a pan with 1 litre (1¾ pints) of the water, bring them to the boil and simmer until tender. Pass the mixture through a sieve and return it to the heat; bring to the boil and stir continuously with a spatula until the water has evaporated. Weigh the fruit and weigh out an equal quantity of castor sugar.

Dissolve the castor sugar in 30 cl (½ pint) of the water over a medium heat and cook the syrup to the hard-ball stage [*pages 10-11*]. Pour the syrup over the fruit and simmer the mixture until it is reduced to a thick paste. Remove the paste from the heat and pour it into cardboard cases or wetted shallow trays, to the depth of a finger's width. Leave the paste in a warm, dry place for several days to dry out. Then cut the paste into 3 by 2 cm (1½ by ¾ inch) pieces.

Dissolve half the granulated sugar in the rest of the water over a medium heat and cook it to the soft-ball stage [*pages 10-11*]. Remove the syrup from the heat and dip the pieces of fruit paste in it, one at a time. Roll them in the rest of the granulated sugar to coat all over and leave them to dry. Store the pieces of fruit paste between sheets of paper, in an airtight tin.

GIUSEPPE SORBIATTI
LA GASTRONOMIA MODERNA

Apricot "Paper"

For this recipe, you will need a promise of three consecutive days of warm sunshine! Once made and wrapped, apricot "paper" will keep indefinitely.

To make two 30 by 90 cm (12 by 36 inch) sheets

1.25 kg	very ripe apricots, stoned and cut into small pieces	2½ lb
175 g	granulated sugar	6 oz

In a large, heavy saucepan, combine the apricots and the sugar. Cook them over a low heat until the mixture comes to just below boiling point. Do not boil. Using a blender or food processor, process the fruit a little at a time, until it is completely puréed. Let the purée cool to lukewarm.

Place a table outdoors where it will get maximum full sunlight. Take two 30 cm (12 inch) widths of very heavy quality plastic film and lay them side by side on the table. Put weights on the corners if necessary. When the fruit purée is tepid, pour a puddle of it into the centre of each sheet of plastic; spread it with a spatula until there is a layer about 5 mm ($\frac{1}{4}$ inch) thick. To be sure flies do not get into the fruit, put a tall bottle in the centre of the table and drape a large piece of muslin or cheesecloth over it, fastening the muslin under the edges of the table with tape.

Leave the purée in the sunlight for one day. The purée will then be firm enough for you to slip baking sheets under the plastic film. Carry the sheets of apricot purée inside for the night. Place them in the sunshine again the next day. After three days of sun drying, you will be able to pull the apricot "paper" from the plastic. Roll it into cones or cylinders; wrap each cone or cylinder in plastic wrap. To eat, tear pieces off.

MIRIAM LOWENBERG
CREATIVE CANDY MAKING

Oriental Apricot Balls

Orientalische Aprikosenkugeln

These apricot balls can also be stuffed. Make a deep indentation with your finger in each ball and fill the cavity with a mixture of chopped pistachio nuts, ground almonds and sugar. Put the stuffed balls into individual paper cases, so that they cannot tip over and spill the stuffing.

To make about 600 g (1$\frac{1}{4}$ lb)

500 g	dried apricots	1 lb
About 150 g	icing sugar, sieved	About 6 oz
90 g	pistachio nuts, skinned	3 oz

Rub the apricots with a damp cloth; they should not be soaked or washed or they will get too moist. Chop the apricots finely and put them in a bowl. Add at least 125 g (4 oz) of icing sugar (the exact amount depends on your taste and the sweetness of the apricots). Wet your hands and knead the mixture until it forms a paste. If necessary, dip your hands in water while working. Shape the paste into small balls. Roll the balls in the rest of the icing sugar and leave them to dry on racks overnight. Garnish each ball with a pistachio nut.

MARGRET UHLE AND ANNE BRAKEMEIER
KONFEKT ZUM SELBERMACHEN

Banana Sweet

Kela Halva

To make about 850 g (1$\frac{3}{4}$ lb)

6	ripe bananas	6
125 g	granulated sugar	4 oz
30 cl	water	$\frac{1}{2}$ pint
125 g	*ghee* or butter, melted	4 oz
60 g	walnuts, chopped or almonds, blanched and chopped	2 oz
3	cardamom pods, seeds extracted and crushed	3
$\frac{1}{4}$ tsp	saffron (optional)	$\frac{1}{4}$ tsp

Lightly oil or butter a flat dish. Mash the fruit to a pulp and place it in a saucepan with the sugar and water; stir the mixture over a low heat until the sugar has dissolved, then boil it rapidly for 5 minutes. Take the pan off the heat and gradually stir in the *ghee* or melted butter. Replace the pan on the heat and stir constantly until the mixture begins to form a firm ball in the pan, about 10 to 15 minutes. Stir in the chopped nuts and crushed cardamom seeds, colour if desired with the saffron and turn the mixture out on to the flat dish. When cool, cut the paste into 4 cm (1$\frac{1}{2}$ inch) squares.

GOOD HOUSEKEEPING INSTITUTE (EDITOR)
GOOD HOUSEKEEPING'S WORLD COOKERY

Orange Balls

Pallottole d'Aranci

To make about 500 g (1 lb)

6	large oranges, peel thickly pared	6
250 g	granulated sugar	8 oz
1 tsp	vanilla extract	1 tsp
	castor sugar	
125 g	mixed nuts, finely chopped	4 oz

Soak the orange peel in cold water for 24 hours. Drain and weigh the peel; there should be about 250 g (8 oz). Place the peel in a saucepan, and cover it with cold water. Bring the water to the boil. Cook the peel for about 10 minutes, or until it is soft. Drain. Chop the orange peel finely and mix it with the granulated sugar. Stir the mixture slowly over a low heat until the sugar dissolves, then continue to cook it for about 10 minutes or until a small quantity dropped into cold water forms a soft ball [*pages 10-11*]. Add the vanilla extract and mix thoroughly. Remove the pan from the heat and cool the mixture. Shape it into balls about the size of small walnuts. Roll the balls in the castor sugar and then in the nuts.

MARIA LO PINTO AND MILO MILORADOVICH
THE ART OF ITALIAN COOKING

Carrot and Citrus Paste

Pâte de Fruit à la Carotte

To make about 750 g (1½ lb)

1 kg	young carrots, peeled	2 lb
500 g	castor sugar	1 lb
3	tangerines, juice strained	3
2	oranges, juice strained	2
125 g	granulated sugar	4 oz

Simmer the carrots in boiling water until very tender, about 30 minutes. Drain the carrots and leave them to dry out overnight on wire racks.

On the following day, put the carrots through a food mill. Mix the carrot purée with the sugar and the tangerine and orange juice. Cook the mixture over a gentle heat, stirring frequently, until it thickens into a paste. This may take up to 30 minutes. Leave the paste to cool, then roll it into little balls. Coat the balls with the granulated sugar.

MARIE-THÉRÈSE CARRÉRAS AND GEORGES LAFFORGUE
LES BONNES RECETTES DU PAYS CATALAN

Carrot Balls

Kulki z Marchwi

To make about 1.5 kg (3 lb)

1 kg	carrots, finely grated	2 lb
500 g	granulated sugar	1 lb
12.5 cl	water	4 fl oz
1	lemon, juice strained, rind grated	1
	castor sugar	

Lightly oil a work surface. Dissolve the granulated sugar in 3 tablespoons of the water in a heavy pan set over a medium heat. Stir in the grated carrots and cook the mixture, without stirring, until the carrots are tender—about 10 to 15 minutes. Add the rest of the water, the lemon juice and rind, and cook the mixture until it thickens. Pour the mixture on to the oiled work surface and leave it to cool for a few minutes until it can be handled. Dip your hands in cold water and form the mixture into little balls. Roll the balls in castor sugar and put them into individual paper cases.

JAN CZERNIKOWSKI
CIASTA, CIASTKA, CIASTECZKA

Indian Carrot Paste

Gajjar Barfi

To make 500 g (1 lb)

500 g	carrots, grated	1 lb
125 g	butter	4 oz
4	cardamom pods, seeds extracted and crushed	4
60 cl	full-cream milk	1 pint
150 g	granulated sugar	5 oz
60 g	blanched almonds, halved, 30 g (1 oz) of them slivered	2 oz
30 g	pistachio nuts, chopped	1 oz
30 g	sultanas	1 oz

Butter a large flat plate. In a heavy pan, heat the butter, add the crushed cardamom seeds and stir for 2 to 3 minutes over a low heat. Add the grated carrots, increase the heat to medium and cover the pan. Cook the mixture until the carrots are soft and the moisture has evaporated, about 15 minutes. Add the milk, and continue to cook, stirring constantly to prevent the milk boiling over or sticking to the pan, until all the milk has been absorbed. Add the sugar, the slivered almonds and chopped pistachio nuts, and half the sultanas. Continue to cook, stirring and scraping the sides of the pan, until butter collects at the sides of the pan. Spread the mixture evenly on the buttered plate in a layer about 1 cm (½ inch) thick. Decorate the mixture with the rest of the almonds and sultanas. When the paste is completely cold, cut it into cubes.

KAILASH PURI
RASOI KALA (COOKERY BOOK)

Carrot Sweetmeat

To make about 500 g (1 lb)

125 g	carrots, freshly grated	4 oz
90 cl	milk	1½ pints
150 g	granulated sugar	5 oz
90 g	*ghee* or clarified butter	3 oz
2 tbsp	sultanas (optional)	2 tbsp
1 tsp	desiccated coconut	1 tsp
2 tbsp	finely sliced mixed nuts	2 tbsp
1 tsp	crushed cardamom seeds or grated nutmeg	1 tsp

Using a large, heavy aluminium frying pan, put the milk and grated carrots to boil on a medium heat. Keep boiling until the mixture thickens, stirring frequently. This should take about 45 minutes. Add the sugar and keep stirring for another 15 minutes, then add the *ghee*. Lower the heat, and keep cooking and mixing until almost all the fat has been absorbed; this should take less than 10 minutes. Add the sultanas, if using, and mix thoroughly.

Remove the pan from the heat and pour the sweetmeat on to a buttered 20 cm (8 inch) square dish or tin. Spread it thickly, and decorate it with the desiccated coconut, mixed nuts and the crushed cardamom seeds or grated nutmeg. When cool, cut it into about 15 squares.

SAVITRI CHOWDHARY
INDIAN COOKING

Prune Sausage

Pflaumenwurst

The technique of making vanilla sugar is shown on page 15.

To make about 500 g (1 lb)

150 g	prunes, stoned and finely chopped	5 oz
150 g	icing sugar	5 oz
100 g	almonds, blanched and ground	3½ oz
50 g	crystallized fruit, finely chopped	2 oz
1	egg yolk	1
1 tbsp	rum	1 tbsp
1 tbsp	vanilla sugar	1 tbsp

Mix the icing sugar with the prunes, ground almonds, candied fruit, egg yolk, rum and vanilla sugar, and work the mixture into a paste. Sprinkle a work surface with additional icing sugar and shape the paste into a sausage. Leave it to dry out for at least 3 hours before slicing it for serving.

MÁRIA HAJKOVÁ
MÚČNIKY

Cherry Paste

Conserve de Cerises

This recipe is from a book of jam and confectionery recipes written in 1698 by Louis XIV's cook. Massialot gives a similar recipe for redcurrant paste, in which the fruit is boiled and the pulp is sieved and added to the juice. He suggests that this method is also suitable for raspberries. Instead of putting these fruit pastes into moulds, they may be spread out on a cold work surface, dusted with icing sugar and left to dry before being cut into shapes. The shapes may be rolled in sugar before storing. The first cooking method given below is suitable for Kentish cherries, the second for the juicier Morello cherries. The drained juice from the second method may be used to make fruit jellies (page 52).

To make about 1 kg (2 lb)

1 kg	cherries, stoned	2 lb
About 500 g	granulated sugar	About 1 lb
3 tbsp	water	3 tbsp

This is for new cherries. Put the cherries into a saucepan and cook them on a low heat, crushing them with a wooden spoon. Stir the fruit regularly. When the juice has evaporated and the mixture is fairly dry, after 20 to 30 minutes, remove the pan from the heat.

Dissolve the sugar in the water and cook the mixture to the soft-crack stage [*page 10*]. Add the cherry pulp, mixing it thoroughly with the syrup so that it is completely blended. Stir the mixture until the surface of the syrup begins to cloud. Then remove the pan from the heat and turn the paste out into wet moulds: your paste is done.

When the cherries are in full season, stew them until they give up their juice—about 20 minutes. Then throw them on to a drum sieve; when they have drained, pound them in a mortar, then put the pulp into a saucepan and cook it over a gentle heat until the remaining juice has evaporated—about 10 minutes. Cook a sugar syrup to the soft-crack stage, as above. Then mix the syrup with the cherry pulp and stir the mixture until it clouds, as described above.

NOUVELLE INSTRUCTION POUR LES CONFITURES,
LES LIQUEURS ET LES FRUITS

Fig Balls

Bolas de Figo

To make about 750 g (1½ lb)

270 g	dried figs, stems removed	8¾ oz
270 g	almonds, blanched and roasted	8¾ oz
7.5 cm	strip orange rind	3 inch
50 g	plain chocolate, broken into pieces	1¾ oz
270 g	granulated sugar	8¾ oz
7 tbsp	water	7 tbsp
	castor sugar	

Put the figs, almonds, orange rind and chocolate through the fine disc of a meat grinder. Dissolve the sugar in the water and boil to a thick syrup [*soft-ball stage, pages 10-11*]. Remove the pan from the heat and mix in the minced ingredients. Leave the mixture to cool, then form it into little balls and roll the balls in castor sugar.

CAROL WRIGHT
PORTUGUESE FOOD

Fig Bonbons

Bomboms de Figo

To make about 400 g (14 oz)

250 g	moist dried figs, minced	8 oz
90 g	toasted blanched almonds	3 oz
About 125 g	granulated sugar	About 4 oz

Mix the minced figs and the almonds. Pinch off pieces of the mixture and shape them into about sixteen 2 to 2.5 cm (¾ to 1 inch) balls. Roll the balls in the granulated sugar to coat them. Leave them to stand until the sugar is partly absorbed, about 10 to 15 minutes. Roll them in the sugar again. Wrap each sweet in foil if you wish.

SHIRLEY SARVIS
A TASTE OF PORTUGAL

Mulberry or Blackberry Paste

Mûres, Pâte

To make about 2 kg (4 lb)

1 kg	mulberries or blackberries, washed in acidulated water, damaged fruit and stems discarded	2 lb
About 1 kg	castor sugar	About 2 lb
¼ litre	water	8 fl oz
	granulated sugar (optional)	

Thoroughly oil a 20 cm (8 inch) cake tin. Weigh the fruit and put it through a food mill. Put the fruit pulp into a preserving pan. Add an equal weight of sugar and ¼ litre (8 fl oz) of water for every 1 kg (2 lb) of sugar. Put the pan on a low heat and simmer the mixture, using a skimmer to remove the small seeds that rise to the surface. After the mixture begins to thicken, stir constantly for about 40 minutes, until the wooden spatula leaves a trail as it is moved through the paste.

Turn the fruit paste into the cake tin. Cover it with a kitchen towel and leave it to set for 48 hours. Unmould the paste. If you want to keep the paste whole, wrap it in aluminium foil. Otherwise, cut it into pieces, roll each piece in granulated sugar, if using, and store in an airtight container.

CÉLINE VENCE
ENCYCLOPÉDIE HACHETTE DE LA CUISINE RÉGIONALE

Mulberry or Blackberry Candies

Conserva di More

To make about 750 g (1½ lb)

500 g	mulberries or blackberries	1 lb
60 g	red grapes	2 oz
500 g	granulated sugar	1 lb
17.5 cl	water	6 fl oz

Line a 38 cm (15 inch) square tin with oiled greaseproof paper. Crush the mulberries or blackberries with the grapes. Strain the mixture through a cloth to remove the pips and skin. Put the strained pulp into a pan. Cook it over a medium heat for 30 to 40 minutes until the excess liquid has evaporated and the purée has the consistency of a thick jam. Dissolve the sugar in the water and boil it to the hard-crack stage [*pages 10-11*]. Remove the pan from the heat, stir in the fruit purée and cook over a low heat, stirring constantly until the surface begins to cloud. Pour the mixture into the tin and, when the mixture has almost set, mark it into 2.5 cm (1 inch) squares. When cold, unmould and separate the pieces.

IPPOLITO CAVALCANTI, DUCA DI BUONVICINO
CUCINA TEORICO-PRATICA

Peach Leather

This is a speciality from Charleston, South Carolina. The strips of fruit paste should be left in a warm, dry place to dry out for 12 hours or overnight before you roll them up.

To make 1.5 kg (3 lb)

500 g	dried peaches	1 lb
1 kg	dried apricots	2 lb
175 to 200 g icing sugar		6 to 7 oz

Put the dried peaches and apricots through a meat grinder twice, using the finest disc. Sprinkle a board thickly with icing sugar and put the fruit mixture on it. Pat and roll the mixture until it is 3 mm (⅛ inch) thick. Cut it into strips 3 by 5 cm (1¼ by 2 inches). Roll each strip into a tight cylinder. Store the leather in a tightly closed box.

FANNIE MERRITT FARMER
THE FANNIE FARMER COOKBOOK

Peach Toffee

Although this is called a toffee, it is really a fruit paste.

To make 750 g (1½ lb)

500 g	stoned peaches, sieved	1 lb
500 g	granulated sugar	1 lb
1 tbsp	slivered blanched almonds	1 tbsp
10	cardamom pods, seeds extracted and ground	10
1 tbsp	*ghee* or clarified butter	1 tbsp

Butter a large dish or 20 cm (8 inch) square tin. Heat the fruit gently in a pan until the moisture begins to evaporate and the purée thickens. Stir in the sugar, almonds and cardamom seeds and continue stirring until the mixture becomes thick and smooth and comes away from the sides of the pan. Add the *ghee*. Stir it in well. Turn the mixture out into the buttered dish or tin. Flatten the paste and allow it to cool. Cut the paste into 2.5 cm (1 inch) squares. Store it in an airtight container.

JACK SANTA MARIA
INDIAN SWEET COOKERY

Korean Date Balls

To make about 500 g (1 lb)

36	dates, stoned	36
3 tbsp	granulated sugar	3 tbsp
1 tsp	ground cinnamon	1 tsp
60 g	pine-nuts, finely crushed	2 oz

Put the dates into the top half of a steamer and steam them over boiling water for 20 minutes. Remove them from the pan, then mash them or push them through a sieve. Mix the sugar and cinnamon with the date purée and shape the mixture into about 18 bite-sized balls. Roll the balls in the pine-nuts.

WILLIAM HARLAN HALE AND THE EDITORS OF HORIZON MAGAZINE
THE HORIZON COOKBOOK

Red Grape Candies

Conserva di Uva Rossa

To make about 1 kg (2 lb)

750 g	red grapes, stems removed	1½ lb
35 cl	water	12 fl oz
500 g	granulated sugar	1 lb

Line a 38 cm (15 inch) square tin with oiled greaseproof paper. Put the grapes in a copper pan with half of the water and boil them until their juice begins to flow—about 15 minutes. Press the pulp through a jelly bag or a sieve lined with a muslin cloth to remove the skin and pips. Put the strained pulp back in the pan. Boil for a further 15 minutes or until the mixture is reduced to a thick jam.

Meanwhile, heat the sugar and the remaining water until the sugar dissolves, then boil the syrup to the hard-crack stage [*pages 10-11*]. Remove the pan from the heat, add the strained pulp and stir well until the surface begins to cloud. Pour the mixture into the tin and when it has almost set, mark it into 2.5 cm (1 inch) squares. Separate the pieces when cold.

IPPOLITO CAVALCANTI, DUCA DI BUONVICINO
CUCINA TEORICO-PRATICA

Pastilles of Fruit

The technique for making this type of fruit paste is shown on page 50. Other fruits—such as pears, plums, apricots or raspberries—can be used to make pastilles. If soft fruit is used, there is no need to cook it before puréeing it.

To make about 1.5 kg (3 lb)

1.5 kg	quinces or apples, each cut into 8 pieces	3 lb
30 cl	water	½ pint
1 kg	granulated sugar	2 lb
100 g	ground almonds, hazelnuts, walnuts or pistachio nuts (optional)	3½ oz
1½	lemons or 1 orange, rind grated	1½
½ tsp	ground cinnamon	½ tsp
	icing sugar	

Butter two baking sheets, two large dishes or two 20 cm (8 inch) square tins. In a covered pan, stew the quinces or apples in the water until they are soft, about 30 minutes. Keeping the pan covered, leave the fruit to cool completely. Purée the fruit through a sieve or food mill and combine the purée with the granulated sugar in a large, shallow pan. Stirring frequently, simmer the mixture gently over a low heat until it becomes very thick and stiff and crackles when a sample is dropped into iced water, or until a spoon drawn across the bottom of the pan leaves a trail in the mixture. This will take from 30 minutes to 1 hour, depending on the amount of moisture in the fruit. Stir in the nuts, if used, the lemon or orange rind and the cinnamon.

Turn the fruit paste out on the buttered baking sheets, dishes or tins and spread it in a layer 1 cm (½ inch) thick. Chill the paste or leave it to set at room temperature. Use biscuit cutters to cut it into fancy shapes or, with a knife, cut it into about sixty 2.5 cm (1 inch) squares. Leftover scraps may be rolled between sheets of wax paper then cut into shapes or squares. Roll the pieces of paste in icing sugar and store them between wax paper in an airtight container.

WILLIAM HARLAN HALE AND THE EDITORS OF HORIZON MAGAZINE
THE HORIZON COOKBOOK

Quince Lowzina

Lowzina mal Haiwah

To make 4.5 kg (10 lb)

3 kg	large quinces	6 lb
12.5 cl	water	4 fl oz
About 2 kg	granulated sugar	About 4 lb
3 tbsp	lemon juice	3 tbsp
350 g	almonds, blanched and ground	12 oz
½ tsp	ground cardamom (optional)	½ tsp

Wash the unpeeled quinces and cut them into 1 cm (½ inch) slices. Remove the cores and rinse the quinces again. Put the quinces into a large heavy-bottomed, stainless-steel saucepan, add the water, cover the pan and simmer the fruit over a low heat for about 1½ hours or until tender. Stir the fruit occasionally and, if it begins to dry out, add a little more water. Remove the pan from the heat and stir. There should be about 2 kg (4 lb) of fruit. Cover the pan and let the fruit stand overnight so that it becomes dark red in colour. (If the paste is made immediately, without leaving the fruit to stand overnight, it will be pale and less attractive.)

The next morning, sieve the fruit pulp to remove the skins. Measure the pulp and add an equal measure of sugar. Cook the mixture over a low heat for 2½ to 3 hours, stirring occasionally with a wooden spoon to prevent sticking and burning. When the paste thickens and comes away from the bottom of the pan, test a spoonful on a plate to be sure it holds its shape and is not sticky when it cools. Add the lemon juice and mix well for 1 to 2 minutes. Remove the pan from the heat and let the mixture stand, stirring occasionally, until almost cold.

Mix the ground almonds with the cardamom, if used, and spread about half of the almonds on a large tray or baking sheet, covering the tray evenly. Pour the fruit mixture into the centre and spread a handful of the remaining almonds on top. Press the paste by hand or with a rolling pin, adding more almonds to keep the fruit from sticking to your hand or the rolling pin, until the confection is about 1 cm (½ inch) thick. Spread the remaining almonds on top and let the sweet stand overnight, covered with wax paper.

The next day, cut the paste with a sharp knife into diamond shapes about 1 cm (½ inch) long, then turn the pieces upside-down for 2 to 3 hours to dry thoroughly. Arrange the pieces in tin boxes, placing wax paper between the layers. Cover the boxes tightly and store them in the refrigerator or in the freezer; the frozen sweets will keep well for a year if the box is wrapped in a plastic bag.

DAISY INY
THE BEST OF BAGHDAD COOKING

Quince Paste

Marmelada

The paste can also be dried out in a warm, dry place for 24 hours. It should be sliced and dusted with icing sugar or castor sugar before being wrapped in wax paper for storing.

Guava paste, *goiabada*, is made in the same way, substituting guavas for quinces in the recipe below.

To make about 3 kg (7 lb)		
12	quinces, peeled and cored, seeds reserved	12
2	lemons, juice strained	2
About 2 kg	granulated sugar	About 4 lb

Soak the quince seeds in just sufficient cold water to cover. Put the quinces into a deep, heavy-based pan with cold water to cover. Add the lemon juice. Cover the pan and simmer until the quinces are soft, about 40 minutes to 1 hour. Drain the quinces and press the pulp through a sieve to purée it.

Weigh the pulp and to each 500 g (1 lb) of fruit add 750 g (1½ lb) of sugar and the water strained from the seeds. Stir the mixture thoroughly and cook it over a low heat, stirring constantly, until it makes a soft ball when a little is tried in cold water [*pages 10-11*]. At this point, take the pan from the heat and beat the contents for 10 minutes. Turn the mixture into a wetted 30 by 20 by 3 cm (12 by 8 by 1¼ inch) tin to cool. Slice the cool paste and dry it in the sun. It will keep indefinitely if the pieces are wrapped in wax paper.

CORA, ROSE AND BOB BROWN
THE SOUTH AMERICAN COOK BOOK

Quince Candy

Bomboms

To make about 1.5 kg (3 lb)		
1 kg	quinces, peeled, cored and quartered	2½ lb
30 cl	water	½ pint
About 850g	granulated sugar	About 1¾ lb
1 tsp	vanilla or almond extract	1 tsp

Cook the quinces in the water over a low heat until they are tender, about 20 to 30 minutes. Sieve the pulp and weigh it.

In a heavy-based saucepan, mix the pulp with an equal weight of sugar and, stirring constantly, simmer the mixture until it is quite thick and pulls away from the sides of the pan. Add the vanilla or almond extract and pour the mixture into a buttered 30 by 20 by 3 cm (12 by 8 by 1¼ inch) tin. Put the tin into a 130°C (250°F or Mark ½) oven for about 30 minutes to harden the candy. Cut the candy into 1 cm (½ inch) squares and wrap the squares in wax paper.

E. DONALD ASSELIN, M.D.
A PORTUGUESE-AMERICAN COOKBOOK

Assemblies and Dipped Confections

Full Figs

Figos Recheados

You can buy these figs almost anywhere in the Algarve, wrapped in fringed paper and strung together into a rope.

To make 24 figs		
24	moist, dried figs	24
30 g	semi-sweet chocolate, grated	1 oz
6 tbsp	ground almonds	6 tbsp

Snip the stem from each fig and gently pull it open to form a cavity in the centre. Mix the grated chocolate and ground almonds, and fill the cavities in the figs as fully as possible with the mixture. Close up the cavities with your fingers.

Place the figs on a baking sheet and bake them in a preheated 150°C (300°F or Mark 2) oven for 5 minutes. Turn the figs over and bake them for another 5 minutes. Remove them from the oven and leave them to cool before storing.

SHIRLEY SARVIS
A TASTE OF PORTUGAL

Stuffed Figs

To make about 560 g (1 lb 2 oz)		
250 g	large dried figs	8 oz
12.5 cl	orange juice	4 fl oz
2 tbsp	granulated sugar	2 tbsp
1 tsp	lemon juice	1 tsp
60 g	maraschino cherries, halved	2 oz
60 g	pecan nuts, broken into pieces	2 oz
	castor or icing sugar	

Heat the orange juice with the granulated sugar and the lemon juice and cook the figs in it on a very low heat, turning and basting them until they are tender and all the cooking liquid has been absorbed, about 40 minutes. Remove the figs from the pan and leave them to drain and cool on a wire rack. When the figs are cold, slit each one open and stuff it with halved cherries and pecan nut pieces. Close up the figs, press them back into shape and roll them in castor or icing sugar.

MRS. SIMON KANDER (EDITOR)
THE SETTLEMENT COOK BOOK

Syrian Stuffed Figs

Teen Mihshee

To make about 850 g (1¾ lb)

500 g	whole dried figs, stems trimmed	1 lb
¼ litre	orange juice	8 fl oz
1 tbsp	lemon juice	1 tbsp
1 tbsp	grated lemon rind	1 tbsp
150 g	granulated sugar	5 oz
150 g	blanched almonds or pecan nuts	5 oz

In a saucepan, combine the orange juice, the lemon juice, the lemon rind and 3 tablespoons of the sugar. Add the figs and heat the mixture to boiling point. Lower the heat, cover the pan and simmer the fruit until it is tender—30 minutes to 1 hour. Drain the figs well and leave them to cool. Pierce the stem end of each fig with a sharp knife and stuff an almond or pecan nut into the hole. Close the opening by pinching with your fingers, and roll the figs in the rest of the sugar. Arrange the figs on racks and dry them overnight before storing them in an airtight container between layers of wax paper.

HELEN COREY
THE ART OF SYRIAN COOKERY

Stuffed Dates and Walnuts

Dattes et Noix Farcies

To make about 1.75 kg (3½ lb)

500 g	dates, stoned	1 lb
250 g	walnut halves	8 oz
	Almond paste	
500 g	almonds, blanched	1 lb
500 g	castor sugar	1 lb
5 tbsp	white rum	5 tbsp
	green or pink colouring	
1 tbsp	strong black coffee	1 tbsp

To make the almond paste, pound the almonds and the castor sugar together in a mortar or grind them in an electric coffee grinder. If you use an electric grinder, put in only 4 tablespoons of the mixture at a time and count to 20 before switching off the motor. To stuff the dates, moisten half the paste with 3 tablespoons of the rum and a few drops of green or pink colouring. To stuff the walnuts, flavour the rest of the paste with 2 tablespoons of the rum and the black coffee.

To stuff the dates, roll a little paste into a ball and use it to fill the cavity left by the stone. To stuff the walnuts, roll the paste into a ball and sandwich it between two walnut halves.

LOUIS GINIÉS
CUISINE PROVENÇALE

French Candy

French candy, or what was called French candy, was made in Charleston, South Carolina, from an early date.

To make 750 g (1½ lb)

30 g	dried figs, cut into large pieces	1 oz
30 g	dates, stoned and halved	1 oz
30 g	prunes, stoned and halved	1 oz
60 g	mixed nuts, halved	2 oz
500 g	icing sugar	1 lb
1 tsp	vanilla extract	1 tsp
2	small egg whites	2

In a mixing bowl, mix the icing sugar with the vanilla extract and egg whites to make a stiff paste. Turn the mixture out on to wax paper or a work surface lightly dusted with icing sugar. Roll it out to about 3 mm (⅛ inch) thickness. Cut this sugar "pastry" into pieces big enough to wrap round the individual fruits and nuts. Press the edges of the coating together gently with your fingertips. Store the candies in an airtight box lined with wax paper, between layers of wax paper. The candies will keep for a week.

MORTON G. CLARK
FRENCH-AMERICAN COOKING

Apricots Stuffed With Almond Paste

Albicocche Marzapane

To make about 1 kg (2½ lb)

500 g	dried apricots	1 lb
250 g	ground almonds	8 oz
250 g	icing sugar	8 oz
	almond extract (optional)	
1	egg white, stiffly beaten	1
	lemon juice (optional)	
	castor sugar	

Soak the dried apricots in hot water overnight. The next day, cook them on a very low heat for about 20 minutes in the water in which they were soaked. Do not let them break up. Drain the apricots and leave them to cool.

Mix together the ground almonds, icing sugar and—if a stronger flavour is liked—two or three drops of almond extract. Add the egg white, mixing in well. If the paste is too stiff, add a few drops of lemon juice. Fill each apricot with almond paste. Roll the apricots in castor sugar. Leave them to dry on racks in a cool place overnight.

BERYL GOULD-MARKS
THE HOME BOOK OF ITALIAN COOKERY

Candied Walnuts

Noci al Caramello

The technique of making almond paste is shown on page 56 and that of making marzipan is shown on page 58. The marzipan may also be flavoured if desired. The technique of making candied walnuts is shown on page 72.

To make 1 kg (2½ lb)		
250 g	walnut halves	8 oz
500 g	almond paste or marzipan	1 lb
	green colouring	
500 g	granulated sugar	1 lb
12.5 cl	water	4 fl oz
1 tbsp	liquid glucose or a pinch of cream of tartar	1 tbsp

Lightly oil or butter a sheet of wax paper or a baking sheet. Knead a few drops of green colouring into the marzipan to colour it pale green. Shape the marzipan into small balls the size of cherries and place each ball between two walnut halves, pressing the halves together firmly.

In a small, heavy saucepan, dissolve the sugar in the water with the glucose or cream of tartar and cook the sugar syrup to the hard-crack stage or to a light caramel [*pages 10-11*]. Remove the pan from the heat and dip the filled walnut sandwiches one at a time into the syrup. Align the walnuts on the wax paper or baking sheet and leave them to dry and cool completely, then place them in paper confectionery cases.

LUIGI CARNACINA
GREAT ITALIAN COOKING

❖

Pistachio Olives

Les Pistaches en Olive

If you do not have fine-screen racks for drying the sweets, the toothpicks or cocktail sticks can be stuck into a potato, a piece of polystyrene foam or any similar material which will hold them firmly in place while the sweets dry in the air.

To make about 625 g (1⅓ lb)		
250 g	shelled pistachio nuts, blanched and finely ground	8 oz
About 375 g	castor sugar	About 12 oz
2 to 3 tbsp	water	2 to 3 tbsp

Dust a piece of greaseproof paper with castor sugar. Put the pistachio nuts in a pan with 125 g (4 oz) of the sugar. Gently heat the mixture, stirring and beating it with a wooden spoon until the paste no longer sticks to the sides of the pan. Remove the paste from the heat and empty it on to the paper; leave it to

cool until it is just warm to the touch. Pinch off a small piece of the mixture at a time and roll it between your palms into the shape of an olive. Stick a small wooden stick into one end of each olive-shaped sweet.

In a pan, over a medium heat, dissolve the remaining sugar in the water, stirring until the sugar dissolves. Increase the heat and boil the syrup until it begins to caramelize [*light caramel, pages 10-11*]. Remove the pan from the heat. Dip each olive-shaped sweet into the caramel and stick the free end of each wooden stick into the mesh of fine-screen racks, so that the sweets can dry in the air. Serve the sweets in a porcelain dish decorated with a paper frill.

PIERRE JOSEPH BUC'HOZ
L'ART DE PRÉPARER LES ALIMENTS

Stuffed Prunes

Prugne Farcite

The technique of making almond paste is shown on page 56 and that of making marzipan is shown on page 58. A paste made of 300 g (10 oz) of freshly grated coconut and 175 g (6 oz) of fondant (page 166) may be substituted for the almond paste or marzipan, as shown on page 72. The technique of making fondant is shown on page 34.

Make sure that the syrup dipping is done in a non-steamy kitchen, or the hard sugar coating will melt and soften.

To make about 2 kg (4 lb)		
36	small, sun-dried prunes	36
500 g	almond paste or marzipan	1 lb
500 g	granulated sugar	1 lb
12.5 cl	water	4 fl oz
½ tbsp	liquid glucose or honey	½ tbsp

Lightly butter two strips of wax paper or two baking sheets. Slit each prune carefully down one side, remove the stone and fill each cavity with a generous amount of the almond paste or marzipan, smoothing down the exposed portion of the paste with the back of a wetted spoon.

Cook the sugar, water and glucose or honey in a deep, heavy saucepan until the mixture reaches the hard-crack stage [*pages 10-11*]. The moment it is ready, remove the pan from the heat and place it in a large pan filled with water to arrest the cooking process. Using tongs or an oiled fork, dip each prune into the syrup. Align the coated prunes on the wax paper or baking sheets, making sure that the prunes do not touch each other. Let them cool for about 2 hours before placing them in pleated paper confectionery cases.

LUIGI CARNACINA
GREAT ITALIAN COOKING

Prunes Stuffed with Pistachios

Pruneaux Farcis

The pine-nuts can be replaced by 125 g (4 oz) of leftover fragments of crystallized chestnuts.

To make about 750 g (1½ lb)

15	large prunes, stones removed	15
50 g	pine-nuts	2 oz
1	egg white	1
50 g	castor sugar	2 oz
2 tbsp	kirsch	2 tbsp
15	pistachio nuts	15
150 g	lump sugar	5 oz
12.5 cl	water	4 fl oz

Slit the prunes on one side and remove the stones without spoiling the shape of the prunes. In a mortar, pound the pine-nuts with the egg white, add the castor sugar and pound them together. Add the kirsch and mix, pounding with the pestle. Put this paste into a small saucepan and heat it gently, stirring continually, until it becomes slightly stiffer. Remove the pan from the heat and leave the paste to cool.

Shape the paste into 15 small olive shapes. Stuff the prunes with the paste olives, sticking a whole pistachio nut into the part of the olive visible through the slit in the prune; the pistachio nuts must be visible.

In a pan, dissolve the lump sugar in the water and cook it to the hard-crack stage [*pages 10-11*]. Remove the pan from the heat. Put a stuffed prune on to a fork and dip it in the syrup. Slide it off the fork on to an oiled marble slab and leave it to dry. Repeat the dipping process with the rest of the prunes. When they are cooled, put them into individual paper cases.

MME. JEANNE SAVARIN (EDITOR)
LA CUISINE DES FAMILLES

Sugared Walnuts

The author also suggests dipping the walnut kernels into melted chocolate before coating them with icing. In this case, the icing should not be baked, but the walnuts should be left in a warm, dry place for the icing to dry. The technique of dipping nuts in chocolate is shown on page 74.

To make about 250 g (8 oz)

18	walnuts, shelled, separated into halves and skinned	18
About 125 g	icing sugar	About 4 oz
1	egg white, lightly beaten	1

To dry the walnut halves, arrange them on a sheet of grease-proof paper and place them in a preheated 130°C (250°F or Mark ½) oven, leaving the door of the oven open. Remove the

walnuts after about 20 minutes.

Mix the icing sugar with the egg white to make an icing which will just coat the back of a spoon. Dip the walnut halves in the icing and place them on a baking sheet lined with greaseproof paper. Place the baking sheet in a preheated 180°C (350°F or Mark 4) oven and bake the walnuts until light brown in colour, about 5 to 10 minutes. Take them out of the oven, leave them to cool and, when cold, remove them from the paper. Serve the walnuts piled on a glass dish.

OSCAR TSCHIRKY
"OSCAR" OF THE WALDORF'S COOK BOOK

Glacéed Orange Sections

Spicchi di Arance Canditi

A temple orange is a cross between an orange and a tangerine. Temple oranges are imported from Israel and are available from December to March.

These glacéed fruits should be served no more than 3 to 4 hours after they have been dipped in the syrup or dampness will cause the coating to melt. For the same reason, do not store them in the refrigerator. They are perfect served with vanilla ice cream.

To make about 1.25 kg (2½ lb)

4	navel oranges, tangerines or temple oranges, peeled, separated into segments, white membrane removed	4
750 g	granulated sugar	1½ lb
¼ litre	water	8 fl oz
½ tbsp	liquid glucose	½ tbsp

Lightly oil a baking sheet. Place the orange or tangerine segments on a plate. Put the sugar, water and glucose in a small, deep, heavy saucepan. Place the pan over a medium heat and stir until the sugar is dissolved. Allow the syrup to cook until it almost caramelizes—143°C (290°F) on the sugar thermometer. Remove the pan from the heat and place it in a larger pan filled with boiling water; this arrests the cooking process, yet keeps the syrup hot and liquid. Using tongs or a fork, dip the orange segments in the hot syrup one at a time, coating each well, and then align them on the oiled baking sheet. Serve the orange segments as soon as the sugar coating has hardened and cooled.

LUIGI CARNACINA
GREAT ITALIAN COOKING

Toffee Apples

Any toffee mixture boiled to the hard-crack stage can be used to coat apples to make toffee apples. An alternative toffee suitable for making toffee apples is shown on page 30.

To make about 8 toffee apples

750 g	apples	1½ lb
500 g	Demerara sugar	1 lb
250 g	black treacle	8 oz
125 g	butter	4 oz
1 tbsp	vinegar	1 tbsp

Butter a baking sheet or wax paper. Stirring constantly, dissolve the sugar in the black treacle with the butter and vinegar over a medium heat. Boil the mixture to the hard-crack stage [*pages 10-11*].

Push sticks into the cores of the apples from the stem. Dip the apples into the toffee, twirl them round for a few seconds, then leave them to cool on the buttered surface.

LIZZIE BOYD (EDITOR)
BRITISH COOKERY

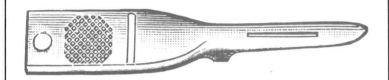

Crystallized Dates

Dattes Glacées au Caramel

To make about 500 g (1 lb)

250 g	dates, partially slit open and stoned	8 oz
125 g	icing sugar	4 oz
125 g	blanched almonds	4 oz
	kirsch	
	green colouring	
350 g	granulated sugar	12 oz
15 cl	water	¼ pint
	fine brown sugar or icing sugar, sieved	

Pound the icing sugar and the almonds together, moistening whilst pounding with sufficient kirsch to produce a stiffish paste; colour the paste with a little green colouring to give it a light green tint. Rub the mixture through a fine sieve.

Place some of this paste inside each date and fold the halves together in such a way as to show a 5 mm (¼ inch) strip of green paste down the slit. Stick a thin wooden toothpick into each date. Dissolve the sugar and water to make a sugar syrup, and boil it to the hard-crack stage [*pages 10-11*]. Dip the dates in the syrup. Dry the dates in the air by sticking the toothpicks into a basin of sieved fine brown or icing sugar, arranging them at an angle so that the dates will drain outside the basin.

When the dates are dry and have cooled completely, remove them from the toothpicks and put them singly into oval paper bonbon cases.

JULES GOUFFÉ
THE BOOK OF PRESERVES

Strawberry Delight

Deser-e Toot Farangi

To make about 1.7 kg (3½ lb)

1.2 kg	strawberries, stems left on	2 lb 7 oz
500 g	granulated sugar	1 lb
12.5 cl	water	4 fl oz
2 tbsp	rose-water or 2 tsp vanilla extract	2 tbsp

Line two or three baking sheets with wax paper. Drain the strawberries on paper towels. Dissolve the sugar in the water over a medium heat. Add the rose-water or vanilla extract and, with a slotted spoon, skim any foam from the surface. When the syrup reaches the soft-ball stage [*pages 10-11*], spread the strawberries out on the wax paper and pour 1 teaspoon of syrup over each berry. When the berries have cooled, loosen each one from the wax paper with the tip of a knife. Arrange the strawberries on paper doilies.

NESTA RAMAZANI
PERSIAN COOKING

Glazed Chestnuts

Kasztany w Cukrze

The technique of peeling and cooking chestnuts is explained on page 56.

The glaze will keep no longer than 24 to 48 hours; the chestnuts must therefore be prepared for immediate use.

To make 750 g (1½ lb)

500 g	chestnuts, peeled and cooked	1 lb
500 g	granulated sugar	1 lb
12.5 cl	water	4 fl oz

Butter two baking sheets. Over a medium heat, dissolve the sugar in the water and cook the syrup to the hard-crack stage or to a pale caramel [*pages 10-11*]. Stick a toothpick into each chestnut and dip it into syrup, then immediately into a bowl of iced water. Leave the chestnuts on the baking sheets until the glaze is dry, a few minutes.

MARJA OCHOROWICZ-MONATOWA
POLISH COOKERY

Fondant-Dipped Cherries

Cerises Déguisées

Although this recipe calls for brandied cherries, fresh cherries can also be fondant-dipped. If using fresh cherries, substitute a sugar syrup cooked to the thread stage (page 10) or water for the liquor. Whichever type of cherry is used, the skins must be absolutely dry before they are dipped or the fondant will not stick. The technique of fondant-dipping is shown on page 70. The coated cherries can be dipped in castor sugar as soon as the excess fondant has drained off. To make brandied cherries, put the cherries with their stalks into a glass jar. Add ½ litre (16 fl oz) of brandy and 75 g (2½ oz) of sugar and seal the jar. Shake it about once a week. Leave the cherries in the brandy for four to five months before using them.

The same recipe can be used for coating other kinds of fruit preserved in brandy or spirit. If the fruit has no stalk, stick a wooden cocktail stick into one end. If you do not have paper confectionery cases, dry the fruit on aluminium foil covered with a dusting of icing sugar.

To make about 500 g (1 lb)

40 to 50	brandied cherries, with stalks	40 to 50
250 g	fondant (*page 166*)	8 oz
1 to 2 tbsp	liquor from the brandied cherries	1 to 2 tbsp
3 or 4 drops	pink colouring	3 or 4 drops

Drain the cherries, reserving the liquor, and take great care not to detach them from their stalks. Making sure they are not touching each other, lay them on wire racks to dry for several hours or overnight.

In a small saucepan, melt the fondant over a very low heat. Add 1 tablespoon of the cherry liquor and use a dropper to add the pink colouring. Stir the mixture, which will become very liquid when heated. Do not heat it to more than 40° to 45°C (104° to 113°F). If at this point the fondant is not liquid enough, add a further tablespoon of liquor.

Remove the pan from the heat. Hold each cherry by the stalk and dip it into the fondant so that it is completely coated. Work without haste, putting each cherry into an individual paper confectionery case as it is coated.

JACQUELINE GÉRARD
BONNES RECETTES D'AUTREFOIS

Caramelized Brandied Cherries

Cerises Glacées au Caramel

To preserve cherries in brandy, put them in a glass jar with ½ litre (16 fl oz) of brandy and 75 g (2½ oz) of sugar. Seal the jar tightly and shake it once a week. Allow it to stand for four to five months before using.

To make about 1 kg (2 lb)

500 g	brandied cherries	1 lb
600 g	granulated sugar	1¼ lb
	cochineal	

Drain the cherries. Dissolve 250 g (8 oz) of the sugar in 1 tablespoon of water and cook the syrup to the thread stage [*page 10*]. Leave the syrup to cool. Pour the cold syrup into a bowl and add the cherries. Remove the cherries and drain them again. Arrange them on racks so that they do not touch each other and leave them in a warm, dry place, such as an airing cupboard, to dry for at least 24 hours.

Boil the rest of the sugar and 15 cl (¼ pint) of water to the hard-crack stage [*pages 10-11*] and remove from the heat. Add a few drops of cochineal. Stick a wooden cocktail stick into each cherry; hold each cherry by the stick and dip them one by one in the syrup then lay them on a lightly oiled baking sheet. Leave them to dry for at least 10 minutes. When they are cold and dry, remove the cocktail sticks and put the cherries into small, round bonbon cases.

JULES GOUFFÉ
THE BOOK OF PRESERVES

Raspberry Brandies

To make brandied raspberries, put the raspberries into a jar with 60 g (2 oz) of granulated sugar and cover them with about 60 cl (1 pint) of brandy. Seal the jar tightly and leave it for four to six weeks before opening it.

The technique of making these chocolates is shown on page 86. The authors recommend storing the chocolates for four or five days after they have been made to allow the centres to become well impregnated with the brandy.

To make 500 g (1 lb)

24	brandied raspberries	24
250 g	plain dipping chocolate	8 oz
175 g	fondant (*page 166*)	6 oz
2 tsp	brandy from the raspberries	2 tsp

Drain the raspberries well. Melt the dipping chocolate and use a teaspoon to pour it into 24 foil cups. Swirl the chocolate around inside each cup to coat it completely and pour off the

excess by inverting the cup over the bowl of dipping chocolate. Leave the chocolate to harden for a few minutes.

In a bowl over hot water, melt the fondant with the brandy. Use a teaspoon to pour a small quantity of fondant into each chocolate cup, so that the cup is not more than one-third full. Add a brandied raspberry, then fill the cup almost to the rim with more melted fondant. Leave the fondant to harden for 5 minutes. Then use a teaspoon to spoon enough melted dipping chocolate over each cup to cover the fondant completely. Swirl the chocolate over the fondant to seal the edges and leave the chocolate to harden. Serve the chocolates in the foil cups.

L.M. RAITH
HAND-MADE CONTINENTAL CHOCOLATES AND PRALINES

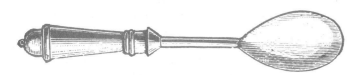

Crystallized Brandy Liqueurs

The equipment and techniques for starch-casting and chocolate-dipping are shown on pages 80-83. It is is advisable to practise the starch-casting technique before filling the moulds with liqueur mixture. After each experiment, the cornflour must be warmed and sieved on to the tray again.

Rum or whisky liqueurs are made in the same way. Whatever the spirit or liqueur used, the quantity must be exact—8 cl (3 fl oz) to each 500 g (1 lb) of sugar used to make the syrup. The chocolates can be dipped twice for extra strength.

To make 750 g (1½ lb)		
500 g	granulated sugar	1 lb
12.5 cl	water	4 fl oz
8 cl	brandy	3 fl oz
250 g	dipping chocolate	8 oz
3.5 to 4.5 kg cornflour		8 to 10 lb

Spread the cornflour on trays and dry it out in a warm place, such as an oven with a pilot light or an airing cupboard. Make the starch moulds, or modelling block, by sticking equal-sized shapes at regular intervals on to a strip of wood.

Dissolve the sugar in the water and bring it to the boil in accordance with the sugar-boiling procedure [*pages 8-9*]. When the sugar is completely dissolved, boil it quickly to a temperature of 108°C (227°F) [*pages 10-11*]. When the correct temperature has been reached, dip the base of the pan into cold water to stop the boil, allow it to cool for 5 minutes or so, then tip in the brandy. Cover the pan with a damp cloth and a lid and allow the syrup to cool until it is tepid—about 49°C (120°F). If desired, the pan can again be dipped into cold water for a few moments.

Use a box or tin not more than 4 cm (1½ inches) deep to make a starch tray. Sieve enough of the cornflour in a mound in the centre of the tray to fill the tray completely when levelled off. Use the back of the starch moulds or a ruler to flatten the cornflour, and make sure the surface is absolutely level. Reserve the surplus cornflour and keep it warm. Press the starch moulds into the starch tray, spacing the impressions evenly. Use a swift, upward movement to lift the moulds out of the tray to keep the impressions sharp. Take care that when a length of moulds is pressed into the cornflour, there is no disturbance which could press the existing impressions out of shape. This can be done by using two sets of moulds and keeping one in the impressions while the other one is used to make further impressions in a leap-frog fashion.

Take a V-shaped funnel and fit a wooden spoon handle into it. Pour the cooled syrup into the funnel. Fill each of the impressions in the starch tray with the syrup, drop by drop, controlling the flow by means of the spoon handle in the funnel. Sieve the reserved cornflour over the entire surface of the tray in a 3 mm (⅛ inch) layer. Leave the tray undisturbed for at least 6 hours. By this time a crystalline shell should have formed at the base of the liqueurs and to some extent up the sides, but hardly at all on the top. Therefore, the liqueurs have to be turned upside down so that the shell can be encouraged to form evenly all round. This must be done in one quick flip. A chocolate dipping fork or ordinary household fork can be used. The liqueurs should be left in the cornflour for another 6 hours at least, until they have formed a complete shell. They can even be left for much longer.

Melt the chocolate in a bowl set inside a saucepan of hot water. Remove each liqueur individually from the starch tray, dust it carefully with a pastry brush and dip it in the melted chocolate. Be careful not to let the liqueur shell break while dipping, as this will ruin the chocolate for future use.

ALEC LEAVER
MAKING CHOCOLATES

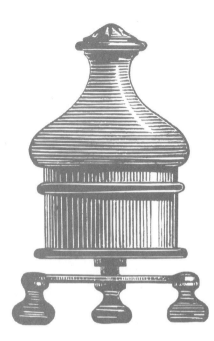

Montmorency Truffles

The technique for hand-dipping in chocolate to give a rough finish is shown on page 78.

To make about 3 kg (6 lb)

1.5 kg	plain chocolate, coarsely chopped	3 lb
60 cl	double cream	1 pint
1	vanilla pod	1
125 to 175 g	butter, softened	4 to 6 oz
	chocolate powder or icing sugar	
About 750 g	dipping chocolate, melted	About 1½ lb
	kirsch	

Boil the cream with the vanilla pod; remove the pod and stir in the plain chocolate. Stir the mixture until it is smooth. Chill the mixture until it begins to set, then beat in the butter until the mixture is light and fluffy. Use a piping bag to pipe lumps of the mixture of equal size on to sheets of greaseproof paper. Allow the mixture to set a little, then dust the lumps with the chocolate powder or icing sugar and roll them into balls.

Allow the balls to harden, then give them a preliminary coating of dipping chocolate by hand. Add a few drops of kirsch to the dipping chocolate and dip the chocolates again. Place the chocolates on a coarse sieve. As soon as the chocolate coating has begun to set, roll the chocolates over evenly, to give the characteristic zigzag appearance to the outside.

WALTER BACHMANN (EDITOR)
CONTINENTAL CONFECTIONERY

Chocolate Chips

If light-coloured molasses is not available, use golden syrup. The technique of melting chocolate is shown on page 74.

To make about 300 g (10 oz)

175 g	soft brown sugar	6 oz
12.5 cl	light-coloured molasses	4 fl oz
15 g	butter	½ oz
1½ tsp	vanilla extract	1½ tsp
125 g	dipping chocolate	4 oz

Butter a marble slab or work surface. In a saucepan, place the brown sugar, molasses and butter. Cook over a low heat, stirring constantly, until the sugar has dissolved. Bring the mixture to the boil and boil to the hard-crack stage [*pages 10-11*]. Remove the pan from the heat and flavour the mixture with 1 teaspoon of the vanilla extract.

Pour the toffee mixture on to the marble slab or work surface. When the mixture is cool enough to handle, pull it into several long thin strips. Cut the strips into small pieces. Leave them until cold.

Melt the dipping chocolate and add the rest of the vanilla extract to it. Dip the pieces of toffee into the dipping chocolate. Leave them on the marble slab to cool and set before storing.

MARY M. WRIGHT
CANDY-MAKING AT HOME

Milan Nut Chocolates

The technique of fondant-dipping is shown on page 70. The technique of chocolate-dipping is shown on page 74.

To make about 1 kg (2½ lb)

850 g	granulated sugar	1¾ lb
30 cl	water	½ pint
125 g	liquid glucose	4 oz
175 g	finely ground almonds	6 oz
175 g	finely ground walnuts	6 oz
6 tbsp	kirsch	6 tbsp
750 g	fondant (*page 166*)	1½ lb
125 g	walnuts, halved, or almonds, blanched and halved	4 oz
175 g	plain dipping chocolate, melted	6 oz

Boil the sugar, water and glucose together until they reach a temperature of 122°C (252°F) [*hard-ball stage, pages 10-11*]. Remove the pan from the heat and stir in the ground almonds

and walnuts, to make marzipan. At this stage, the marzipan will be quite soft. Pour the marzipan out on to a marble slab and leave it to cool. When the marzipan is cold, it becomes quite hard. Crush it to a powder with a rolling pin, then mix it with 3 to 4 tablespoons of kirsch to form a stiff paste. Roll out to a thickness of about 8 mm ($\frac{1}{3}$ inch) and cut it into ovals.

Gently melt the fondant with the rest of the kirsch. When it is well warmed and liquid, remove it from the heat and dip the oval marzipan shapes into the fondant. Place half a walnut or almond on the top at once. When the fondant has set, dip the lower half of each sweet into the plain dipping chocolate.

WALTER BACHMANN (EDITOR)
CONTINENTAL CONFECTIONERY

Delicieuse

Confectioner's bars are illustrated on page 19.

To make about 1.5 kg (3 lb)

1 kg	plain chocolate, coarsely chopped	2 lb
20 cl	double cream	7 fl oz
350 g	granulated sugar	12 oz
6 or 7	egg yolks	6 or 7
250 g	butter, softened	8 oz
3	oranges, juice strained	3
1 tsp	finely grated orange rind	1 tsp
750 g to 1 kg	milk dipping chocolate, melted	1½ to 2 lb

Heat the cream. Mix the sugar well with the egg yolks and add the butter. Combine this with the hot cream and the orange juice and rind. Heat to boiling point, stirring constantly.

Add the plain chocolate, stir the mixture well and pour it out on to greaseproof paper. Hold the mixture in place with confectioner's bars. Leave the mixture to cool. When it has set, use a circular cutter to cut out 2.5 cm (1 inch) rounds. Dip these in the milk dipping chocolate.

WALTER BACHMANN (EDITOR)
CONTINENTAL CONFECTIONERY

Locarno Rocks

The technique of making marzipan is shown on page 58.

To make about 350 g (12 oz)

175 g	marzipan (*page 167*)	6 oz
125 g	preserved ginger, finely chopped	4 oz
1 to 2 tbsp	icing sugar, sieved	1 to 2 tbsp
60 g	desiccated coconut	2 oz
30 g	plain chocolate, melted	1 oz

Mix the marzipan and ginger together. If the mixture is too sticky to handle, add some or all of the icing sugar. Wrap the paste and leave it in a cool place for 24 hours.

Roll the marzipan mixture into 2.5 cm (1 inch) sausage shapes and cut them into slices or, if you like, roll the paste into little balls or roll it out and cut it into squares, triangles, diamonds or bars. Mix the coconut with the melted chocolate. Coat the marzipan shapes with the chocolate and coconut. Place the shapes on wax paper to dry.

SONIA AGNEW
SWEET-MAKING FOR EVERYWOMAN

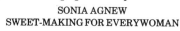

Honey Nougat Chocolates

Although the author calls this a nougat, the result resembles a caramel or toffee. Confectioner's bars are shown on page 19.

To make about 1.5 kg (3 lb)

900 g	honey	1 lb 14 oz
12.5 cl	liquid glucose	4 fl oz
½ litre	double cream	16 fl oz
625 g	almonds, blanched, slivered and lightly toasted	1 lb 4 oz
750 g	plain dipping chocolate, melted	1½ lb
About 500 g	almond halves, toasted (optional)	About 1 lb

In a copper pan, heat the honey, glucose and cream. Boil the mixture to the firm-ball stage [*pages 10-11*]. Add the slivered almonds and pour the nougat on to an oiled marble slab, between confectioner's bars. When the mixture is almost cold, cut it into small triangles and dip it in the chocolate. A lightly toasted almond half may be added as decoration.

WALTER BACHMANN (EDITOR)
CONTINENTAL CONFECTIONERY

Eugénies

The technique of crystallizing fruit peel is shown on page 49. The technique of chocolate-dipping is shown on page 74. The rind can also be served undipped. Instead of peeling the oranges as described below, they may also be peeled in long spirals. An alternative method of drying crystallized peel is to put it in an oven heated only by its pilot light for about 3 hours.

You can prepare these sweets in advance and store them for a week in the refrigerator, completely buried in cocoa powder.

To make about 175 g (6 oz)

2	oranges, weighing 200 g (7 oz) each	2
650 g	castor sugar	1 lb 7 oz
3½ litres	water	6 pints
150 g	plain chocolate, coarsely chopped	5¼ oz
60 g	cocoa powder	2 oz

With a small sharp knife, slice both ends off the oranges so you can sit them comfortably on a work surface. Then cut the skin from top to bottom in 2.5 cm (1 inch) strips taking great care that no white pith comes away with the orange rind. The peeled oranges can be used for some other purpose. Cut the rind strips into diamonds of roughly the same size—about 2.5 to 4 cm (1 to 1½ inches) across.

Put 1 litre (1¾ pints) of water to boil in a saucepan, then plunge the pieces of orange rind into it for 3 minutes. Refresh them in cold water. Repeat twice more, using fresh water each time. This is to remove as much bitterness as possible from the rind. Drain the rind in a colander.

Empty and rinse the saucepan and put in the rest of the water and the sugar. Bring the mixture to the boil, stirring constantly with a fork to dissolve the sugar, and add the drained orange rind. Cook for 3 hours on a low heat; the surface of the liquid should be barely shivering.

Take out the pieces of rind with a skimmer and lay them on a wire rack to drain off excess syrup. Let them dry out in the air for 3 hours.

Melt the chocolate slowly in a second saucepan standing in a bain-marie at about 30°C (85°F), stirring continually with a wooden spatula to make it really smooth. Lift up one piece of candied orange peel at a time on a fork, without piercing it, and dip it in the melted chocolate. Put the coated pieces on the cake rack to allow the chocolate to set a little and, after a few minutes, roll them in a plateful of the cocoa powder until they are completely coated. Let them cool in the cocoa and pick them out with your fingers, shaking each piece gently to dust off any excess cocoa.

Pile them in a crown on a plate covered with a white paper doily, and offer them as an extremely elegant accompaniment to coffee at the end of a meal.

MICHEL GUÉRARD
MICHEL GUÉRARD'S CUISINE GOURMANDE

Standard Preparations

Fondant

If the fondant is to be made into confections (*pages 34-37*), cook it until a sugar thermometer registers 116°C (240°F). If it is to be used for dipping, cook it to 113°C (236°F). Colourings and flavourings suitable for fondant are discussed on page 14.

To make about 350 g (12 oz)

500 g	granulated sugar	1 lb
15 cl	water	¼ pint
1 tbsp	liquid glucose	1 tbsp

Sprinkle a marble slab or large dish with water. Put the ingredients into a heavy pan, preferably made of untinned copper, and stir them over a medium heat. While the sugar is dissolving, use a wet pastry brush to brush down any crystals that form on the sides of the pan; alternatively, put a lid on the pan for a minute to allow the steam from the syrup to wash down the sides. As soon as the sugar has completely dissolved, stop stirring and put a sugar thermometer in the pan. Bring the syrup to the boil over a high heat and cook it to the soft-ball stage [*pages 10-11*]. Remove the pan from the heat and quickly dip the base into cold water to stop the cooking.

Pour the syrup on to the marble slab or dish. Leave it to cool for a few minutes. With a dampened metal scraper, turn the sides of the mixture towards the middle to ensure that the syrup cools evenly. When the syrup has a yellowish tinge and becomes viscous, work it with the scraper or a wooden spatula, using a figure-of-eight motion. The syrup will thicken and become whiter. Continue to work the syrup until it becomes completely opaque and crumbly, about 5 to 10 minutes. Wet your hands and form the mixture into a smooth ball. Knead it with your hands for about 10 minutes until it is smooth, white and plastic. The fondant will be easier to shape if it is covered with a damp cloth and left overnight.

Fondant can be wrapped in wax paper or plastic film and stored in a tightly sealed jar in the refrigerator, where it will keep almost indefinitely.

Praline

Praline can be made with any hard, dry nuts, such as almonds, peanuts, pecan nuts or pistachio nuts. The nuts may be toasted or plain, skinned or unskinned, chopped, halved or whole. If you intend to crush the praline into a powder, make it with skinned nuts.

To make about 750 g (1½ lb)

500 g	granulated sugar	1 lb
15 cl	water	¼ pint
350 g	nuts	12 oz

Place the nuts on a baking sheet and put them in a preheated 180°C (350°F or Mark 4) oven for about 5 minutes to warm. Thoroughly oil or butter a marble slab or two 30 by 20 by 3 cm (12 by 8 by 1¼ inch) tins.

In a heavy saucepan over a medium heat, dissolve the sugar in the water, stirring constantly. Use a wet pastry brush to brush down any crystals that form on the sides of the pan; alternatively, place a lid on the pan for a short time to allow the steam from the syrup to wash down the crystals. As soon as the sugar has dissolved, stop stirring and put a sugar thermometer in the pan. Bring the syrup to the boil over a high heat and boil it to a light caramel colour—160° to 170°C (320° to 338°F). Remove the pan from the heat and immediately dip the base into cold water to stop the cooking process.

Immediately add the warmed nuts and stir the mixture very gently to mix them into the syrup. Pour the syrup on to the oiled or buttered slab or into the tins. When it is completely cold, break the praline into pieces.

Praline powder: to make the praline into praline powder, put pieces of praline into a plastic bag and crush them with a rolling pin into a fine powder.

Nut brittle: this is a variation of praline which uses a smaller proportion of nuts to sugar—250 to 350 g (8 to 12 oz) of nuts to 500 g (1 lb) of sugar. The nuts should be skinned. Pour the sugar syrup and nut mixture on to an oiled or buttered slab or baking sheet. With an oiled spatula, spread the mixture evenly. As soon as it is cool enough to handle, generously coat your hands with oil or butter and gently stretch the solidifying mixture at the edges, pulling it until it forms a thin sheet. When the brittle is completely cold, break it into pieces.

Nut Paste

Nut paste can be made from ground, blanched almonds, hazelnuts, pistachio nuts, Brazil nuts or pecan nuts, or a mixture of these; coconuts, peanuts and tiger nuts are not suitable. When a nut paste is made entirely from almonds, it is sometimes called marzipan. The ratio of sugar to nuts can be varied according to taste, and can be as high as two parts of sugar to one part of nuts. One variation is to use equal parts of ground nuts and soft, dark brown sugar.

Nut pastes can be bound with egg yolks or whole eggs instead of with egg whites. Yolks or whole eggs will make the paste richer, and darker in colour. Suitable flavourings for nut pastes include vanilla, brandy, rum, a liqueur or a teaspoon of finely grated orange rind. Flavourings and colourings are discussed on page 14.

To make about 1 kg (2 lb)

500 g	icing sugar, sieved	1 lb
250 g	almonds, blanched and ground	8 oz
250 g	hazelnuts, skinned and ground	8 oz
2 to 3	egg whites, lightly beaten	2 to 3
	flavouring and colouring (optional)	

In a large bowl, mix the icing sugar and ground nuts. Stirring constantly, gradually add enough of the egg whites to make the mixture moist enough to cohere. Knead the mixture gently with your hands until it is smooth and thick. To store the paste, wrap it well in several layers of wax paper or plastic film and refrigerate it. It will keep for two months.

To flavour and colour the paste, dust a cool surface with more sieved icing sugar and put the paste on it. Knead in a few drops of the desired flavouring and colouring. If the mixture becomes too moist, knead in a little more icing sugar; if the mixture dries out during kneading, add a little lightly beaten egg white. To use the paste for making confections, roll it out with a rolling pin dusted with icing sugar, then cut it into shapes or mould it by hand.

Recipe Index

English recipe titles are listed by categories such as "Chocolate", "Crystallized Confections", "Honey", "Marzipan", "Pulled Sugar Sweets" or "Walnuts", and within those categories alphabetically. Foreign recipe titles are listed alphabetically without regard to category.

General Index/Glossary

Included in this index are definitions of many of the culinary terms used in this book: definitions are in italics. The recipes in the Anthology are listed in the Recipe Index on page 168.

Recipe Credits

The source for the recipes in this volume are shown below. Page references in brackets indicate where the recipes appear in the Anthology.

Agnew, Sonia, *Sweet-Making for Everywoman*. Published in 1936 by Herbert Joseph Ltd., London. By permission of Herbert Joseph (*pages 89, 145 and 165*).

Allison, Sonia, *The Dairy Book of Home Cookery*. © Milk Marketing Board of England and Wales 1977. Published by the Milk Marketing Board, Thames Ditton, Surrey. By permission of the Milk Marketing Board (*pages 89, 90, 106 and 146*).

American Heritage, the Editors of, *The American Heritage Cookbook*. Copyright © 1964 by American Heritage Publishing Co., Inc. Published by American Heritage Publishing Co., Inc., New York. By permission of American Heritage Publishing Co., Inc. (*pages 102, 109*).

Arsdale, May B. Van and Emellos, Ruth Parrish Casa, *Candy Recipes & Other Confections*. Published by Dover Publications, Inc., New York, in 1975. First published in 1941 by M. Barrows & Company, Inc. under the title "Our Candy Recipes & Other Confec-

tions". By permission of Dover Publications, Inc. (*pages 96, 112, 119 and 122*).

Art of Cookery, Made Plain and Easy, The. By a Lady. London, 1747 (*page 141*).

Artusi, Pellegrino, *La Scienza in Cucina e l'Arte di Mangiar Bene*. Copyright © 1970 Giulio Einaudi editore S.p.A., Torino. Published by Giulio Einaudi editore S.p.A. (*page 92*).

Asselin, M. D., E. Donald, *A Portuguese-American Cookbook*. Copyright in Japan, 1966, by The Charles E. Tuttle Company, Inc. Published by The Charles E. Tuttle Company, Inc., Tokyo. By permission of The Charles E. Tuttle Company, Inc. (*page 157*).

Bachmann, Walter (Editor), *Continental Confectionery*. First edition 1955. Published by Maclaren & Sons Ltd., London (*pages 164, 165*).

Beard, James, *James Beard's American Cookery*. Copyright © 1972 by James A. Beard. First published by Little, Brown and Company, Boston. Published in 1974 by Hart-Davis MacGibbon Ltd./Granada Publishing Ltd., St. Albans, Hertfordshire. By permission of Granada Publishing Ltd. (*page 148*).

Becker, Fritz, *Das Kochbuch aus Mecklenburg, Pommern & Ostpreussen*. Copyright © 1976 by Verlagsteam Wolfgang Hölker. Published by Verlag Wolfgang Hölker, Münster. Translated by permission of Verlag Wolfgang Hölker (*page 134*).

Bellin, Mildred Grosberg, *The Jewish Cook Book*. Copyright 1941 by Bloch Publishing Co., Inc. Pub-

lished by Bloch Publishing Co., Inc., New York, 1947. By permission of Bloch Publishing Co., Inc. (*pages 96, 110 and 116*).

Blanquet, Mme. Rosalie, *Le Pâtissier des Ménages*. Librairie de Théodore Lefèvre et Cie./Émile Guérin, Éditeur, Paris, 1878 (*page 100*).

Bonekamp, Gunnevi, *Scandinavian Cooking*. Copyright © 1973 Spectator Publications Ltd., London. Published by Spectator Publications Ltd. By permission of Spectator Publications Ltd. (*pages 98, 147*).

A Book of Famous Old New Orleans Recipes. Copyright Peerless Printing Co., Inc., New Orleans. Published by Peerless Printing Co., Inc. By permission of Peerless Publishing Co., Inc. (*pages 94, 115 and 127*).

Booker, Esmé Gray, *Sweets that have Tempted me*. © Esmé Gray Booker 1959. Published by Mills & Boon Ltd., London. By permission of Mills & Boon Ltd. (*pages 109, 132 and 147*).

Bookmeyer, Mary B., *Candy and Candy-Making*. Published by Chas. A. Bennett Co., Inc., c. 1930. By permission of The University of Nebraska Foundation, Lincoln, Nebraska (*page 124*).

Borer, Eva Maria, *Tante Heidi's Swiss Kitchen*. English text copyright © 1965 by Nicholas Kaye Ltd. Published by Kaye & Ward Ltd., London. First published under the title "Die Echte Schweizer Küche" by Mary Hahns Kochbuchverlag, Berlin W., 1963. By permission of Kaye & Ward Ltd. (*page 111*).

Boyd, Lizzie (Editor), *British Cookery*. © 1976 by

British Tourist Authority and British Farm Produce Council. Published by Croom Helm Ltd., London. By permission of the British Tourist Authority, London (*page 161*).

Břízová, Joza and Klimentová, Maryna, *Tschechische Küche*. Published by PRÁCE, Prague and Verlag für die Frau, Leipzig, 1977. Translated by permission of DILIA, Theatrical and Literary Agency, Prague, for the authors (*pages 142, 147*).

Brown, Cora, Rose and Bob, *The South American Cook Book*. First published by Doubleday, Doran & Company, Inc. in 1939. Republished in 1971 by Dover Publications, Inc., New York (*pages 110, 114 and 157*).

Buc'hoz, J.-P., *L'Art de Préparer les Aliments*. Second edition. Published by the author, Paris, 1787 (*pages 136, 159*).

Buckeye Cookbook: Traditional American Recipes, The. As published by the Buckeye Publishing Company in 1883. Republished in 1975 by Dover Publications, Inc., New York (*page 97*).

Byron, May (Editor), *Puddings, Pastries, and Sweet Dishes*. Published in 1929 by Hodder & Stoughton Ltd., London. By permission of Hodder & Stoughton Ltd. (*pages 88, 100*).

Calera, Ana Maria, *Cocina Catalana*. © Ana Maria Calera 1974. Published in 1974 by Editorial Bruguera, S.A., Barcelona. Translated by permission of Editorial Bruguera S.A. (*pages 114, 125*).

Carnacina, Luigi, *Great Italian Cooking*. Edited by Michael Sonino. Published in English by Abradale Press Inc., New York and The Hamlyn Publishing Group Ltd., London. By permission of Aldo Garzanti Editore S.p.A. (*pages 159, 160*).

Carréras, Marie-Thérèse and Lafforgue, Georges, *Les Bonnes Recettes du Pays Catalan*. © Presses de la Renaissance, 1980. Published by Presses de la Renaissance, Paris. Translated by permission of Presses de la Renaissance (*page 152*).

Cascante, Maria del Carmen, *150 Recetas de Dulces de Fácil Preparación*. © Editorial De Vecchi, S.A., 1975. Published by Editorial De Vecchi, S.A., Barcelona. Translated by permission of Editorial De Vecchi, S.A. (*page 146*).

Cavalcanti, Ippolito, Duca di Buonvicino, *Cucina Teorico-Pratica*. Tipografia di G. Palma, Naples. Second edition, 1839 (*pages 154, 155*).

Chenoweth, Walter W., *How to Make Candy*. Copyright 1936 by The Macmillan Company. Published in 1936 by The Macmillan Company, New York (*pages 107, 118*).

Chowdhary, Savitri, *Indian Cooking*. Copyright © Savitri Chowdhary 1954, 1975. First published 1954 by André Deutsch Ltd., London. Revised edition published by Pan Books Ltd., London, 1975. By permission of André Deutsch Ltd. (*page 153*).

Clark, Morton G., *French-American Cooking*. Copyright © 1967 by Morton G. Clark. By permission of Harper & Row, Publishers, Inc., New York (*page 158*).

Colquitt, Harriet Ross (Editor), *The Savannah Cook Book*. © 1933 by Harriet Ross Colquitt. © 1960 by Harriet Ross Colquitt. Eighth edition 1974 published by Colonial Publishers, Charleston, South Carolina. By permission of Colonial Publishers (*page 115*).

Corey, Helen, *The Art of Syrian Cookery*. Copyright © 1962 by Helen Corey. Published by Doubleday & Company, Inc., Garden City, New York. By permission of Doubleday & Company, Inc. (*pages 150, 158*).

Czernikowski, Jan, *Ciasta, Ciastka, Ciasteczka*. Published by Wydawnictwo Przemysłu Lekkiego i Spożywczego, Warsaw, 1958. Translated by permission

of Agencja Autorska, Warsaw, for the heiress to the author (*pages 94, 140 and 152*).

Davidis, Henriette, *Praktisches Kochbuch*. Newly revised by Luise Holle. Published in Bielefeld and Leipzig, 1898 (*pages 128, 135*).

Denison, Grace E. (Editor), *The New Cook Book by The Ladies of Toronto and Other Cities and Towns*. Revised edition 1906. Published by Rose Publishing Co., Toronto (*page 106*).

Disslowa, Marja, *Jak Gotować*. Published by Wydawnictwo Polskie R. Wegnera, Poznań, 1938. Translated by permission of Agencja Autorska, Warsaw, for the author (*page 141*).

Elkon, Juliette, *The Chocolate Cookbook*. Copyright © 1973 by Juliette Elkon. Published by The Bobbs-Merrill Co., Inc. By permission of The Bobbs-Merrill Co., Inc. (*pages 94, 145*).

Farmer, Fannie Merritt, *The Fannie Farmer Cookbook*. Eleventh edition, revised by Wilma Lord Perkins. Copyright 1896, 1900, 1901, 1902, 1903, 1904, 1905, 1906, 1912, 1914 by Fannie Merritt Farmer. Copyright 1915, 1918, 1923, 1924, 1928, 1929 by Cora D. Perkins. Copyright 1930, 1931, 1932, 1933, 1934, 1936, 1941, 1942, 1946, 1951 by Dexter Perkins. Copyright © 1959, 1965 by Dexter and Wilma Lord Perkins. Published by Little, Brown & Company, Boston. By permission of The Fannie Farmer Cookbook Corporation (*pages 93, 155*).

Firth, Grace, *A Natural Year*. Copyright © 1972 by Grace Firth. Published by Simon & Schuster, New York. By permission of Simon & Schuster, a Division of Gulf & Western Corporation (*page 132*).

Flexner, Marion, *Out of Kentucky Kitchens*. © Copyright 1949 by Marion Flexner. Published by Bramhall House, a division of Clarkson N. Potter, Inc., by arrangement with Franklin Watts, Inc., New York. By permission of Franklin Watts, Inc. (*pages 105, 108, 114 and 144*).

Gaspero, Josh (Editor), *Hershey's 1934 Cookbook*. Copyright © 1971 by Hershey Foods Corporation. Published by Hershey Foods Corporation, Hershey, Pennsylvania. By permission of Hershey Foods Corporation (*pages 112, 116*).

Gérard, Jacqueline, *Bonnes Recettes d'Autrefois*. © Librairie Larousse, 1980. Published by Librairie Larousse, Paris. Translated by permission of Société Encyclopédique Universelle, Paris (*pages 138, 139, 149 and 162*).

Gillette, Mrs. F. L. and Ziemann, Hugo, *The White House Cookbook*. (Edited and new material supplied by Frances R. Grossman.) New material copyright © 1976 by David McKay Company, Inc. Published by David McKay Company, Inc., New York. By permission of Frances R. Grossman (*page 104*).

Giniés, Louis, *Cuisine Provençale*. Sixth edition. Published by U.N.I.D.E., Paris, 1976. Translated by permission of U.N.I.D.E. (*pages 92, 158*).

Good Housekeeping Institute (Editor), *Good Housekeeping's Picture Cookery*. Published by the National Magazine Company Ltd., London. Revised edition 1954. By permission of the National Magazine Company Ltd. (*page 88*).

Good Housekeeping Institute (Editor), *Good Housekeeping's World Cookery*. © The National Magazine Company Limited, England 1962. Published by Octopus Books Limited, London, 1972. By permission of The National Magazine Company Limited (*page 151*).

Gouffé, Jules, *The Book of Preserves*. Translated from the French "Le Livre de Conserves" by Alphonse Gouffé. Published by Sampson, Low, Son, and Mar-

ston, London, 1871 (*pages 161,162*).

Gould-Marks, Beryl, *The Home Book of Italian Cookery*. © Beryl Gould-Marks 1969. Published by Faber & Faber Ltd., London. By permission of Faber & Faber Ltd. (*pages 122, 124 and 158*).

Graham, Winifred, *Chocolates and Candies for Pleasure and Profit*. Copyright © Winifred Graham 1977. Published by White Lion Publishers Limited, London. By permission of Severn House Publishers Ltd., London (*pages 90, 133*).

Groot, Roy Andries de, *The Auberge of the Flowering Hearth*. Copyright © 1973 by Roy Andries de Groot. Published by The Bobbs-Merrill Company, Inc., Indianapolis/New York. By permission of Robert Cornfield Literary Agency, New York (*page 93*).

Guérard, Michel, *Michel Guérard's Cuisine Gourmande*. © Macmillan London Ltd., 1977, 1978. Published by Macmillan London Ltd. Originally published in French as "La Cuisine Gourmande", © Editions Robert Laffont S.A., Paris, 1978. By permission of Macmillan, London and Basingstoke (*page 166*).

Haitsma Mulier-van Beusekom, C. A. H. (Editor), *Culinaire Encyclopedie*. Published by Elsevier 1957. Revised edition 1971 by Elsevier Nederland B.V. and E.H.A. Nakken-Rövekamp. Translated by permission of Elsevier Nederland B.V. (*page 90*).

Hajková, Mária, *Múčniky*. © Mária Hajková 1974. Published by PRÁCA, Bratislava and Verlag für die Frau, Leipzig. German translation "Backbuch" © 1974 by PRÁCA, Bratislava, CSSR and Verlag für die Frau, DDR-701 Leipzig. By permission of LITA Slovak Agency, Bratislava (*pages 136, 148 and 153*).

Haldar, Mrs. J., *Bengal Sweets*. Fifth edition. Published by Industry Publishers Ltd., Calcutta, 1948 (*page 139*).

Hale, William Harlan and the Editors of Horizon Magazine, *The Horizon Cookbook*. © 1968 by American Publishing Co., Inc. Published by American Heritage Publishing Co. Inc., New York. By permission of American Heritage Publishing Co. Inc. (*pages 130, 155 and 156*).

Hall, Dorothy, *The Book of Herbs*. © Dorothy Hall 1972. First published 1972 by Angus & Robertson Publishers, London. Published in 1976 by Pan Books Ltd., London. By permission of Angus & Robertson (UK) Ltd. (*page 88*).

Heaton, Nell (Editor), *Home-made Sweets*. Copyright Nell Heaton 1949. Published by Faber & Faber Ltd., London, 1949. By permission of Faber & Faber Ltd. (*page 101*).

Henderson, H. H. F., *Het Nieuwe Kookboek*. © 1948/1972 Zomer & Keuning-Wageningen. Published by Zomer & Keuning-Wageningen. Translated by permission of Zomer & Keuning B.V., Ede (*pages 141, 144 and 145*).

Hewitt, Jean, *The New York Times Southern Heritage Cookbook*. Copyright © 1972 and 1976 by The New York Times Company. Published by G. P. Putnam's Sons, New York. By permission of Curtis Brown Ltd., New York (*page 129*).

Horvath, Maria, *Balkan-Küche*. Copyright © 1963 by Wilhelm Heyne Verlag, München. Published by Wilhelm Heyne Verlag, Munich. Translated by permission of Wilhelm Heyne Verlag (*page 126*).

How to Make Candy. Published by N. P. Fletcher and Company, Hartford, Conn., 1875 (*page 102*).

Hutton, D. F. and Bode, E. M., *Simple Sweetmaking*. © D. F. Hutton and E. M. Bode 1965. Published by Faber & Faber Ltd., London, 1965. By permission of Faber & Faber Ltd. (*pages 89, 119, 123 and 129*).

Iny, Daisy, *The Best of Baghdad Cooking*. Copyright

© 1976 by Daisy Iny. Published by Saturday Review Press/E. P. Dutton & Co. Inc., New York. By permission of Jean V. Naggar Literary Agency, for the author (*pages 95, 136 and 156*).

Irwin, Florence, *The Cookin' Woman.* Published by Oliver and Boyd, London, 1949 (*page 96*).

Jerome, Helen, *Sweet-making for All.* Published by Thomas Nelson & Sons Ltd., London, 1955. By permission of Thomas Nelson & Sons Ltd. (*pages 120, 134*).

Junior League of Jackson, Mississippi (Editor), *Southern Sideboards.* Copyright © 1978 by Junior League of Jackson, Mississippi. Including recipes from The Southern Junior League Cookbook © 1977 by Junior League of Jackson, Mississippi. By permission of Junior League of Jackson (*pages 91, 116, 120 and 150*).

Junior League of New Orleans, The, *The Plantation Cookbook.* Copyright © 1972 by The Junior League of New Orleans, Inc. Published by Doubleday & Company, Inc., Garden City, New York. By permission of Doubleday & Company, Inc. (*page 113*).

Kander, Mrs. Simon (Editor), *The Settlement Cook Book.* Copyright © 1965, 1976 by The Settlement Cookbook Company. By permission of Simon & Schuster, a Division of Gulf & Western Corporation, New York (*pages 100, 157*).

Kasdan, Sara, *Love and Kishkes.* Published in England by Arco Publications Ltd., London, 1957. Originally published in U.S.A. as "Love and Knishes" by Vanguard Press, Inc., New York. Copyright © 1956 by Sara Kasdan. By permission of Curtis Brown Ltd., New York (*pages 91, 94 and 95*).

King's College Hospital Book of Cooking Recipes, The *(Being a Collection of Recipes contributed by Friends of the Hospital).* Published by Longmans, Green and Co., London, 1911. By permission of Friends of King's College Hospital (*pages 99, 133 and 142*).

Kollist, E. J., *French Pastry, Confectionery and Sweets.* Published by Cassell & Company Ltd., London, 1929 (*pages 127, 133*).

Land, Mary, *New Orleans Cuisine.* © 1969 by A. S. Barnes & Co., Inc. Published by A. S. Barnes & Co., Inc., South Brunswick and New York. By permission of A. S. Barnes & Co., Inc., San Diego (*pages 117, 135*).

Leaver, Alec, *Making Chocolates.* © 1975 by Alec Leaver. Published by Michael Joseph Ltd., London. By permission of Michael Joseph Ltd. (*pages 143, 163*).

Leyel, Mrs. C. F., and Hartley, Miss Olga, *The Gentle Art of Cookery.* Copyright The Executors of the Estate of Mrs. C. F. Leyel 1925. Published by Chatto & Windus Ltd., London, 1925. By permission of Chatto & Windus Ltd. (*page 107*).

Lowenberg, Miriam, *Creative Candy Making.* Copyright © 1979 by Ottenheimer Publishers, Inc. Published by Weathervane Books under arrangement with Ottenheimer Publishers, Inc. By permission of Ottenheimer Publishers, Inc., Baltimore (*pages 95, 103, 108 and 150*).

Magyar, Elek, *Kochbuch für Feinschmecker.* © Dr. Magyar Bálint. © Dr. Magyar Pál. Originally published in 1967 under the title "Az Ínyesmester Szakácskönyve" by Corvina, Budapest. Translated by permission of Artisjus, Literary Agency, Budapest (*page 137*).

Manders, Beatrice and Millner, E. M., *The Art of Sweet-Making,* Fouth Edition, greatly enlarged and revised. Published by the Confectionery and Cookery School, London, 1923 (*pages 101, 103*).

Mathiot, Ginette, *La Pâtisserie pour Tous.* © 1938

Albin Michel, Éditeur, Paris. Published by Albin Michel, Éditeur. Translated by permission of Éditions Albin Michel (*page 131*).

McBride, Mary Margaret, *Harvest of American Cooking.* © 1956, 1957 by Mary Margaret McBride. Published by G. P. Putnam's Sons, New York. By permission of G. P. Putnam's Sons (*pages 104, 111*).

McCormick, *Spices of the World Cookbook.* Copyright © 1979 by McCormick & Co., Inc. Published by McGraw-Hill Book Company, New York. By permission of McGraw-Hill Book Company (*page 116*).

Menichetti, Piero Luigi, and Panfili, Luciana Menichetti, *Vecchia Cucina Eugubina.* Published by Tipolitografia Rubini & Petruzzi, Città di Castello, 1976. Translated by permission of Piero Luigi Menichetti, Gubbio (*page 128*).

Menon, *La Cuisinière Bourgeoise.* Published by Guillyn, Paris, 1746 (*page 135*).

Meyer, Carolyn, *Lots and Lots of Candy.* Text copyright © 1976 by Carolyn Meyer. Published by Harcourt Brace Jovanovich, Inc., New York. By permission of Joan Daves, New York, for the author (*pages 120, 130*).

Miller, Gloria Bley, *The Thousand Recipe Chinese Cookbook.* Copyright © 1966 by Gloria Bley Miller. Published by Grosset & Dunlap, Inc., New York, 1970. By permission of the author (*page 138*).

Montagné, Prosper, *New Larousse Gastronomique.* Originally published under the title "Nouveau Larousse Gastronomique". © Copyright Librairie Larousse, Paris 19. 1960. © Copyright English text The Hamlyn Publishing Group Limited 1977. Published by The Hamlyn Publishing Group Limited, London. By permission of The Hamlyn Publishing Group Limited (*page 137*).

Nichols, Nell B. (Editor), *Homemade Candy.* Copyright © 1970 by Farm Journal, Inc. Published by Barnes & Noble Books, a division of Harper & Row, Publishers, by arrangement with Doubleday & Co., Inc., 1974. By permission of Farm Journal, Inc., Philadelphia (*pages 106, 108, 109 and 113*).

Norberg, Inga (Editor), *Good Food from Sweden.* Published by Chatto & Windus, London, 1935. By permission of Curtis Brown Ltd., London, agents for the author (*page 90*).

Norwak, Mary, *Toffees, Fudges, Chocolates and Sweets.* © Mary Norwak 1977. Published by Pelham Books Ltd., London, 1977. By permission of Pelham Books Ltd./Michael Joseph Ltd., London (*pages 107, 142*).

Nostredame, Michel de, *Excellent & Moult Utile Opuscule.* Published by Antoine Volant, Lyons, 1556 (*page 115*).

Nouvelle Instruction pour les Confitures, les Liqueurs et les Fruits. Attributed to Massialot. Second edition, Paris, 1698 (*pages 128, 153*).

Ochorowicz-Monatowa, Marja, *Polish Cookery.* Translated by Jean Karsavina. © 1958 by Crown Publishers, Inc. Published by Crown Publishers, Inc., New York. By permission of Crown Publishers, Inc. (*pages 130, 161*).

Oliver, Michel, *Mes Recettes.* © Plon, 1975. Published by Librairie Plon, Département des Presses de la Cité, Paris. Translated by permission of Librairie Plon (*page 146*).

Petits Propos Culinaires 6, October 1980. © Prospect Books 1980. Published by Prospect Books, London and Washington, D.C. By permission of the publisher (*page 97*).

Philippou, Margaret Joy, *101 Arabian Delights.* Copyright © Margaret Joy Philippou. Published in

1969 by Clifton Books, Brighton and London (*page 95*).

Picayune's Creole Cook Book, The, Copyright, 1900, by The Picayune, New Orleans (*pages 92, 112, 127 and 128*).

Pinto, Maria Lo, and Miloradovich, Milo, *The Art of Italian Cooking.* Copyright 1948 by Doubleday & Company, Inc. By permission of McIntosh & Otis, Inc., New York (*page 151*).

Point, Fernand, *Ma Gastronomie.* Translated and adapted by Frank Kulla and Patricia Shannon Kulla. English language edition © 1974, Lyceum Books, Inc., Wilton, Conn., USA. Published by Lyceum Books, Inc. By permission of Lyceum Books, Inc. (*page 143*).

Puri, Kailash, *Rasoi Kala (Cookery Book).* First edition, 1959. Published by Hind Publishers Ltd., Jullundur, Punjab, India. Translated by permission of the author (*pages 139, 152*).

Raith, L. M., *Hand-made Continental Chocolates and Pralines.* Translated from the original by "The British Baker" staff. By permission of Applied Science Publishers Ltd., London (*page 162*).

Ramazani, Nesta, *Persian Cooking.* Copyright © 1974 by Nesta Ramazani. Published by Quadrangle/The New York Times Book Company, New York. By permission of the author (*pages 99, 138 and 161*).

Rattray, Mrs. M. E., *Sweetmeat-Making at Home.* Published by C. Arthur Pearson, Ltd., London, 1904. By permission of The Hamlyn Publishing Group Ltd., Feltham, Middx. (*page 111*).

Ripoll, Luis, *Nuestra Cocina. 600 Recetas de Mallorca, Menorca, Ibiza y Formentera.* © by Luis Ripoll. Published by Editorial H.M.B., S.A., Barcelona, 1978. Translated by permission of the author (*pages 138, 141*).

Roth, June, *Old-Fashioned Candymaking.* Copyright © 1974 by June Spienwak Roth. Published by Henry Regnery Company, Chicago. By permission of Toni Mendez, Inc., New York, for the author (*page 149*).

Roy-Camille, Christiane, and Marie, Annick, *Les Meilleures Recettes de la Cuisine Antillaise.* © Jean-Pierre Delarge, Éditions Universitaires, 1978. Published by Jean-Pierre Delarge, Éditeur, Paris. Translated by permission of Jean-Pierre Delarge, Éditeur (*page 140*).

Santa Maria, Jack, *Indian Sweet Cookery.* © Jack Santa Maria 1979. Published by Rider & Co., London. By permission of Rider & Co. (*pages 114, 155*).

Sarvis, Shirley, *A Taste of Portugal.* Copyright © 1967 Shirley Sarvis. Published by Charles Scribner's Sons, New York. By permission of the author (*pages 154, 157*).

Savarin, Mme. Jeanne (Editor), *La Cuisine des Familles (Magazine).* 16th July, 1905, 9th February, 1908, 8th March, 1908 (*pages 130, 140 and 160*).

Schuler, Elizabeth, *Mein Kochbuch.* © Copyright 1948 by Schuler-Verlag, Stuttgart-N. Translated by permission of Schuler Verlagsgesellschaft mbH., Herrsching (*pages 117, 142 and 144*).

Skuse's Complete Confectioner. Tenth edition. Published by W. J. Bush & Co., Ltd., London, c.1920 (*page 99*).

Sorbiatti, Giuseppe, *La Gastronomia Moderna.* Second edition. Published by Tip. Boniardi-Pogliadi di Ermenegildo Besozzi, Milan, 1866 (*page 150*).

Southern Living Magazine, The Editors of, *The Cookies and Candy Cookbook.* Copyright © 1976 Oxmoor House, Inc. Published by Oxmoor House, Inc., Birmingham, Alabama. By permission of Oxmoor House, Inc. (*page 121*).

Stechishin, Savella, *Traditional Ukrainian Cookery.*

Copyright 1957, 1959 by Savella Stechishin. Tenth edition, 1979. Published by Trident Press Ltd., Winnipeg, Canada. By permission of Trident Press Ltd. (*pages 92, 122 and 148*).

Stuber, Hedwig Maria, *Ich helf dir kochen.* © BLV Verlagsgesellschaft mbH., München, 1976. Published by BLV Verlagsgesellschaft mbH., Munich. Translated by permission of BLV Verlagsgesellschaft mbH. (*page 143*).

Szathmáry, Louis (Editor), *Fifty Years of Prairie Cooking.* Copyright © 1973 by Arno Press Inc. Published by Arno Press Inc., a New York Times Company, New York, 1973. By permission of Arno Press Inc. (*pages 113, 121*).

Taylor, Demetria, *Apple Kitchen Cook Book.* Copyright © 1966, 1971 by International Apple Institute. Published by Popular Library, The Fawcett Books Group of CBS Inc., New York. By permission of The Fawcett Books Group of CBS Inc. (*page 149*).

Tibbott, S. Minwel, *Welsh Fare.* © National Museum of Wales, Welsh Folk Museum. Published by National Museum of Wales, Welsh Folk Museum, St. Fagans, Cardiff, 1976. By permission of National Museum of Wales, Welsh Folk Museum (*pages 104, 105*).

Toklas, Alice B., *The Alice B. Toklas Cook Book.* Copyright 1954 by Alice B. Toklas. By permission of Harper & Row, Publishers, Inc., New York (*page 145*).

Toupin, Elizabeth Ahn, *Hawaii Cookbook and Backyard Luau.* © 1964, 1967 by Elizabeth Ahn Toupin. © 1967 by Silvermine Publishers, Inc. Published by Bantam Books, 1967, by arrangement with Silvermine Publishers, Inc. By permission of Silvermine Publishers, Inc., Norwalk, Conn. (*page 132*).

Tschirky, Oscar, *"Oscar" of the Waldorf's Cook Book.* Published in 1973 by Dover Publications, Inc., New York. First published by The Werner Company in 1896 under the title "The Cook Book by 'Oscar' of the Waldorf" (*pages 125, 160*).

Turkbas, Ozel, *The Turkish Cookbook.* Copyright © Ozel Turkbas 1977. Published by Nash Publishing, New York. By permission of Edward J. Acton, Inc. (*page 126*).

Uhle, Margaret and Brakemeier, Anne, *Konfekt zum Selbermachen.* © Droemersche Verlagsanstalt Th. Knaur Nachf., München/Zürich 1976. Translated by permission of Droemersche Verlagsanstalt Th. Knaur Nachf. GmbH. & Co., Munich (*pages 118, 124 and 151*).

Vence, Céline, *Encyclopédie Hachette de la Cuisine Régionale.* © Hachette 1979. Published by Hachette, Paris. Translated by permission of Hachette (*pages 93, 111 and 154*).

Wannée, C. J. (Editor), *Kookboek van de Amsterdamse Huishoudschool.* Published by H. J. W. Becht's Uitgevers Mij., Amsterdam. Translated by permission of H. J. W. Becht's-Uitgevers-Mij. B.V. (*pages 101, 118 and 119*).

Widenfelt, Sam (Editor), *Favorite Swedish Recipes.* Published by Dover Publications, Inc., New York, 1975. By permission of Dover Publications, Inc. (*pages 97, 102*).

Woman's Day Collector's Cook Book. (Prepared and edited by the Editors of Woman's Day.) Copyright © 1970, 1973 by Fawcett Publications, Inc. Published by Simon & Schuster, New York. By permission of CBS Publications, New York (*pages 98, 113, 121 and 123*).

Woodroof, Ph.D., Jasper Guy, *Coconuts: Production Processing Products.* © Copyright 1970 by The Avi Publishing Co., Inc., Westport, Connecticut. Published by The Avi Publishing Co., Inc., second edition, 1979. By permission of The Avi Publishing Co., Inc. (*page 110*).

Wright, Carol, *Portuguese Food.* © Text, Carol Wright, 1969. Published by J. M. Dent & Sons Ltd., London. By permission of Deborah Rogers Ltd., Literary Agency (*page 154*).

Wright, Mary M., *Candy-Making at Home.* Copyright 1915 by The Penn Publishing Company. Published by The Penn Publishing Company, Philadelphia, 1915 (*pages 131, 164*).

Acknowledgements and Picture Credits

The Editors of this book are particularly indebted to Werner Krattiger, London; Ann O'Sullivan, Deya, Mallorca; and Dr. R. H. Smith, Aberdeen.

They also wish to thank the following: Mary Attenborough, Chelmsford, Essex; The British Sugar Bureau, London; Butterfield Laboratories Ltd., King's Lynn, Norfolk; Lesley Coates, Ilford, Essex; Emma Codrington, Richmond, Surrey; Neyla Freeman, London; Fritzsche Dodge & Olcott (UK) Ltd., Wellingborough, Northamptonshire; Annie Hall, London; Mary Harron, London; Maggi Heinz, London; International Flavours & Fragrances (GB) Ltd., Haverhill, Suffolk; Pippa Millard, London; Sonya Mills, Canterbury, Kent; Wendy Morris, London; Michael Moulds, London; Elizabeth Pickford, Long

Colour separations by Gilchrist Ltd.—Leeds, England
Typesetting by Camden Typesetters—London, England
Printed and bound by Brepols S.A.—Turnhout, Belgium.

Ashton Research Station, Bristol; Baker Smith (Cake Decorations) Ltd., Farnham, Surrey; Fiona Tillett, London; Tina Walker, London; Williams (Hounslow) Ltd., Hounslow, Middlesex.

Photographs by Tom Belshaw: 8 to 10, 11—top right, centre and bottom, 12, 13, 15—top and bottom right, 16—right, 17—top and bottom middle, 18—top and bottom right, 19, 23—top left, 24—top left, 26 to 31, 37—top, 38, 39—top and bottom left, 40, 41, 42—top left, 46—top left and bottom right, 47—top left, 49—top, 50—top left and bottom, 51—bottom, 52, 53, 58, 59, 60—top, 61, 64 to 68, 70—bottom left, 71—top right and bottom left, 72 to 77, 78—bottom, 79—bottom left, 80 to 84, 85—top, bottom left and right, 86.

Other photographers (alphabetically): Alan Duns: Cover, 15—top left and middle, centre, bottom left and middle, 16—left and middle, 17—bottom left and right, 18—bottom left, 20, 34 to 36, 39—bottom right, 44, 46—bottom left, 47—bottom right, 48—top, bottom left and middle, 71—top left, 79—bottom right. John Elliott: 11—top left, 78—top, 79—top, 85—bottom middle. Louis Klein: 2. Bob Komar: 4, 22, 23—top middle and right and bottom, 24—top right and bottom, 25, 32, 33, 37—bottom, 42—top right and bottom, 43, 46—top right, 47—top middle and right and bottom left, 48—bottom right, 49—bottom, 50—top right, 51—top, 54 to 57, 60—bottom, 62, 63, 70—top right and bottom right, 71—bottom right.

All line cuts from Mary Evans Picture Library and private sources.